SMIL™ For Dummies

Defining Your Media

Media Elements	Attributes	Definition
<animation />		Animation file
<audio />		Audio file
<img />		Image file
<param />		Media initialization
<ref />		Any type of media file
<text />		Text file
<textstream />		Streaming text
<video />		Video file
	alt	Alternative text
	begin	Begin playing
	end	End playing
	dur	Playing duration
	left	Left edge
	top	Top edge
	width	Object width
	height	Object height
	src	Object address

Controlling the Timeline

Element	Definition
<excl> ... </excl>	Exclusive media
<priorityClass> ... </priorityClass>	Set priority for exclusive media
<par> ... </par>	Parallel media
<seq> ... </seq>	Sequential media
<prefetch> ... </prefetch>	Fetch media in advance
<switch> ... </switch>	Switch between display options

Tips for Designing SMIL

- Before you begin creating your presentation, create a list of all the media that you want to use; then actually create all the media.
- Decide how your presentation will be navigated and create any media pieces you need for navigation.
- Draw a storyboard of your presentation at each major stage of the production.
- Figure out the timing for all media elements so that your presentation flows smoothly.
- Put the pieces together using SMIL code or one of the SMIL editors.
- Test the SMIL presentation in all the major viewers including RealPlayer, QuickTime, and Internet Explorer 5.5.

BESTSELLING
BOOK SERIES

SMIL™ For Dummies®

Cheat
Sheet

Animations, Transformations, and Links

Element	Attribute	Definition
<a> ... </a>		Link from entire object
<area> ... </area>		Link from part of object
	href	Link address
	shape	Link shape
	cords	Link coordinates
<animate />		Generic attribute animation
<animateColor />		Animate object color
<animateMotion />		Move object along path
<set />		Set values of an attribute
	attributeName	Animated attribute name
	to	Animation destination
	from	Animation origin
	begin	Animation start
	dur	Animation duration
<transform> ... </transform>		Control transformations
	type	Transformation type
	subtype	Transformation subtype
	begin	Transformation start
	dur	Transformation duration
	end	Transformation end

Web Sites to Keep Handy

- World Wide Web Consortium's SMIL Documentation: www.w3.org/AudioVideo
- Real Networks Tutorial on Using SMIL: www.realnetworks.com/devzone/howto/contentcreation/smiltips/index.html
- Helio's SMIL Tutorial: www.helio.org/products/smil/tutorial
- WebReviews SMIL Tutorial: webreview.com/wr/pub/1999/03/12/feature/index.html
- WebTechniques SMIL Tutorial: www.webtechniques.com/archives/1998/09/bouthillier

IDG
BOOKS
WORLDWIDE

TM

References for the Rest of Us ®

BESTSELLING BOOK SERIES

Are you intimidated and confused by computers? Do you find that traditional manuals are overloaded with technical details you'll never use? Do your friends and family always call you to fix simple problems on their PCs? Then the *...For Dummies*® computer book series from IDG Books Worldwide is for you.

...For Dummies books are written for those frustrated computer users who know they aren't really dumb but find that PC hardware, software, and indeed the unique vocabulary of computing make them feel helpless. *...For Dummies* books use a lighthearted approach, a down-to-earth style, and even cartoons and humorous icons to dispel computer novices' fears and build their confidence. Lighthearted but not lightweight, these books are a perfect survival guide for anyone forced to use a computer.

> *"I like my copy so much I told friends; now they bought copies."*
>
> — Irene C., Orwell, Ohio

> *"Quick, concise, nontechnical, and humorous."*
>
> — Jay A., Elburn, Illinois

> *"Thanks, I needed this book. Now I can sleep at night."*
>
> — Robin F., British Columbia, Canada

Already, millions of satisfied readers agree. They have made *...For Dummies* books the #1 introductory level computer book series and have written asking for more. So, if you're looking for the most fun and easy way to learn about computers, look to *...For Dummies* books to give you a helping hand.

IDG
BOOKS
WORLDWIDE ®

SMIL™

FOR

DUMMIES®

by Heather Williamson

IDG Books Worldwide, Inc.
An International Data Group Company

Foster City, CA ◆ Chicago, IL ◆ Indianapolis, IN ◆ New York, NY

SMIL™ For Dummies®

Published by
IDG Books Worldwide, Inc.
An International Data Group Company
919 E. Hillsdale Blvd.
Suite 300
Foster City, CA 94404
www.idgbooks.com (IDG Books Worldwide Web site)
www.dummies.com (Dummies Press Web site)

Library of Congress Control Number: 00-105685

ISBN: 0-7645-0753-2

Printed in the United States of America

10 9 8 7 6 5 4 3 2 1

1O/QR/QS/QR/IN

Distributed in the United States by IDG Books Worldwide, Inc.

Distributed by CDG Books Canada Inc. for Canada; by Transworld Publishers Limited in the United Kingdom; by IDG Norge Books for Norway; by IDG Sweden Books for Sweden; by IDG Books Australia Publishing Corporation Pty. Ltd. for Australia and New Zealand; by TransQuest Publishers Pte Ltd. for Singapore, Malaysia, Thailand, Indonesia, and Hong Kong; by Gotop Information Inc. for Taiwan; by ICG Muse, Inc. for Japan; by Intersoft for South Africa; by Eyrolles for France; by International Thomson Publishing for Germany, Austria and Switzerland; by Distribuidora Cuspide for Argentina; by LR International for Brazil; by Galileo Libros for Chile; by Ediciones ZETA S.C.R. Ltda. for Peru; by WS Computer Publishing Corporation, Inc., for the Philippines; by Contemporanea de Ediciones for Venezuela; by Express Computer Distributors for the Caribbean and West Indies; by Micronesia Media Distributor, Inc. for Micronesia; by Chips Computadoras S.A. de C.V. for Mexico; by Editorial Norma de Panama S.A. for Panama; by American Bookshops for Finland.

For general information on IDG Books Worldwide's books in the U.S., please call our Consumer Customer Service department at 800-762-2974. For reseller information, including discounts and premium sales, please call our Reseller Customer Service department at 800-434-3422.

For information on where to purchase IDG Books Worldwide's books outside the U.S., please contact our International Sales department at 317-572-3993 or fax 317-572-4002.

For consumer information on foreign language translations, please contact our Customer Service department at 1-800-434-3422, fax 317-572-4002, or e-mail rights@idgbooks.com.

For information on licensing foreign or domestic rights, please phone +1-650-653-7098.

For sales inquiries and special prices for bulk quantities, please contact our Order Services department at 800-434-3422 or write to the address above.

For information on using IDG Books Worldwide's books in the classroom or for ordering examination copies, please contact our Educational Sales department at 800-434-2086 or fax 317-572-4005.

For press review copies, author interviews, or other publicity information, please contact our Public Relations department at 650-653-7000 or fax 650-653-7500.

For authorization to photocopy items for corporate, personal, or educational use, please contact Copyright Clearance Center, 222 Rosewood Drive, Danvers, MA 01923, or fax 978-750-4470.

is a registered trademark under exclusive license to IDG Books Worldwide, Inc., from International Data Group, Inc.

About the Author

Heather Williamson has spent the last five years designing and developing HTML documents for both corporate intranets and public Internet sites. When corporate mergers forced her to look for alternative forms of employment, she started a small Web development and consulting company that provides a variety of programming and development services to companies in the Pacific Northwest, New York, and Arizona. These services include Web page development, e-commerce solutions, graphic design, developing computer-based training, and application development. Somewhere along the way, she wrote the 1,400-page *HTML Master Reference* for IDG Books, drawing a new line in the sand marking the makeup of a complete reference book.

In her free time, between writing and raising her family, Heather raises American Quarter Horses, moves cattle, and generally metamorphoses from your typical techno-nerd into a downright tomboyish, country-raised farm kid.

ABOUT IDG BOOKS WORLDWIDE

Welcome to the world of IDG Books Worldwide.

IDG Books Worldwide, Inc., is a subsidiary of International Data Group, the world's largest publisher of computer-related information and the leading global provider of information services on information technology. IDG was founded more than 30 years ago by Patrick J. McGovern and now employs more than 9,000 people worldwide. IDG publishes more than 290 computer publications in over 75 countries. More than 90 million people read one or more IDG publications each month.

Launched in 1990, IDG Books Worldwide is today the #1 publisher of best-selling computer books in the United States. We are proud to have received eight awards from the Computer Press Association in recognition of editorial excellence and three from Computer Currents' First Annual Readers' Choice Awards. Our best-selling ...For Dummies® series has more than 50 million copies in print with translations in 31 languages. IDG Books Worldwide, through a joint venture with IDG's Hi-Tech Beijing, became the first U.S. publisher to publish a computer book in the People's Republic of China. In record time, IDG Books Worldwide has become the first choice for millions of readers around the world who want to learn how to better manage their businesses.

Our mission is simple: Every one of our books is designed to bring extra value and skill-building instructions to the reader. Our books are written by experts who understand and care about our readers. The knowledge base of our editorial staff comes from years of experience in publishing, education, and journalism — experience we use to produce books to carry us into the new millennium. In short, we care about books, so we attract the best people. We devote special attention to details such as audience, interior design, use of icons, and illustrations. And because we use an efficient process of authoring, editing, and desktop publishing our books electronically, we can spend more time ensuring superior content and less time on the technicalities of making books.

You can count on our commitment to deliver high-quality books at competitive prices on topics you want to read about. At IDG Books Worldwide, we continue in the IDG tradition of delivering quality for more than 30 years. You'll find no better book on a subject than one from IDG Books Worldwide.

John Kilcullen
Chairman and CEO
IDG Books Worldwide, Inc.

Eighth Annual Computer Press Awards ≥1992

Ninth Annual Computer Press Awards ≥1993

Tenth Annual Computer Press Awards ≥1994

Eleventh Annual Computer Press Awards ≥1995

IDG is the world's leading IT media, research and exposition company. Founded in 1964, IDG had 1997 revenues of $2.05 billion and has more than 9,000 employees worldwide. IDG offers the widest range of media options that reach IT buyers in 75 countries representing 95% of worldwide IT spending. IDG's diverse product and services portfolio spans six key areas including print publishing, online publishing, expositions and conferences, market research, education and training, and global marketing services. More than 90 million people read one or more of IDG's 290 magazines and newspapers, including IDG's leading global brands — Computerworld, PC World, Network World, Macworld and the Channel World family of publications. IDG Books Worldwide is one of the fastest-growing computer book publishers in the world, with more than 700 titles in 36 languages. The "...For Dummies®" series alone has more than 50 million copies in print. IDG offers online users the largest network of technology-specific Web sites around the world through IDG.net (http://www.idg.net), which comprises more than 225 targeted Web sites in 55 countries worldwide. International Data Corporation (IDC) is the world's largest provider of information technology data, analysis and consulting, with research centers in over 41 countries and more than 400 research analysts worldwide. IDG World Expo is a leading producer of more than 168 globally branded conferences and expositions in 35 countries including E3 (Electronic Entertainment Expo), Macworld Expo, ComNet, Windows World Expo, ICE (Internet Commerce Expo), Agenda, DEMO, and Spotlight. IDG's training subsidiary, ExecuTrain, is the world's largest computer training company, with more than 230 locations worldwide and 785 training courses. IDG Marketing Services helps industry-leading IT companies build international brand recognition by developing global integrated marketing programs via IDG's print, online and exposition products worldwide. Further information about the company can be found at www.idg.com.   1/26/00

Dedication

To everyone on the W3C that pushes and strives for excellence in all things they create. . . .

Author's Acknowledgments

My hat goes off to the great teams at IDG Books and Studio B for their constant faith in me throughout the long arduous task of getting this book published. I definitely couldn't have done it without all their help. Thanks to Ed Adams, Carol Sheehan, Jodi Jensen, Nicole Laux, Stephen Kraushaar, Neil Salkind (at Studio B), and all the great production and editorial crew whom I never saw nor heard from but witnessed the wondrous results of their work in my writing. And I don't want to forget the illustrators, binders, papermakers, and others who worked on this book — I might not know your names, but my thanks go out to all of you.

On a more personal note, I want to thank you, Ann, for making Mommy (me) get off the computer and play with you. You will always be a constant source of fun and love in my life. Just don't become a teenager too fast! And Luis . . . babe . . . I really appreciate you not calling when I'm working, but I *can* take a break every now and again!

Publisher's Acknowledgments

We're proud of this book; please send us your comments through our IDG Books Worldwide Online Registration Form located at www.dummies.com.

Some of the people who helped bring this book to market include the following:

Acquisitions, Editorial, and Media Development

Project Editors: Jodi Jensen, Linda Morris

Associate Acquisitions Editor: Carol Sheehan

Copy Editor: Nicole A. Laux

Proof Editor: Sarah Shupert

Technical Editor: Stephen Kraushaar

Senior Permissions Editor: Carmen Krikorian

Media Development Specialist: Travis Silvers

Media Development Coordinator: Marisa E. Pearman

Editorial Manager: Kyle Looper

Editorial Assistant: Jean Rogers

Production

Project Coordinator: Leslie Alvarez

Layout and Graphics: Amy Adrian, LeAndra Johnson, Jeremey Unger

Proofreaders: Andy Hollandbeck, Carl Pierce, Linda Quigley, and York Production Services, Inc.

Indexer: York Production Services, Inc.

Special Help
Teresa Artman

General and Administrative

IDG Books Worldwide, Inc.: John Kilcullen, CEO; Bill Barry, President and COO; John Ball, Executive VP, Operations & Administration; John Harris, CFO

IDG Books Technology Publishing Group: Richard Swadley, Senior Vice President and Publisher; Mary Bednarek, Vice President and Publisher; Walter R. Bruce III, Vice President and Publisher; Joseph Wikert, Vice President and Publisher; Mary C. Corder, Editorial Director; Andy Cummings, Publishing Director, General User Group; Barry Pruett, Publishing Director

IDG Books Manufacturing: Ivor Parker, Vice President, Manufacturing

IDG Books Marketing: John Helmus, Assistant Vice President, Director of Marketing

IDG Books Online Management: Brenda McLaughlin, Executive Vice President, Chief Internet Officer; Gary Millrood, Executive Vice President of Business Development, Sales and Marketing

IDG Books Packaging: Marc J. Mikulich, Vice President, Brand Strategy and Research

IDG Books Production for Branded Press: Debbie Stailey, Production Director

IDG Books Sales: Roland Elgey, Senior Vice President, Sales and Marketing; Michael Violano, Vice President, International Sales and Sub Rights

◆

The publisher would like to give special thanks to Patrick J. McGovern, without whom this book would not have been possible.

◆

Contents at a Glance

Cartoons at a Glance

By Rich Tennant

page 9

page 53

page 283

page 183

page 99

page 313

page 243

Cartoon Information:
Fax: 978-546-7747
E-Mail: richtennant@the5thwave.com
World Wide Web: www.the5thwave.com

Table of Contents

Introduction

* *

*N*ever before has the Internet been so lively, fun, full of sound, and packed with video animation. No, I'm not talking about a bunch of plugins that other software companies are trying to sell to you. I'm talking about one of the latest developments in the *multimediation* of the World Wide Web: *S*ynchronized *M*ultimedia *I*ntegration *L*anguage (*SMIL*), which you can use to create dynamic multimedia for software, such as RealNetworks RealPlayer and Apple QuickTime. SMIL has even been incorporated into Web browsers, such as Internet Explorer 5.5 and Netscape Navigator 6. SMIL is the solution that Web and presentation developers have been seeking for a long time.

If you've ever built your own Web page, you know how easy that can be with the right tools. Sorry, but SMIL doesn't really have the "right" tools yet, if you like to do WYSIWG (*What You See Is What You Get*) editing and not hand-coding. A few editors are available that really help you develop your SMIL presentations, but you're still required to know SMIL before you can make your presentations function exactly as you intend. Think of it as exploring the frontier with the *Star Trek* crew. The current crop of SMIL tools offers adventures to pique your interest, stretch your brain, and maybe push you into that next raise at work!

About This Book

This book doesn't take a direct approach to your presentation development projects. You'll find no diary of elements and their attributes included here in long droning text. You will find, however, coverage of each of the primary parts of the latest SMIL 2.0 specification and how to make all those parts work together. In *SMIL For Dummies,* my goal isn't to answer every question that you may have but to help you start using SMIL in your daily presentation development projects.

The World Wide Web Consortium (W3C), located on the Web at www.w3.org, provides constantly updated specifications for Internet-related languages and technologies. SMIL is one of these. In 1997, the W3C released SMIL 1.0. This specification included just the basic commands for controlling timing and placement of objects on your SMIL presentations. With the SMIL 2.0 specification, you get everything that SMIL 1.0 had to offer (watch out for a few syntax changes) plus:

- ✔ Animation controls for moving and altering objects (Chapter 14)

- ✔ Transformation controls for fading in, or wiping in, objects (Chapter 14)

- ✔ More options for controlling the timing of your presentation (Chapters 8, 9, 10, and 11)

- ✔ Increased storage capabilities through use of metadata (Chapter 4)

- ✔ New controls for creating layouts, viewports, and regions (Chapters 6 and 7)

HTML developers can pick up SMIL very quickly. When using SMIL, all a Web developer has to do is pick up a few new tags/elements and get to work. *SMIL For Dummies* gives you the tools that you're missing.

Conventions Used in This Book

Keeping things consistent makes them easier to understand. In this book, those consistent elements are *conventions*. Notice how the word *conventions* is in italics? In this book, I put new terms in italics and then define them so that you know what they mean. When you have to type something in a text box (very rare around here), I put it in **bold** type.

When I type URLs (Web addresses) within a paragraph, they look like this: `www.w3.org`. All the sample code that I've included in this book also appears in this `code font`. All the names of SMIL elements, attributes, and their values appear in the code font so that you can spot them easily amidst the rest of the text. That's about it for the conventions used in the book!

Oh yeah! I almost forgot. Within many of the code examples you'll find lines of `bold code`. This is to help you spot the specific lines of code that I'm discussing in the accompanying text. And, if you ever see a word in code that's also italicized (like this: `systemBitrate=<integer>`), it means that the word is a placeholder. You must specify a particular value in place of the italicized word.

You — The Adventurous Audience

Most people make assumptions about the people they meet, and I've made some assumptions about you as I've written this book. I know . . . "Assumptions are the devil of a thorough job," or so my grandmother used to tell me. But I've done the best I can to write this book for you without actually meeting you in person. Just so you know what I'm assuming about you, I'll tell you:

✓ **You're familiar with your own computer.** I'm assuming that you can turn your computer on and off and know at least how to start some type of text editor. Oh, and I also assume that you know how to type and use your mouse. I don't care if you're God's gift to touch-typing or if you're a two-fingered hunt-and-peck artist; the end results are the same.

✓ **You have a basic understanding of Web pages.** Did I go too far with this one? No, you don't have to understand HTML fully to get a lot out of this book, but it's nice if you understand the basics. I spend a lot of time comparing SMIL to HTML, so even if you aren't an HTML expert, you'll know it a little better by the time you finish reading *SMIL For Dummies* — whether you want to or not.

✓ **You have a working connection to the Internet.** You don't actually have to be on the Internet to get the samples in this book to work. You do, however, need access to the Internet if you want to check out some of the Web sites referred to throughout this book. In addition, you'll want to download new versions of the software after the ones included on the CD become outdated. Given the current rate of change for the Internet, that could well be less than six months after you buy this book.

✓ **You want to create SMIL presentations.** Did I guess wrong? Hmm . . . maybe you need to get the latest murder mystery instead of this book. Or maybe you don't want to read about SMIL, but your boss is making you. Well, even in that case, this book is a great place to start. Maybe you can even have some fun with this SMIL adventure while you try to keep the paychecks coming.

Assuming that I've made the right guesses, and you are this book's intended audience, my grandmother will be happy and not give me any more castor oil. All you need now is an idea of what you want to build and you're ready to get started. But even if you don't have your own idea, you can borrow one of mine; I have a few extras.

How This Book Is Organized

This book contains seven major parts, each of which helps you understand a specific aspect of SMIL. You don't need to read each chapter, or part, in order — you can use the Table of Contents and the index as your keys to finding the information, commands, and concepts that you're interested in at any specific point of your journey.

The following shows a breakdown of each of the parts and their contents.

Part I: SMILs, Everyone, SMILs: An Overview

In Part I, you can find your answers to how SMIL should be used, what type of media it supports, and in general how it works. It's in this part that I tell you what SMIL is, what it can do, how it affects the Web as we know and love it, and where it comes from. You can see how SMIL is integrated into HTML documents and why they work together the way that they do. You also see a description of the standard image, text, video, and audio file types that work with SMIL.

By the time you're done with Part I, you'll know what SMIL is and what it works with. Throughout the rest of the book, I show you how to put SMIL together to make a presentation.

Part II: Putting SMIL to Work

At this point, you can see how to set up the basic framework for a SMIL document so that your browser or a SMIL player knows how to use the information that you've given it. In this part, you figure out exactly what role each part of the SMIL document plays, including the following:

- ✔ `<smil>`, which identifies the entire SMIL document.
- ✔ `<head>`, which identifies the heading information, including the instructions on how to lay out the SMIL document.
- ✔ `<body>`, which identifies the meat of your SMIL document, such as the timing and media elements.
- ✔ `<meta>` and `<metadata>`, which provide information about your SMIL presentation to other computers that ask for it.
- ✔ `<switch>`, which provides you a way to control which computers see which parts of your presentation.

If you read Part II, you'll have the foundation of your SMIL presentation and be ready to start adding media, timing, and layout areas to your document.

Part III: A Time and Place for Everything

Placement of your SMIL media elements is of vital importance. So in this part, I show you how to ensure that all your media elements are placed exactly where you want them by using the `<layout>`, `<root-layout>`, `<region>`, and `<view-port>` elements. I also discuss the concept of absolute positioning so that you know what happens to the rest of your elements as you create documents and add to your layout area. In this section, you learn what happens to various elements that are too large for your specified layout area. Be sure to read this section when you're using images and video so that you can be sure that it all appears just as you want it to.

After you get your layout perfected, you're ready to add all the timing elements to your SMIL presentation. This is a biggie. Who wants to have their soundtrack a few seconds off from their video, or have text appear when an image is supposed to? In the chapters in which I discuss the `<seq>`, `<excl>`, and `<par>` elements, I help you deal with all the potential timing nightmares of working with complex presentations.

At the end of this part, you'll be ready to start linking your presentation to other resources so that your presentation viewers can get access to all the proper text, audio, and images when they're visiting your place.

Part IV: Linking Up

Networking may be the foundation of getting someplace in the business world, but *linking* is the core of the Internet. You can create complex links in SMIL that enable you to jump from one location to another, load additional information into your presentation, start another presentation at a particular point, or simply pause your presentation so that you can go get a cup of coffee. Using SMIL Links, the possibilities are seemingly endless — especially when you compare them to HTML.

In this part, I also give you an introduction to the animation and transformation effects that are literally the frosting on the cake for SMIL. Using these preprogrammed effects, you no longer have to spend hours programming JavaScript, or some other scripting language, to create specific effects or to move your objects around your screen for you.

At the end of this part, you'll be ready to create some complete SMIL projects. You'll have seen a bit of everything that SMIL has to offer. This book doesn't cover everything that SMIL has to offer in the depth you may need to develop SMIL professionally, but it gets you started and should keep you and your boss happy — if that's what's important to you!

Part V: Multimedia from the Ground Up

And if you're wondering — I didn't forget the examples. Every chapter includes examples of creating SMIL documents using those little pieces that you've been exploring, but this part is *all* examples. Take a look at these three simple examples of what you can do with SMIL and just a little bit of time:

> ✔ A little radio station that plays my favorite kind of music.
>
> ✔ A short silent movie that, unlike the classic oldies from Hollywood, is in color.
>
> ✔ A cartoon that doesn't keep you entertained for long, but gives you an example of how difficult it is to get the timing right.

Part VI: The Part of Tens

In true *For Dummies* style, I've included a Part of Tens in this book. In these chapters, I introduce lists of ten items about a variety of topics. Here you find additional resources, hints, and tips, plus other gold nuggets of knowledge. The Part of Tens is a resource you can turn to again and again.

Part VII: Appendixes

I save some of the more detailed information for last. In the appendixes, you find information that can add depth to your understanding and use of SMIL. Appendix A is a listing of the SMIL 2.0 supporting editors and players that you can find on the Internet and then use to create and view SMIL documents. Appendix B includes copies of the detailed Document Type Definition (DTD) information that's used by all XML-based languages to control how SMIL commands interact. This appendix is more useful as you delve further into SMIL and its wide variety of options.

My grandfather used to tell me that you couldn't really know a person until you knew his family. And he was right. So in Appendix C, I included a short and sweet history of SMIL's ancestors: XML, XML Namespaces, and the various other multimedia specifications that are available from the World Wide Web Consortium. Appendix D gives you all the details about how to use the cool stuff on the CD-ROM that comes with this book.

Finally, every book has its limits, and this one didn't have quite enough pages for me to fit in some other useful material that I wanted to share with you. So you'll find Appendixes E and F on the CD. Appendix E provides a list of all the SMIL elements and their attributes so that you don't have to search through the entire book just to find the name or spelling of an element or attribute whose function you already know. Appendix F is a directory of RealText and RealPix terminology that works with SMIL as it's implemented within RealPlayer — the most popular SMIL-viewing software. So be sure to pop in the CD and check out these appendixes!

Icons Used in This Book

 This icon signals technical details that are informative and interesting but not critical for writing your SMIL documents. These snippets of information are useful as you continue to create SMIL presentations (so be sure to come back and read them later).

 This icon flags useful information that makes the creation of your SMIL presentations easier and helps you to avoid pitfalls that may otherwise trap you.

 This icon points out information that you really need to remember as you continue along your SMIL adventure. These little gems of information may make the next leg of your journey that much easier.

 Definitely don't skip this portion of your adventure. These warnings help you see what you shouldn't do or at least help explain why you shouldn't have done what you already did.

 Don't miss out on the information that the World Wide Web has to offer. I can't put it all in this book. If I did, IDG Books wouldn't be able to afford the paper or the shipping. This icon helps you spot important references to information on the Internet that may help you advance your SMIL studies in the future.

 Be sure to check out these other books, which include related information about SMIL from other talented IDG Books authors.

 And finally, this icon marks all the samples, images, and perks that I've placed on the CD, just for you.

Where to Go from Here

Do you know where you're headed now? You don't have to start at the beginning; you can jump in anywhere that you want. If you want to find out about placing media in SMIL, take a look at that first. If you want to see how timing works, go ahead and read that information. The beginning of an adventure is a very personal thing. Some people start at the beginning; others parachute down and work their way from the middle to the end. Still others jet their way to the end, and then work their way back as they figure out what they missed. However you want to start your adventure, I hope you do one thing . . . *enjoy the journey!*

Part I

SMILs, Everyone, SMILs: An Overview

In this part . . .

1f you're unfamiliar with SMIL and what it can do for you and your organization, you need to read this part. First you find out exactly what SMIL is, how it can help you, and where it came from. Then you can read about each type of media that's used within a SMIL presentation: images, animations, audio, video, and text. I also show you how to identify these media types.

At the end of this part, you find a quick discussion of how to design and develop your SMIL presentations. Throughout, I discuss a number of multimedia design rules and conventions, including some timesaving tips for creating rich multimedia presentations.

Chapter 1

SMIL, It's Not Candid Camera

In This Chapter

▶ Checking out what SMIL can do for you

▶ Understanding how SMIL can help you create rich multimedia

▶ Finding out where SMIL came from

*Y*ou probably have an inkling about what SMIL is, or you wouldn't have picked up this book in the first place. Maybe you want to add some multimedia to your Web site and heard that SMIL can help you do that. Well, you've come to the right place.

SMIL, *Synchronized Multimedia Integration Language* (pronounced *smile*), is a markup language similar to *HTML* (*H*ypertext *M*arkup *L*anguage) that enables you to add tags to a text document so that you can easily combine and synchronize text, still images, animations, audio, and video. You can then turn that document into a lively new Web site with enough bells and whistles to impress even the most skeptical friends or customers.

You can store SMIL pages on the Web, but you don't need a T1 line running into your house or your office to view them, as you would need if you were creating high-end multimedia documents in most other programs. Folks using 28.8 modems can view SMIL documents as easily as those with faster equipment. And SMIL isn't just for Web pages. You can use SMIL to enhance multimedia presentations on CD-ROM, as a way to spruce up a computer-based training session, or for its pure entertainment value in a RealPlayer multimedia presentation. You can apply SMIL to any type of project as long as you have the SMIL software (such as RealPlayer 8) available to read the document.

Why Do You Need SMIL?

Many possibilities are open to you when you add multimedia to your Web site: You can offer your customers a video demonstration of your latest product, either on your Web site or by creating a multimedia CD; you can provide a walk-through tour of the house that you're trying to sell; or you can put together multimedia help files and product tutorials as technical support for your customers. And you can even use multimedia when you plan that big roast for your boss on his 50th birthday. Figure 1-1 shows an example of a SMIL presentation.

You can apply SMIL to a document in which you don't want all the elements of the presentation to be visible from the beginning. SMIL gives you the capability to time when certain events take place so that you can vary what the viewer is seeing at a particular spot in the presentation. And SMIL isn't just for HTML documents and the Internet. If you have a text editor, such as Windows Notepad or BBEdit on a Macintosh, you can use SMIL to create slide shows, photo journals, and music videos.

SMIL lets you create top-quality presentations as long as the pieces you're putting into the presentation are top quality as well. If your videos are well done and your sound is clean and clear, your SMIL presentation carries the same quality. Because SMIL simply directs the playing of each of your presentation's parts, it doesn't interfere with the existing quality of your media files nor does it add any degradation to the files due to playing and positioning instructions.

Where else can you develop broadcast-quality interactive multimedia presentations without the use of a full television studio? The Internet can make anything happen.

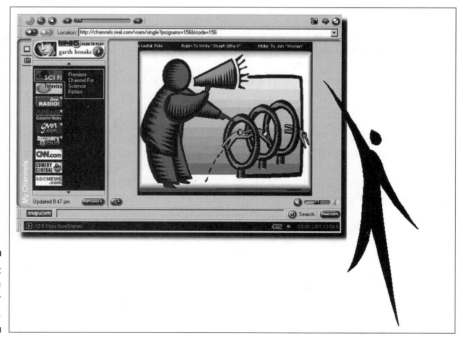

Figure 1-1:
Just one
idea for
using SMIL.

SMIL Support

SMIL attracts more support every month. A perfect example of this is RealNetworks constant development of new tools that both play and create SMIL documents. Apple QuickTime has joined the bandwagon by increasing its support for SMIL in the QuickTime 4.1 version of the software. Other small, relatively unknown, companies are also adding support for, or developing products for, SMIL.

SMIL players

A variety of SMIL players are ready for user prime time, and many more are on their way. Here are some players that are currently available:

> ✔ **RealNetworks RealPlayer 7 (**www.real.com**):** This player, shown in Figure 1-2, shows both RealPlayer proprietary video and audio documents, and lets you play SMIL files containing RealVideo and RealAudio multimedia content. The goal of RealNetworks is to make its player the global player, supporting all the nonproprietary types of multimedia used on the Internet.

Figure 1-2:
The RealPlayer software is one of the most popular on the Internet; its basic version is automatically installed with many Internet-related software packages.

✔ **Apple QuickTime 4.1** (www.apple.com/quicktime/): Apple QuickTime, shown in Figure 1-3, runs proprietary QuickTime video files as well as SMIL documents containing QuickTime-supported files.

Figure 1-3: Apple QuickTime is one of the original movie players that has grown with technology and now supports the latest multimedia standards and files.

✔ **Oratrix GRiNS** (www.oratrix.com/GRiNS/index.html): This player and authoring software enables you to create both RealPlayer G2 and SMIL files quickly and easily using a very simple development interface.

✔ **Internet Explorer 5.5** (msdn.Microsoft.com/downloads/): Internet Explorer 5.5 provides support for SMIL 1.0 and partial support for SMIL 2.0 — the latest release of the SMIL standard from the World Wide Web Consortium (www.w3.org).

SMIL editors

The capability to watch SMIL action has often been offset by the difficulty of creating it. SMIL editors are now available that enable you to create content quickly and easily without having to remember the entire new language. In the future, it will only get better; but for now, you can choose from the following SMIL editors:

✔ **Allaire Homesite** (www.allaire.com)

Homesite now provides direct support for adding SMIL applets into HTML documents and creating the SMIL document itself.

✔ **Veon's Studio** (www.veon.com)

This authoring software uses a series of wizards as well as a comfortable interface to develop SMIL documents quickly and easily. This program incorporates JavaScripts to help increase the functionality of the product and the resulting documents.

✔ **RealNetworks RealSlideshow 2** (www.real.com)

You can now create SMIL documents that incorporate e-mail, MP3 files, and PNG and GIF images. All the documents created with RealSlideshow, shown in Figure 1-4, are playable in the RealPlayer G2 and the RealPlayer 7 products that are also available through RealNetworks.

Figure 1-4:
RealSlide-
show 2
enables you
to create
slide shows
of images
and text
playable in
either
RealPlayer G2
or
RealPlayer 7.

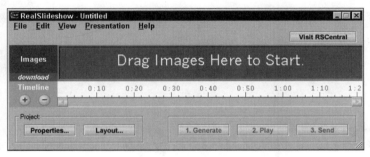

✔ **Sausage Software's SMIL Composer**
(www.sausage.com/supertoolz/toolz/stsmil.html)

The SMIL composer, shown in Figure 1-5, focuses on developing SMIL-based multimedia content for play within the RealSystems G2 or 7 player. It enables you to define your SMIL content without having any knowledge of SMIL syntax and elements.

✔ **Oratrix GRiNS** (www.oratrix.com/GRiNS/index.html)

This author and player software enables you to create both RealPlayer G2 and SMIL files quickly and easily using a very simple development interface.

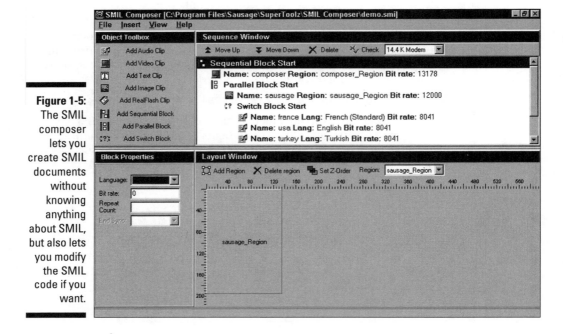

Figure 1-5:
The SMIL
composer
lets you
create SMIL
documents
without
knowing
anything
about SMIL,
but also lets
you modify
the SMIL
code if you
want.

What SMIL Can Do for You

Whether you're a Web content developer or just want to add some zip to a computer-based training CD, SMIL can make your life easier. SMIL can stand on its own, so you don't have to use it with HTML or XML. And you don't have to be an experienced Web designer or a video and sound guru to use SMIL. You just have to want to create small, fast-running, multimedia presentations. Figure 1-6 shows an example of SMIL code.

When you use SMIL for your multimedia presentations, your Web viewers aren't forced to download a special tool to view the sound or video on your site. With other technologies, you have to use a particular multimedia format for each type of player. You must have Flash to make Flash movies, and your visitor must also have the Flash viewer installed to view the movies. Just a few years ago, you had to have RealPlayer, QuickTime, Microsoft Media Player, a Wav player, and a MIDI player to access all the information on the Web. Sometimes, even all these programs didn't do the trick. Next thing you know, you're downloading a particular browser plug-in just to access a sound or video from a certain Web site.

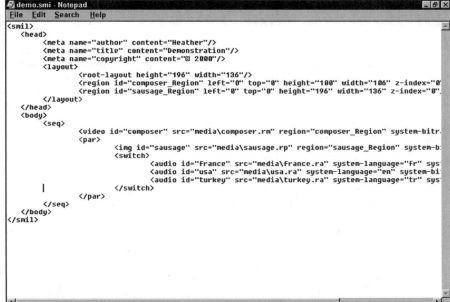

Figure 1-6:
SMIL is
a simple
text-based
language
that creates
elaborate
multimedia
presenta-
tions in
software as
basic as
Windows
Notepad.

Fortunately, SMIL is becoming so widely supported that viewers no longer have to get a new tool to look at SMIL-based Web sites. If visitors don't have a fairly recent browser version, or a recent version of RealPlayer or QuickTime, they may have to download an additional program — but at least it's only *one* program.

You can view SMIL documents in a variety of multimedia players. The most popular of these players is either of the RealPlayer versions offered for free download by RealNetworks or the QuickTime 4.1 player developed by Apple Inc. In addition to these players, SMIL support is included in Microsoft Internet Explorer 5.5 and is rumored to be part of the upcoming release of Netscape Navigator.

Even if Microsoft Internet Explorer and Netscape Navigator do support SMIL directly, they may not support all the video and audio file types — such as RealPlayer's proprietary movie files — that you can manipulate using SMIL. This leaves you resorting to programs like RealPlayer and QuickTime to view that particular movie file.

HTML, XML, and SMIL

SMIL didn't appear out of thin air — it has a whole family of markup languages behind it. SMIL is a close cousin to the familiar HTML language that serves as the foundation for the exchange of documents on the Internet. SMIL gets much of its scalability and ease of use from the *Extensible Markup Language* (XML) family. XML, specifically designed to create Web documents and control Web data, is a simplified subset of the *Standard Generalized Markup Language* (SGML). If you've worked with HTML, programming with SMIL will be a breeze. You can learn SMIL practically overnight.

The HTML/SMIL resemblance

If you look at an HTML and a SMIL document side-by-side (see Table 1-1), you can see a number of similarities.

Table 1-1	Comparing HTML to SMIL
HTML Document	*SMIL Presentation*
<html>	<smil>
<head>	<head>
<meta>	<meta/>
</head>	</head>
<body>	<body>
Content of document	Content of presentation
</body>	</body>
</html>	</smil>

As you can see, the documents are almost identical. Like HTML, SMIL uses a series of *elements* (or tags) to identify each section of the presentation, such as the <head> and <body>, and each item that is added to the document, such as a particular piece of video or a text blurb. Elements are simply placeholders on the document that tell the SMIL player, or the Web browser, what type of information it's reading and how to display that information.

The only major difference in the primary document structure is that you start with a `<smil>` element instead of with an `<html>` tag. Otherwise, the format of these languages is the same in the following aspects:

- ✔ All element names are enclosed in angle brackets (< >).
- ✔ Each element has an opening and closing element marker.
- ✔ The closing element marker has an additional forward slash (/) that identifies it as the close of a preceding tag.

Okay, you need to know *one* other difference between SMIL element formatting and HTML element formatting. SMIL requires that you close the `<meta>` element with a forward slash, as shown in Table 1-1, before the closing angle bracket. In HTML documents, that slash isn't necessary and actually causes some Web browsers to display documents incorrectly if you include it in your HTML element formatting. SMIL's XML foundations dictate this strict requirement.

The XML foundation

In a nutshell, XML enables developers to create a specialized markup language to describe the content and formatting requirements specific to their own projects. Individuals working on projects can share XML document definitions with others working on similar projects all over the world. Chemists can share documents using the CML language, based on XML, that enables them to more easily write and display complex chemical equations. Mathematicians can share documents with complex math equations using their MathML language, also based on XML. Chemists and mathematicians, as well as others, never had the option of sharing simple text documents before because they had no way to write complex multilayered equations, such as those used in chemistry and mathematics.

SMIL is simply a derivative of XML that's focused on supplying a means of designing and controlling the timing of complex presentations that include text, still images, animations, audio, and video objects. You can read more about the XML parentage of SMIL in Appendix C.

For more information on XML, check out *XML For Dummies* by Ed Tittel and Frank Boumphrey (published by IDG Books Worldwide, Inc.).

The SMIL world

Think about HTML for a second. HTML is a specification from the World Wide Web Consortium (W3C) — the primary standards organization for the Internet. The W3C works hard to make the Internet a more user-friendly and active place to be. HTML is supported, for the most part, by all the major Web browsers available both commercially and privately. SMIL, also a specification that the W3C has developed, is gaining popularity every day. More and more improvements are being made to the software that has been created to read and play SMIL presentations, and new companies are jumping on the bandwagon every day.

So, it's a great time to become familiar with this fairly simple, but powerful, markup language for multimedia, and this book can help you find out just what you need to know.

Chapter 2

All About Media Types

SMIL(e), you're ready to explore the world of multimedia *media types*. SMIL adds the feel of rich multimedia content to the Internet. Where else can you combine text, audio, video, still imagery, and animations for nothing more than the cost of storing a few files? You can create a full range of multimedia for any job by using the primary media types that you see every day on the Internet. You may ask, "What are these types of media?" It's simple. If you've built a standard Web page, you're already familiar with many of the standard media types. *Media* is simply a global term that applies to the various types of images, animations, text, sound bytes, and video that can be played and displayed — in this case, on your SMIL presentation.

Projecting Your Visual Image

As you browse the hundreds of thousands of Web pages on the Internet, you may notice a common trait: They all use images to create a pleasing visual atmosphere for your visit. On HTML pages — as with SMIL presentations — these images consist of pictures in a GIF, JPEG, or PNG file format and animations.

To bitmap or draw, that's the question

In creating images for the Internet, you can choose from various types of software. And a few image formats. The two primary types of drawing/painting styles use either bitmap-based tools or vector-based tools. No matter what types of tools you use to draw your image, the majority of the time you're able to save your image in one of the common bitmap formats used on the Internet: GIF, JPEG, or PNG.

You can use either bitmap or draw programs to create the graphics for your SMIL presentation. When you save your graphics as GIF, JPEG, or PNG images, however, all your vector information is lost, and in the future, you'll have to use bitmap tools to work with that image.

You should first consider using bitmap images — by far the most popular format used on the Internet. *Bitmap images* use a variety of colored pixels to fill in the image, which means that lines in the image may have a jagged appearance (see the edges on the top of the letter *A* on the left in Figure 2-1). When you create an image using bitmap-painting tools, you color each pixel individually — and not because you aren't using a good drawing tool. But instead of treating a circle or rectangle as a true shape on the image, a bitmap image tool creates a series of colored pixels in a roughly circular or rectangular pattern. If you want to treat your drawn circles and rectangles as individual maneuverable shapes, you need to find a vector drawing program, which I discuss shortly.

GIF and JPEG images are bitmap images. The process of drawing a bitmap image is similar to painting with oil paint on canvas. After the paint is on the canvas, you can't move it. The only way to remove its effects is to paint over it. As you create or draw shapes by using the bitmap painting program tools, you have to draw those shapes in where the object belongs. You can't drag it around the screen — that shape has been added to your image in the same permanent manner that an artist's brush adds oil to a canvas.

While drawing an angled line in a bitmap program, you may also notice that the edges are either fuzzy (antialiased) or jagged. The bitmap program blends the line into its background, producing the antialiased effect. The pixels are square, and so the jagged effect is created. Think back to your building blocks days. You could create great pyramids, right? But you couldn't make them with smooth walls; they were always terraced. The blocks were square. You always had to deal with the fact that you had no way of creating a smooth angle when all the blocks had to fit within a stacked grid. A variety of bitmap painting programs are available, including Adobe Photoshop and Jasc Paint Shop Pro (which also contains vector-drawing tools). If you're using Windows, you have access to the Paint and Imaging programs that come with the operating system.

Bitmap programs are commonly called *paint* programs, and vector programs are referred to as *draw* programs.

Figure 2-1:
Bitmap images use individual pixels to mark the edges of the image; vector images use mathematical equations to draw images with smooth edges.

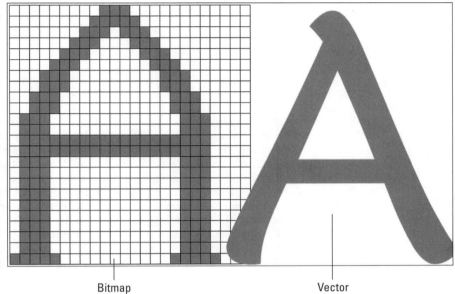

Bitmap   Vector

Vector drawings are based on a series of complex mathematical equations. Each line or circle that you draw — instead of being a series of colored pixels — is actually based on the rules you learned in your high school geometry class. These rules enable you to draw straight lines straight and smooth without the jagged edges you see on bitmap images. Using vector graphics, you can also adjust the sizes of the individual shapes that you place on your illustration — independent of the other shapes in your picture.

Because vector-drawing tools make shapes based on math, they don't work like the tools that you use to create bitmap images. You don't have to worry about your drawn shapes automatically merging into a single layer of an image. The math equations draw the image shapes and provide a unique way of accessing the individual shape as an entity that's separate from the remainder of the image. Because a math equation can take on any dimensions or numbers, as potential values, you can change the shape and size of the image by simply adjusting its location on-screen. The adjustment is automatically fed back to the equation, and the image is updated to reflect your intended adjustment.

Think of a vector image as a series of mathematical-based instructions that control the size, shape, and color of the object you're drawing. For example, referring back to your geometry courses in school, you may remember graphing the center point and radius or diameter of a circle. Vector-drawing programs take that information and input it into a mathematical equation. The outcome is the visible circle you see on-screen, including the width and color of the line and the color filling the interior of the circle.

You have a variety of vector-drawing programs to choose from, including the following:

- ✔ Paint Shop Pro (www.jasc.com)
- ✔ Macromedia Fireworks (www.macromedia.com)
- ✔ Adobe Illustrator (www.adobe.com)

Even if you're drawing images using a vector-drawing program, you can still convert them into bitmap image formats for use on the Internet. Whether you use a vector-drawing program (such as Adobe Illustrator) or a program that includes both bitmap and vector-drawing functions (such as Paint Shop Pro 7) to create your SMIL document images, you just need to export your image to a GIF, JPEG, or PNG file format when you're ready to play with SMIL. Most of the popular graphics programs enable you to automatically save your image in any format you want. With the increasing popularity of the Internet, GIF, JPEG, and PNG images are becoming the standard default selections.

If you're drawing your images using a vector-drawing program, be sure to save your image in that software's native format so that you can manipulate your vector-based objects in the future. After you save your image as a GIF or JPEG, you'll never be able to return to the movable vector state.

Adding illustrations with GIFs

GIF (*G*raphics *I*nterchange *F*ormat) images are probably the most popular images on the Internet. They're bitmap images that provide a very crisp, clean look to pictures using just a limited number of colors and a few, smooth shading effects. GIFs are 256-color images that can include *animations* (see the section, "Putting it all down on paper," later in this chapter) and *transparent* colors.

GIF images are great for illustrations, line drawings, and any other type of image that doesn't require more than 256 colors, as shown in Figure 2-2. In other words, don't count on using GIFs for photographs or images with extensive shading or color variations. GIF images work well for photos *only* if the photo has a limited number of colors.

When creating computer graphics, you can use a technique called *dithering* that allows you to make additional colors and shades from the colors on the existing color palette by interspersing pixels of different colors. Don't dither GIF images — it only adds to the overall size of the image files.

Figure 2-2:
GIF images
have 256
colors and
are great for
creating
small
illustrations.

When using GIF images on the Internet, try to stick to a *Web-safe color palette,* which can create an image (using only 216 colors) that displays safely on any system — no matter the operating system. Many of the popular graphics programs provide the option of saving your images with the Web-safe color palette.

Another reason for the popularity of GIF images on the Internet is that the GIF file format gives you the capability to create transparent images. Because you're often placing an image over a colored background or another image, you want to avoid having sharp borders around your images. GIF images create a transparent effect by assigning a single visible color as the one replaced with the transparency. When selecting a color for the transparency replacement, ensure that it's only used where you want the transparency to be.

If you select white as your transparent color, for instance, and you have white lettering inside a black button that's on a white background, then the white background and the white lettering, when placed on your SMIL document, would both allow the color of the background they were placed over to show through. For instance, if you placed that button on a blue background, the black button would appear to have blue text. If that button were placed over a green background, then the button would appear to have green text.

You have a variety of ways to control the size of GIF images:

✔ **Reduce the number of colors in the image's color palette.** Most types of graphic software allow you to reduce the number of colors on your image palette by editing the palette directly. GIF images give you the added ability of using only selected colors on your color palettes. So, you can easily use only red, blue, and green shades without any white or black colors, if those are the only colors that are included within your image.

✔ **Reduce the number of individual image frames in the image file.** A GIF image can contain multiple images. When displayed on a compatible viewer, each of these images is displayed in order and used to create a complete animation. The removal of individual image frames helps to reduce the overall size of the GIF image.

✔ **Reduce the outside dimensions of the image.** The smaller the outside dimensions of the file, the smaller (typically) the overall file size.

Adding photographs with JPEGs

JPEG (*J*oint *P*hotographic *E*xperts *G*roup) images are also bitmap images. JPEGs, however, aren't limited to 256 colors — they can use up to 16 million. These additional colors tend to make photographs appear much more crisp and clear. JPEGs can't store multiple images so you can't, therefore, animate a JPEG image. They also can't have any transparent areas. The standard JPEG image is a photograph with very little graphical illustration effects, as shown in Figure 2-3. Actually, JPEG files were originally designed for compressing photos, and the JPEG file format does a great job with that task. You can compress an image up to 100 times its original file size using JPEGs, a standard that GIFs just can't compete with. But JPEGs can't compress the clean, bold colors found in illustrations that contain text and still retain a small file size.

Figure 2-3:
JPEG images have 16 million colors and are great for creating full-color photographs.

Photo courtesy Outback Ranch Outfitters

You can easily conserve space when saving JPEG images:

- ✔ **Reduce the outside dimensions of the file.** By shrinking the physical dimensions of the file, you reduce the file size. This also has an effect on the quality of the image. Every time you increase or decrease the outside dimensions of a file, you're either compressing the image or expanding it into a new shape that affects its clarity and crispness.

- ✔ **Reduce the quality of the image.** When using JPEG images, you have control over the quality of the image. Most software programs give you the ability to choose from best quality to a low-quality image. Of course, the better the quality of the image, the larger the file size. Conversely, the lower the quality of the image, the smaller the file size.

Notice that these options are somewhat different from the options available to you for controlling the size of GIF images.

Illustration or photo, try PNG

The *PNG* (*P*ortable *N*etwork *G*raphic) format is no different than the GIF or JPEG formats; PNGs are bitmap images. PNG images use a very tight compression algorithm that enables you to keep the size of a PNG version of JPEG images (for photographs) and GIF images (for illustrations) near the same file size of JPEG and GIF images. They're completely free of all licensing fees, which are applicable for developers of the software that develop GIF images. PNG images can store up to 16 bits of grayscale or 48 bits of color information per pixel. PNGs also support transparencies and text within a picture, without increasing the file size, as happens with JPEG images.

The PNG image file format isn't supported in most 3.0 version and earlier browsers. Internet Explorer and Netscape Navigator 4.x versions both support PNG images. (Only the first 4.0 release of Internet Explorer for the Macintosh operating system does not.)

PNG images are available in two flavors:

- ✔ **PNG-8:** Roughly equivalent to GIFs in that it's best used with illustrations, line drawings, and other images that don't require lots of colors. PNG-8 enables you to reduce the size of illustration type image files to the size of GIF images. Use PNG-8 images for text, buttons, and other flat graphics.

- ✔ **PNG-24:** Roughly equivalent to JPEGs in that it's best used for high-color images, such as photographs. Essentially, PNG-24 is JPEG's competition. This version of PNG is great for working with full-color photographs and complex illustrations that require smooth shading, as shown in Figure 2-4. PNG-24 images have the same, if not better, image quality as JPEG images, but the PNG file size is invariably larger.

PNG-24 does have one primary advantage over JPEG images: PNG-24 supports *multi-level transparencies*. Using multi-level transparencies, you can have complex photographs blended into any variety of background colors on your SMIL pages.

Although PNG doesn't support animations, an up-and-coming file type based on PNG does. The *Multiple-image Network Graphic* (MNG, pronounced ming), currently in the development stage, enables you to create animated images and includes a wide variety of image manipulation capabilities.

Checking out the bandwidth

With the hurry-up-and-wait attitude of most of the multimedia sites you visit, bandwidth and download times are becoming one of the critical make-it or break-it factors on fully animated multimedia sites. Essentially, it comes down to one thing: The larger the files, the longer they take to load. Graphics and animation files can be very large indeed. Huge graphics that take forever to load are likely to chase your visitors away.

Fortunately, you have options for keeping your load times reasonable, as follows:

- **Select your file type carefully.** Choose GIFs for illustrations and JPEGs for photographs.

- **Select your file dimensions carefully.** Be aware that a large portion of your presentation's audience is using 640 x 480 screen resolution, and that an image that is 350 x 400 pixels practically fills the entire monitor.

- **Create thumbnails that link to larger versions of the images.** If you can't see all the detail in an image, create a small version that loads on your presentation automatically. Make it a link, however, so that visitors can see a larger, more detailed version if interested.

- **Select the quality of the image.** With JPEG and PNG images, you can control their compression ratio. The more highly compressed, the smaller the file size, but the worse the visual quality and clarity of the image.

Look at the images shown in Figure 2-5. The image was taken with a digital camera that stored the file originally in JPEG format. Each of the four images is the same size but has been saved in a different format using Paint Shop Pro 5 by Jasc Software. As you can see, in this case, the JPEG image is the best option because it provides the best resolution for the shortest download time.

Figure 2-4:
PNG images have 16 million colors and are great for creating either full-color photographic images or illustrations containing just a few colors.

Look at the top right and lower left of Figure 2-5. They're both JPEG images with the same dimensions, but with radically different file sizes and appearances. The compression ratio, selected when the image was saved, was changed from 15% (top right) to 75% (lower left). With JPEG images, the higher the compression, the smaller the file and the more grainy the resulting picture.

In the images shown in Figure 2-6, you see a simple illustration designed in Paint Shop Pro 5.0 by Jasc Software. The compression ratio has been increased for the JPEG images, which results in more colors but a fuzzier picture. In this example, the PNG image is smaller than the GIF. On other images, this may not be the case. The GIF image, shown in the top left of Figure 2-6 has a file size of 25K with 256 colors, but if you reduce the number of colors in this image to 16, you lose very little detail or crispness, and the file size reduces to 13K. This JPEG image, shown in the top right of Figure 2-6, is 700 x 300 pixels with a file size of 39K, but by shrinking this image's dimensions to 350 x 150, you can reduce the file's size to just 15K.

GIF — 206 x 270 pixels; file size — 45K;
256 colors; 72 pixels/inch resolution

JPEG — 206 x 270 pixels; file size — 14K
at 15% compression; 256 colors;
72 pixels/inch resolution

Figure 2-5:
The three
Web image
formats, GIF,
JPEG, and
PNG, create
different
varying
levels of
quality
images
when
used with
photographs.

JPEG — 206 x 270 pixels; file size — 4K
at 75% compression; 16 million colors;
72 pixels/inch resolution

PNG-24 — 206 x 270 pixels; file size — 88K;
16 million colors; 28 pixels/cm resolution

One of the primary reasons you need to look at a variety of image formats for the Web is that the download time of your page increases dramatically with the size of your image. The longer the download time, the less likely people will stick around to see your presentation. Table 2-1 gives you the download times for four different sizes of files. When you add the size of your SMIL document file into the equation, along with all the other files/images/animations that are used in your presentation, the size of your complete presentation increases dramatically. Check out Chapter 3 for some detailed download times and bandwidth usage scenarios.

GIF — 700 x 300 pixels; file size — 25K; 256 colors; 72 pixels/inch resolution

JPEG — 700 x 300 pixels; file size — 39K at 15% compression; 16 million colors; 72 pixels/inch resolution

Figure 2-6:
For illustrations, GIF beats JPEG, and often PNG files, for quality and file size.

JPEG — 700 x 300 pixels; file size — 17K at 75% compression; 16 million colors 72 pixels/inch resolution

PNG-8 — 700 x 300 pixels; file size — 17K; 256 colors; 118 pixels/cm resolution

Table 2-1	Image Download Times	
File Size (kilobytes)	*Speed (kilobits per second)*	*Time (seconds)*
10	14.4	5.6
	28.8	2.8
	33.6	2.4
	57.6	1.4
	64	1.2
	128	0.6
30	14.4	17
	28.8	8.5
	33.6	7.2
	57.6	4.2

(continued)

Table 2-1 (continued)

File Size (kilobytes)	Speed (kilobits per second)	Time (seconds)
	64	3.7
	128	1.8
60	14.4	34
	28.8	17
	33.6	14.5
	57.6	8.5
	64	7.4
	128	3.6
100	14.4	56
	28.8	28
	33.6	24
	57.6	14
	64	12
	128	6

Putting it all down on paper

Now that you're familiar with the various types of graphics available for use on SMIL documents, you're ready to put them down in SMIL code. Whether your image is a GIF, JPEG, or PNG file, you add it to the presentation using the same SMIL elements.

Not all SMIL elements support the same image types, although GIF and JPEG are supported by most of the available SMIL players.

Showing images with <img>

To add images to your SMIL document, you simply need to use the ⟨img⟩ (which stands for image) element. Using this element, you can insert any image, of any type, into your SMIL document. You can even use ⟨img⟩ to insert animation, although for ease of readability, you should really use the ⟨animation⟩ element, which I discuss in the following section, "Showing animations with <animation>." The format of the ⟨img⟩ element is shown in the following code:

```
<img src = "url"
     alt = "information for reader"
     author = "author name"
     longdesc = "long description"
     region = "RegionName"
     title = "title of image"
     type = "MIME type">
```

You're required to use just two attributes with the <img> element:

- ✔ The src attribute: Identifies the address of the image that is placed in the SMIL presentation. The SMIL player then replaces the <img> element with the actual image. If the image is supposed to be displayed in a region, then the image identified by the src attribute will be displayed in the region specified by the region attribute.

- ✔ The type attribute: Used by many programs to establish a definite identification for the file type placed on the presentation.

Here's an example of the <img> element referencing GIF, JPEG, and PNG images:

```
<img src = "http://www.mydomain.com/smillogo.gif"
     type = "image/gif">
<img src = "http://www.mydomain.com/smillogo.jpg"
     type = "image/jpeg">
<img src = "http://www.mydomain.com/smillogo.png"
     type = "image/png">
```

A variety of other attributes are available for use with the <img> element, which I detail in Table 2-5 (later in this chapter).

Showing animations with <animation>

Animations are simply GIFs that contain multiple images within them — at least as far as standard Internet workable file formats are concerned. The basis of animated GIFs is the inclusion of more than one image within a single GIF file. You create each frame, or image, individually. Then, using some type of GIF animation compilation program, such as Jasc Animation Shop, you place these frames into the proper sequential order and add timing controls. GIF animation software simply combines a series of images, adds timing controls within the image, and then saves the compiled images into a single file.

Take a look at the images shown in Figure 2-7. Each of these images is slightly different. In the first image, the fish isn't even visible. In the second image, the fish's head is just poking out of the water. In image three, the majority of the fish's body is out of the water. Other than a change in the fish's position and the bow of the fishing rod, the images are the same. These images have already been put together in an organized progression showing each image in rapid succession. When viewed as part of a SMIL presentation, the fish jumps out of the water, flops around a few times, and then returns to the water, only to leap from it again.

See `animfish.gif` in the `Examples/Chapter2` folder.

This example is actually quite simple. It has only one animated part and has only one shade of color. The more moving parts and colors the image has, the larger it becomes. You can create quite a few nice, small animations such as this one, which is only 27K. The more practice you have making animations, the better you're able to cut the proper corners to keep your images small yet interesting for more than one cycle of activity.

The code to add an animated GIF to your SMIL presentation is much the same as adding an image, but you use the `<animation>` element instead of `<img>`. You can actually use the `<img>` element if you want to, but for human-readability concerns, the `<animation>` element is much more clear and understandable. The only two attributes necessary for using the `<animation>` element are `src` and `type`.

```
<animation src="url"
    alt="information for reader"
    author = "author name"
    longdesc = "long description"
    region = "RegionName"
    title = "title of image"
    type = "application/gif">
```

The `<animation>` element inserts animated GIF images into your document, but it doesn't create the motion itself. All the animation effects must be stored in your image.

Text: All It's Cracked Up to Be

Adding text to your SMIL document is no more difficult than adding an image. To add text, use either the <text> or the <textarea> elements. These elements enable you to add text to your presentations in whatever shape set up by the region to which they have been applied. You do not need to specify the type attribute for either the <text> or the <textarea> element because the software gets that information from the file extension of the added information.

The most common attributes used for the <text> and <textarea> elements are src (required), id, region, title, and type.

```
<text src = "http://www.mydomain.com/smiltext.txt"
      id = "TextName"
      region = "RegionName"
      title = "TextTitle"
      type = "text/plain">
<textarea src = "http://www.mydomain.com/smil.html"
          type = "text/html">
```

Video Adds to the Look

What would multimedia be without videos? When you think of multimedia presentations, don't you automatically think of the combination of audio, still images, text, and video? You can include as many different types of video in your presentations as you have readers to view it. To make videos for your presentations, you can get software from a lot of places. You can often get video snippets from public domain sites on the Internet, some of which I list a little later.

Finding videos

If you're like me, you figure out how to do something when you're actually doing it yourself, not using something that someone else has already created. So, for all you do-it-yourselfers out there, you can find a variety of software packages on the Internet that enables you to create your own videos. Many of these packages are listed in Table 2-2.

Table 2-2	Video Creation Software	
Software Name	*Web Address*	*What You Find There*
pcworld.com	www.pcworld.com/fileworld/	Select Video, then Video Tools. A full range of software, some of which are listed here.
Microsoft Camcorder	http://support.microsoft.com/ support/Office/content/ Office97/camcorder.asp	Microsoft's video conversion software for standard camcorders. It can use input received through your computer's sound or video card.
Gotcha	www.gotchanow.com	Software to capture images from video.
Flash	www.macromedia.com/ software/flash	One of the best programs for creating your own animation and videos.
RealNetworks	www.realnetworks.com/ developers/index.html	A variety of video- and animation-creating software to fit practically any need.

Okay, so you've tried some of the software allowing you to make your own videos and just don't have the time or patience for it. That's okay! You can hire someone else to make your video, or you can download videos from some of the various Web sites that I list in Table 2-3. (Remember that material you get from other Web sites is often copyrighted, and you need permission to use it in any capitalistic endeavor.)

Using prefabricated videos devalues your presentation. It removes the sense of uniqueness from your presentation, and subjects your presentation to additional critiques from anyone who has viewed your selected video on another site.

Table 2-3	Video Web Sites
Site Name	*Web Address*
Star Wars	www.starwars.com
City Lights	www.foxhome.com/millennium/city.html
Inet Films	www.inetfilm.com
Twisted Humor	www.twistedhumor.com
Movie Gallery	www.moviegallery.com

Twisted Humor contains R-rated clips. The clips are clearly rated from G to R, so you can avoid the R ones if you want to.

Unless it's specifically labeled otherwise, assume that *everything* on the Internet belongs to someone else. If you want to download and use these video files for yourself, feel free. If you want to use them in some commercial endeavor, then you need to have the permission of the company, or individual, that created them.

Adding your <video>

Unlike the <text> and <img> elements, video elements are considered *continuous media* types. Continuous media types have an *intrinsic duration* (a preset time that they run). To add <video> elements to your presentation, use the following SMIL commands:

```
<video src = "http://www.mydomain.com/smillogo.qt"
       id = "VideoName"
       region = "RegionName"
       title = "VideoTitle"
       type = "video/quicktime">
<video src = "http://www.mydomain.com/smillogo.mpg"
       type = "video/mpeg">
```

You can find out more about the variety of attributes associated with the <video> media element in Table 2-5, a bit later in this chapter.

Audio — Rocking to the Beat

Audio files, an integral part of any good multimedia presentation, are becoming more and more popular on the Internet. Take care to ensure that your audio files are pleasant to the ear and that they can be turned off by the listener (there *may* be someone out there who doesn't share in your idea of pleasant). You can find some good audio clips on the Internet. Some of them are great for adding emphasis to your videos or text; others provide the perfect background mood for your presentation.

Be careful to look for audio files that have been placed in the public domain. You can't use audio clips for commercial gain, or even in a commercial endeavor, without the permission of the owner.

Finding audio clips

It's very difficult to find audio files that *aren't* copyrighted. Unless you have the proper hardware — and some musical talent — it's just as difficult to create them. The sites that I've listed in Table 2-4, although not all free, can give you some ideas. You can make audio files from copyrighted material for your own personal presentations. For example, you can record music from the Internet and play it for your grandparent's 50th wedding anniversary (a private affair), but you can't sell that music or play it as a dance DJ. That type of commercial use violates the music's copyright.

Table 2-4	Audio Clip Web Sites
Site Name	*Web Address*
mp3.com	www.mp3.com
avProductions	www.archervalerie.com
Audio Highway	www.audiohighway.com
Bern Clare	www.bernclare.com/sample.htm
MJ Cop	http://users.neca.com/mjcop/audio.htm
The Wanderer	www.wanderers.com/wanderer
Listen	www.listen.com

Playing your <audio>

After you've collected your audio files, you have to add them to your SMIL presentation document. You can easily add sound to your presentation by inserting the <audio> element in your document, as shown in the following code. The src attribute identifies the name and location of the audio file. The id attribute enables you to reference this audio file from other objects. The region attribute provides the name of the region (which I discuss in Chapter 7) that holds the audio file. The title attribute provides a human-understandable title for the audio file. And last, but not least, the type attribute provides the SMIL player with the MIME type — a scheme for identifying the variety of different types of files commonly shared over the Internet — designation for the type of audio file that's playing.

```
<audio src = "http://www.mydomain.com/smilsong.au"
       id = "AudioName"
       region = "RegionName"
       title = "AudioTitle"
       type = "audio/basic">
<audio src = "http://www.mydomain.com/smilspng.wav"
       type = "audio/wav">
<audio src = "http://www.mydomain.com/smilsong.mid"
       type = "audio/midi">
```

Referring to Your Media: <ref>

Sometimes, you may want to add information to your SMIL presentation, but you're not sure which media type you'll use. This can happen frequently, especially if you're using a scripting language to create your SMIL presentations. In this event, SMIL provides you with the <ref> element, which simply refers you to some other media object. When you're using the <ref> element, you provide more than the minimum required attributes. This way, you ensure that your SMIL player knows exactly what to do with the media type that you're adding to your presentation. (See Chapter 1 for a refresher on the various SMIL players.)

```
<ref src = "http://www.mydomain.com/songimg.gif"
     id = "NewImage"
     region = "RegionName"
     title = "Reference Image"
     type = "image/gif">
```

Media types

You can divide the available media types into two categories:

- ✔ **Media types with an intrinsic duration (video, audio):** These types have an intrinsic duration — a specific length of time — that they must play.

- ✔ **Media types without an intrinsic duration (text, image):** These types, also termed *discrete media,* have no further action after they're loaded.

When the SMIL player attempts to define the media type of the object inserted into a presentation, it doesn't rely on the name of the element adding the media object. Rather, the player relies on a combination of the file extension (of the linked file) and the contents of the type attribute.

Even though you have a variety of ways that you can identify media types, you, as the presentation creator, still need to use the appropriate element (`<animation>`, `<audio>`, `<img>`) name in your document. This increases the readability of the presentation.

Media attributes

Languages implementing the SMIL Media Object Module must define which attributes may be attached to media object elements. In all languages implementing the SMIL Media Object Module, media object elements can have the attributes shown in Table 2-5. (To find out more about the `begin`, `clipBegin`, and `clipEnd` attributes, see Chapter 8.)

Table 2-5		SMIL Media Attributes
Name	**Example(s)**	**Description**
abstract	abstract="link to llama packing courses"	Provides a brief description of the content contained within the element.
alt	alt="Llama Packing Instructions"	Provides alternative text information for SMIL players that don't support the particular media type used. This element is strongly recommended for use on all media objects, but the enforcement of this usage has been left in the hands of the SMIL authoring tools.
author	author="Heather"	The name of the person who created this particular media object.
begin	begin="ImgObject.click" begin="5s" begin= "song.begin+2s"	Provides the starting time for the playing of this object or another object by the clock in reference to another object or in response to a user interaction.
clipBegin	clipBegin= "smtpe=01:31:00"	Provides the specific time for beginning the playing of a portion, or clip, of a media object.
clipEnd	clipEnd="song=5s"	Provides the specific time for stopping the playing of a portion, or clip, of a media object.
copyright	copyright="Copyright 2005, H. Williamson"	Provides the copyright of the content that's identified by this media element.

Name	Example(s)	Description
longdesc	longdesc="http://mydomain.com/longdesc.html"	Provides a link to a file that contains a long description of the current media object. If the media object is used as a link to another destination, this attribute often contains the information about that destination.
port	port="1234-1235"	Provides the Real Time Transport Protocol/Real Time Streaming Protocol (RTP/RTSP) port identifier for the media object — if transferred with RTP and not RTSP.
readIndex	readIndex="1"	Provides the indexing value that controls the order in which screen readers read out the text provided in longdesc and alt attributes. The default is 0, with those objects having a positive readIndex value read first from lowest to highest value.
rtpformat	rtpformat="96,98"	Provides a list of media formats that are available to use with the RTP file transfer.
src	src="SMILaudio.au"	Provides the address/URL of the added media object.
stripRepeat	stripRepeat="true"	Removes the built-in repeat value from the media object, preventing animated GIFs from repeating indefinitely and songs from playing more than once.
title	title="SMIL Primary Audio"	Provides the title of the added object. This text is often used as a tool tip on visual SMIL players.
transport	transport ="RTP"	Provides a name for the transport protocol used to deliver the media object.
type	type="audio/basic"	Provides the MIME type (scheme for identifying the variety of different types of files commonly shared over the Internet) of the object that's being added to the SMIL presentation.
xml:lang	xml:lang="en-US"	Provides the natural language of the element.

Although some aren't always necessary or may never be used in your presentation, all these attributes are valid to use with the various media types identified within SMIL presentations.

Chapter 3

Building the Framework

*W*ould a carpenter start building a house without the architect's blueprints? Probably not. Likewise, you shouldn't start building your SMIL presentation without your own set of blueprints. Your planning is critical to creating a complete presentation; you can't skip, skirt, or shorten the planning phase. This is one area of the development stage where you may see shortcuts, but you must ignore them. You need to become an architect for your SMIL presentation, drawing blueprints before you write even one word of your SMIL presentation code.

To create any presentation, you must first plan every stage of the process so that you know what elements you're using, where those elements are going, how you're using the elements, and how the visitors navigate the SMIL presentation. Whew! That's some intensive planning. It's also the only way you can create a completely flawless presentation for any and all of your visitors. In this chapter, I show you how to do that.

Creating a Multimedia Playlist

To plan your presentation, you must first create a list of all the multimedia objects that you want to include. Jot down any information or media type — text, images, video, audio, and animation files — that you plan to use in the presentation. If you have questions about what type of media works best for each topic that you want to include, check out Chapter 2 where you can see what media works best for different types of information. You need to write it all down. If you're out at the local burger joint thinking about your presentation, write your ideas on a napkin — just don't wipe up ketchup with it afterwards!

Table 3-1 shows a simple multimedia playlist for a SMIL presentation created by a company that I'll call *Book Stackers Anonymous* that trains people to stack books properly. You need a list of the information that you want on your SMIL presentation, including what you're calling each type of media, and where that media is currently located.

Table 3-1		Multimedia Playlist	
Media Type	*Name*	*Location*	*Description*
Text	Intro	c:\smil\intro.txt	Book Stacker's Anonymous motto and introduction text.
Video	Stacking	c:\smil\stack.rm	This installation video shows you how to stack books.
Audio	Soundtrack	c:\smil\audio.au	The soundtrack providing background music for the video.
Img	Background	c:\smil\bkgrnd.gif	The background image of the introductory text screen.
Animation	Sliding Scale	c:\smil\slide.gif	Animated GIF of a sliding scale that tracks the progress of the window installation (25% done, 50% done, and so on).
Text	Lesson1	c:\smil\lsn1.txt	The text that accompanies the first step.
Text	Lesson2	c:\smil\lsn2.txt	The text that accompanies the second step.
Text	Lesson3	c:\smil\lsn3.txt	The text that accompanies the third step.
Text	Lesson4	c:\smil\lsn4.txt	The text that accompanies the fourth step.
Img	Logo	c:\smil\logo.gif	The logo for the company that recorded the video.
Text	Copyright	c:\smil\copyr.txt	The text used as a copyright for the presentation as a whole.

This is just a basic list of your presentation's parts. Before you create your SMIL presentation, you can, of course, expound upon it, shrink it down to size, or alter it at your whim. In this list, you may want to incorporate thumbnail versions of the images, animations, and text that you'll show on your presentation. By including the filenames of the media that you're going to use in your presentation, you already may know exactly what each of those pieces looks like, as well as how long the videos last. If you don't know for sure, watch and time the videos before you start putting your presentation together. (In Chapter 8, I emphasize that timing your presentation is one of the most important issues that you need to consider when creating SMIL presentations.) Hopefully, this list can help you organize your information so that you know what information needs to appear and exactly what it's going to look like when it gets there.

Laying the Foundation for Navigation

Just as you may have a dozen ways to drive to the movie theatre across town, you also have a variety of ways to implement a navigation system on your SMIL presentation. The easiest way that you can do this is to create a series of links from one object, such as text or an image, to the presentation part — whether video, audio, image, or text — that you want your viewers to see next. Or, you can use a mouse or keyboard event to load the other parts of the presentation. Using SMIL, you can even use the movement of your mouse or the press of a key to start the playing of a music video or any other type of media that you want to use — again, whether video, audio, image, or text.

One of the first items of your navigation system that you need to attend to is to decide what's loaded on your presentation screen from the first time it starts, what's going to appear later, and how it's going to appear in the first place. You then have to put all that information together with links to ensure that your presentation viewers can easily get from one part of your presentation to another.

Deciding what's going to appear on-screen first — typically the heading, some short intro text, and maybe a short introductory audio file — when your presentation opens is pretty easy. The rest of the loading and unloading of information gets more complicated. So, first things first: Decide how information is going to appear in your presentation. Essentially, you have the following two options:

  ✔ **Timeline:** Just as you schedule meetings for yourself during the day, you can schedule the playing of music or video in your SMIL presentation for your visitors. You can schedule events to start a certain length of time into the presentation, for example, or a certain interval after another event takes place. I cover all the various methods for adding and controlling timing in your SMIL presentations in Chapter 8, but you must keep in mind that time is an integral part of your presentations.

✔ **Visitor interaction:** If you want your visitors to control how and when music, video, and text appear, you need to set up a navigation system based on user interactions.

You have it easy if you're going to control your entire presentation with a timeline. To put it simply — *very* simply — just identify the timing of each media type, whether it's video, animation, or audio, and then time the other objects so that they work with each other. (I discuss this in more detail in Chapter 8.)

For example, suppose that you have a video that starts 20 seconds into the presentation and lasts for 120 seconds. And suppose that you also have two audio files, each lasting 10 seconds, which provide your lead-in and lead-out music to the video. Your presentation would preload both the audio files and the video files so that your SMIL player is ready to display the files immediately when your timeline is ready for them, as you can see in the timeline shown in Figure 3-1. Your opening audio file loads approximately 12 seconds into the presentation, allowing a 2-second overlap with the start of the video. The closing audio file loads approximately 138 seconds into the timeline of the presentation, starting about 2 seconds before the close of the video.

Figure 3-1:
A simple timeline helps you track all the information that's playing in your presentation.

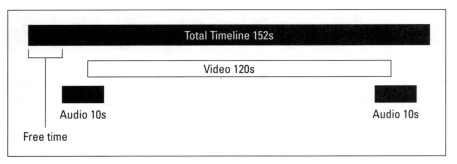

If you want an interactive interface that allows visitors to load information into the presentation based on their own selections, you need to define a complete navigation system with buttons or links to click. Here are some of the components that you can include in this system:

✔ **A series of linked images or text.** Links, shown in Figure 3-2, (see Part 4 for more information about links) are the most obvious means of loading media selections into your SMIL player.

✔ **An image map.** You can use an image map, shown in Figure 3-3, to link to specific portions of your presentation, based on where the presentation visitor clicks the mouse — the areas of the image or video.

✔ **A drop-down list.** Drop-down lists, shown in Figure 3-4, typically need scripts to work, but they give you an easy way to select the next page of text in a story or the specific segments of a video that you want to play. The possibilities are endless, and they don't take up much room on your SMIL presentation screen either. But scripts don't always work across all your potential SMIL players.

After you've determined how you're going to implement your navigational scheme, you must ensure that your design incorporates it smoothly.

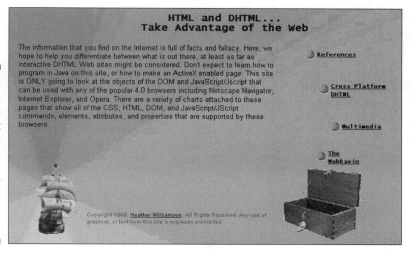

Figure 3-2:
A selection
of text links
on the right
side of this
screen
provides
links to new
information
in the
presentation.

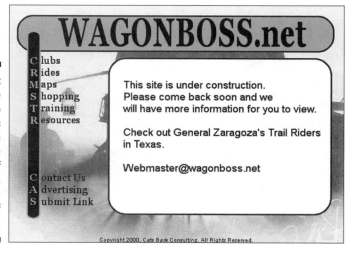

Figure 3-3:
An image
map
provides
links to each
of the
categories of
information
listed on the
left side of
this screen.

Figure 3-4:
Drop-down
lists provide
an easy way
to select the
next page of
text in a
story or the
specific
segments of
a video.

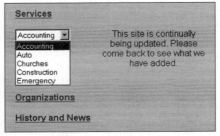

Planning the Layout

If you've definitively identified all the images, text, video, and audio files that
are to appear on your presentation, you're ready to start laying them out on-
screen. The easiest way to plan the actual layout of your screen is the old-
fashioned way — with graph paper and a pencil, as shown in Figure 3-5.

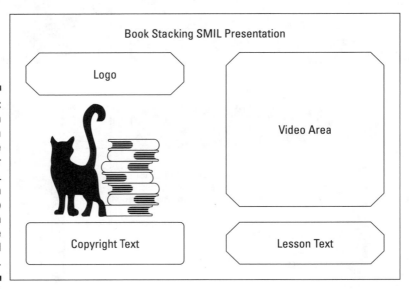

Figure 3-5:
This sketch
shows a
sample
layout for
the SMIL
presentation
(refer to
Table 3-1, in
which I've
identified
the parts).

Graphing your design

After laying out the design of your presentation, you need to fit everything into a grid. The grid used by SMIL elements is in pixels, so you need to convert your grid to pixels when planning your layout. For example, the design shown in Figure 3-5 is laid out on an 80 x 45 grid. By figuring that each block of the grid is a 5 x 5 block of pixels, you can easily create a presentation that's 400 pixels wide x 225 pixels high. This fits on most screens — whether a 640 x 480 resolution monitor or a Web TV screen.

By keeping everything measured in pixels, you need to identify the size of all your media objects within the scope of the pixel dimensions that they're going to require, as shown in Table 3-2.

Table 3-2	Multimedia Object Dimensions		
Media Type	*Name*	*Dimensions*	*Top-Left Corner*
Text	Intro	155w x 40h	0, 0
Video	Stacking	230w x 150h	175, 0
Audio	Soundtrack	n/a	n/a
Img	Background	400 x 25	0, 0
Text	Lessons	230w x 60h	175, 150
Img	Logo	140w x 90h	10, 55
Text	Copyright	140w x 50h	15, 145

After you list the width and height of each object on your presentation, you can easily create the code for the creation of the layout regions for your objects. (See Chapter 6 for more information about the <layout> elements.)

Setting up for interactive images

Start thinking about the various events, such as the clicking of a mouse or the pressing of a key on a keyboard, that can occur within your pages after you've completed the basic design. Those viewing your page use these events to interact with it. The following events are available for all types of media objects enclosed in either an <a> or an <area> element (see Chapter 12 for more about these elements):

- ✔ **onBlur:** Performs an action or runs a script when a visitor moves a mouse pointer over it or unselects it with the Tab key.

- ✔ **onClick:** Performs an action or runs a script whenever a visitor clicks the object. The entire clicking process of the mouse has to be completed within this object in order for this event to fire. In other words, you must both press and release your mouse over this media element for your mouse to be considered clicked by the program.

- ✔ **onDoubleClick:** Performs an action or runs a script whenever a visitor double-clicks the object.

- ✔ **onFocus:** Performs an action or runs a script whenever the object receives the focus of the mouse pointer or the document cursor, such as when a visitor selects it using the keyboard or clicks it with the mouse.

- ✔ **onKeyDown:** Performs an action or runs a script whenever the object has a key pressed within it. This event becomes active when the key is pressed down but not necessarily released. This works quite well for entry fields in documents that combine HTML and SMIL.

- ✔ **onKeyPress:** Performs an action or runs a script whenever the object has a key pressed within it. This event becomes active when the key is pressed and released.

- ✔ **onKeyUp:** Performs an action or runs a script whenever the object has a key released within it. Now, I've never been able to get a key to release in a field without first pressing it there, but if you press a key and hold onto it for a while, this event doesn't actually do anything until you release that key.

- ✔ **onMouseDown:** Performs an action or runs a script whenever a visitor presses the mouse pointer over an object, whether it's been released there or not. This event becomes active before the mouse button is released.

- ✔ **onMouseMove:** Performs an action or runs a script whenever the mouse pointer is moved within an object. This event becomes active when the mouse pointer is moved, not necessarily clicked.

- ✔ **onMouseOut:** Performs an action or runs a script whenever the mouse pointer is moved out from over an object.

- ✔ **onMouseOver:** Performs an action or runs a script whenever a visitor moves the mouse pointer over the linked object.

- ✔ **onMouseUp:** Performs an action or runs a script whenever a visitor releases the mouse button with the pointer over an object. This event becomes active when the mouse button is released, whether or not it was originally pressed over that object.

Sometimes, your visitors change their minds mid-click. I'm sure you've done it: You press your mouse over one button, but before releasing it, change your mind and slide your pointer over another object and release your mouse there. If you use the onMouseUp event rather than the onMouseDown event, you give your visitors a chance to be sure that this is the button they want to click. By the way, if you do this switcho-chango on an element that's monitored by the onClick event, the onClick event won't fire because the mouse wasn't both pressed and released over that one element.

When added to the links encompassing your objects, these events allow your entire SMIL document to appear interactive. You can slide your mouse pointer over an image and have text appear in one field, while sliding your mouse pointer over another image causes it to be replaced with a small video file. In Chapter 14, I spend more time on using these events within actual SMIL code.

Limiting File Size (Or the Band Can't Play On)

As you design your SMIL presentation, you need to keep in mind that there are limits to how much information can be transferred through your Internet connection using today's hardware. You know how long it takes to load a fancy graphics-filled interactive Web site. You don't really want to force your presentation visitors to wait through the download of megabytes after megabytes of information, do you?

Videos and images take up a lot of space. Animations generally don't take up as much space as videos, but it's more than the space used by images. When you add those images, videos, and animations to your SMIL and HTML code, be aware that all that great graphical content dramatically increases the time it takes a visitor to download your presentation, as well as have it play smoothly on all types of systems.

SMIL code

Your SMIL code doesn't take up any more space than a similar HTML document — so that's *one* relief. Because SMIL is all text, you're able to easily keep the size of your presentation file within about 7K. (By the way, 7K is the generally agreed upon optimum for HTML.) A 28.8K Internet connection can download a file this size (7K) within 3 seconds. If your visitors can't wait that long, someone should remind them of the old adage that claims patience is a virtue. When you start adding image files to your presentation, your nice, small 3-second SMIL file download increases by the size of each of the images. As you can imagine, the size of the download of the entire presentation starts growing at a rapid pace.

Multimedia bandwidth

Bandwidth is a term that describes how much time it takes to get the information that you want. Think of the Internet as the bell on a funnel and your modem connection as the hole that all the information has to get through. The faster the modem, the bigger the hole and the more information you get in less time. For example, a high bandwidth connection allows you to view more audio and video faster, and with fewer interruptions, than a lower bandwidth Internet connection.

Your modem, if you're using one, controls how much bandwidth you can get. For instance, if you're using a 28.8K modem, your typical bandwidth is about 26.4K. For a 56K modem, your typical bandwidth is approximately 48K. Images, audio, video, and animations can eat you alive when it comes to bandwidth. You don't have a choice, however, but to use these media types when creating a complete multimedia presentation. You can see how fast their individual file sizes add up in Table 3-3.

Table 3-3	Figuring Download Time for Your Presentation	
Object	*Size (kilobytes)*	*Time, in seconds (28.8K connection)*
SMIL document	7	2.5
Images	30	11
Animations	15	5.5
Video	56	20
Audio	56	20
Total	**164**	**59**

The numbers shown in Table 3-3 are probably below-average estimates for the size of video and audio files. They do, however, give you some idea of how fast your presentation size can grow. I recommend keeping your images and audio files as small as possible to ensure that your visitors have to spend less time downloading the information. Smaller files are also easier and faster to play on your visitors' computers. Generally, when it comes to the Internet — smaller is better.

Part II
Putting SMIL to Work

The 5th Wave   By Rich Tennant

YOU KIDDING!! TRUE INTERACTIVE CONTENT?! ME CAN'T WAIT, PULL LEVER, OPEN SCREEN!

In this part . . .

Here you can take your first plunge into actually creating your own SMIL documents. I first discuss the SMIL elements that you use to start laying out your document. Next, I show you how to control the location of the objects, how to ensure that your multimedia information is visible when you want it to be, and how to allow access only to specific computer configurations so that you can optimize the way the presentation looks for everyone.

Chapter 4

Adding a Little SMIL to Your Web Site

Smile! You're now jumping into the real meat of SMIL. In Chapter 2, I introduce you to the types of elements used within SMIL presentations and in Chapter 3, I discuss the fun challenges of designing and laying out multimedia documents. Now, you're going to emulate the professionals and put text, animation, and sound to work for you in your projects.

Just like every other type of document on the Internet, you need a place to start formatting it. SMIL documents are identified by the `.smi` extension and the opening `<smil>` tag. All in all, the structure of a SMIL document is very similar to the structure of an HTML document. Throughout this chapter, I discuss how the underlying structure of a SMIL document is put together, showing you some of the similarities between SMIL and HTML along the way.

Getting Started with a <smil>

Pssst! Ever use HTML? Remember how every HTML page begins and ends with an `<html>` element? SMIL works the same way. Every SMIL presentation has to start and end with the `<smil>` and `</smil>` elements, as shown in the following lines of code. Without these elements, the software reading the presentation doesn't know whether to treat the commands as HTML, SMIL, or Klingon. This entire section of the document would become unintelligible to the computer.

```
<smil>
</smil>
```

Element primer

To keep your documents intelligible to the computer, you must understand what each part of the language you're using is doing. You have a series of *elements* within SMIL, such as the `<smil>`, `<head>`, and `<body>` elements, which I discuss in this chapter. Each of these elements defines a portion of your document. If you're familiar with HTML, you already know the purpose each of the following elements serves (because they serve the exact same purpose in SMIL as they do in HTML):

- `<smil>`: This element provides a structure for the entire SMIL document and identifies the contents as SMIL information.

- `<head>`: This element creates a structure that holds information about the SMIL presentation, including the information for formatting regions to contain the media elements that you're using in the presentation.

- `<body>`: This element holds the references to all the media and timing elements that you're using within the presentation.

All of these elements have a required *opening element* and a required *closing element* (or *end tag*). The opening element is simply the name of the element enclosed within angle brackets, while the closing element has an additional forward slash (/) that precedes the name within the angle brackets:

- Opening elements: `<smil>`, `<head>`, `<body>`
- Closing elements: `</smil>`, `</head>`, `</body>`

Attribute primer

Each element has a series of *attributes* associated with it. An attribute provides additional information about the element. For example, an attribute of your head is hair. Each attribute has a *value* that defines the existing state of the attribute. For example, the value of the hair attribute of your head can be brunette or blond. To place this in the constructs of your SMIL document, an attribute of your `<head>` element is `title`, which may have the possible value of *Fred's Dance Video*.

Several attributes are available to use with the `<smil>` element:

- `id`
- `class`
- `xml:lang`

    ✔ profile

    ✔ title

    ✔ xmlns

Each of these attributes has values that provide additional information about the entire SMIL presentation. For example, the id attribute has a value that identifies the name of the element. In the SMIL document that follows, the id attribute of the <smil> element is "fredvideo". When you're adding values to your attributes, you need to include the values within quotation marks. The quotation marks set the values apart from the rest of the element, and, in addition, they're required by the SMIL specification as an official part of the SMIL statement's syntax.

The six attributes that you use with the <smil> element each have their own purpose in defining the entire SMIL presentation. For an example, check out the sample code that follows. In it, the values of each of the attributes provide some information about the document (see Table 4-1 for an explanation of each attribute from the code and what it does):

    ✔ The value of the id attribute is "fredvideo", identifying a name for the SMIL document itself.

    ✔ The value of the class attribute is "smil-media", providing another way of identifying the type of media being used and allowing a group classification for the presentation.

    ✔ The value of the xml:lang attribute is "en-US", referencing the particular version of English spoken in the United States.

    ✔ The title of the SMIL presentation is "Fred's Video Debut", which provides your visitors and the SMIL-playing software a human-readable and understandable name for the presentation.

    ✔ The last two attributes, xmlns:smil and xmlns:fred, reference two different documents that provide descriptions for the type of elements and attributes that you can use in this particular SMIL presentation.

```
<smil id="fredvideo"
      class="smil-media"
      xml:lang="en-US"
      title="Fred's Video Debut"
      xmlns:smil="http://www.w3.org/SMIL-Boston.dtd"
      xmlns:fred="http://www.fredvideo.com/Fred-Video.dtd">
</smil>
```

Table 4-1		\<smil\>, \<head\>, and \<body\> attributes	
Attribute	*Example*	*Element*	*What It Does*
id	id="fredvideo"	\<smil\>, \<head\>, \<body\>	Provides a uniquely identifiable name for the SMIL content. It's imperative to use the id attribute when you include SMIL content within another document and plan on using scripting languages to manipulate it dynamically from within SMIL players (see Chapter 1).
class	class="smil-media"	\<smil\>, \<head\>, \<body\>	Provides a way of identifying SMIL content as part of a group. For example, you can have three \<smil\> sections in a single HTML document, each having the class smil-media attribute. (The id attribute identifies individual smil-media class elements.)
xml:lang	xml:lang="en"	\<smil\>, \<head\>, \<body\>	An XML-based attribute that identifies the language used in an element. A variety of language codes are available, such as "en" for English, with variations such as "en-GB" for Great Britain's English (or the King's English) and "en-US" for the American version.
profile	profile="http://www.w3.org/TR/SMIL-Boston"	\<head\>	Identifies the current set of definitions that identifies the Document Type Definition (DTD) to which this SMIL document is matched. DTDs provide a detailed list of the elements and attributes that you can use in a specific type of document. The SMIL DTD provides definitions of all the elements and attributes that you can use within SMIL documents. The DTD identified in this statement may or may not be the same as one of your xmlns: statements located in the \<smil\> element. See Appendix B for more about the SMIL DTDs.

Attribute	Example	Element	What It Does
title	title="Fred's Video Debut"	\<smil\>, \<head\>, \<body\>	Provides additional information about the \<smil\> object providing a page title for the software's title bar. It may be used by the SMIL player or Web browser or ignored entirely. You can place long strings of text here or a simple identifier, such as "Fred's movie". The use of this attribute almost entirely depends on the SMIL player viewing the document.
xmlns	xmlns:smil="http://www. w3.org/SMIL-Boston.dtd"	\<smil\>	Identifies the XML Namespace (a means of identifying the origin of all the elements in a document) used by SMIL. In other words, an XML Namespace provides the address of the document that specifies the individual elements used within the SMIL document. You can use this attribute as many times in the document as you have element origins.

Go to the World Wide Web Consortium site at `www.w3.org/TR/REC-xml-names` for more information on XML Namespaces and XML elements and attributes.

Although you may use each of the attributes in Table 4-1 with the ⟨smil⟩ element, you're not required to use any of them.

The easiest place to start working on your first SMIL document is in a simple text editor. Open a text editor, such as Windows Notepad, and type in the sample code given previously. This code shows all the available attributes applied to the ⟨smil⟩ element.

You should never apply an attribute to a closing element. They aren't allowed and cause SMIL players to create lots of nasty errors that prohibit playing your presentation.

Two other elements are required within the root ⟨smil⟩ element. I discuss these elements, the ⟨head⟩ and the ⟨body⟩, in the following sections.

Using Your <head>

The <head> element probably looks familiar if you've ever done any HTML development. In SMIL presentations, the <head> element serves a similar function as the <head> element in an HTML document. The <head> element provides a place for storing additional information about the information in the document by using <meta> and <metadata> elements. It also controls the physical location of the presentation's content using the <switch> and <layout> elements.

The elements that exist within another element are called *child elements*. If you think of the format of your SMIL document code as a family tree, you see the <head> element underneath the <smil> element. This is the position of a child on a standard family tree. The verbiage has crossed over to include the same relationship in SMIL documents. In other words, the <head> element is a child of the <smil> element, and the <smil> element is the parent of the <head> element.

The <head> element has children of its own, including the <meta>, <metadata>, <switch>, and <layout> elements. Other elements can reside within the <head> element, such as <transform>, which I discuss in other chapters. These four, <meta>, <metadata>, <switch>, and <layout>, are the primary elements used in almost all SMIL presentations. In Figure 4-1, you can see how all these elements are stacked together.

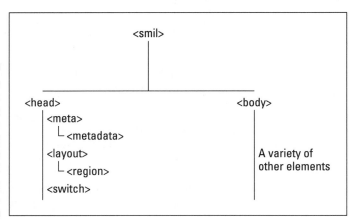

Figure 4-1:
Each document creates a tree of elements nested within each other.

- ✔ <meta>: Identifies information about the SMIL presentation.
- ✔ <metadata>: Identifies additional information about the information used to describe the presentation.

> ✓ `<switch>`: Provides a way to select different layout and media objects for use with different computer systems.
>
> ✓ `<layout>`: Provides a structure for laying out the different areas of your SMIL presentation that are filled with media.

You can't use the `<head>` for controlling the timing of the presentation, but you can use the `<switch>` and `<layout>` elements to control the location of the visible content contained within the page. For more information on the `<switch>` and `<layout>` elements, see Chapters 5 and 6, respectively.

In addition to using child elements, the `<head>` supports many of the same attributes as the `<smil>` element. These shared attributes are: `id`, `class`, `xml:lang`, and `title`. The `<head>` element has one additional attribute that isn't used with the `<smil>` element: the `profile` attribute. You can read all about the attributes that the `<head>` element supports in Table 4-1.

<head> attributes

You can apply each of these attributes (`id`, `class`, `xml:lang`, `profile`, and `title`) to the `<head>` element, but you aren't required to add any for the document to function properly. The following example code, also shown in Figure 4-2, creates the `<head>` element of the basic SMIL document that you're creating:

```
<head id="Fred-Head"
      class="smil-head"
      xml:lang="en"
      title="Fred's Video-Meta Data"
      profile="http://www.w3.org/SMIL-Boston.dtd">
</head>
```

<head> child elements

The `<head>` element has four primary children. I discuss the `<switch>` and `<layout>` elements in Chapters 5 and 6. The primary child elements that I focus on right now are the `<meta>` and `<metadata>` elements.

The <meta> element

The SMIL `<meta>` element works like the `<meta>` element in an HTML document and follows the same structure as `<meta>` elements in XML and HTML documents. It provides *metadata*, or additional information about the information in the SMIL presentation. You can store information about the presentation's author, description, copyright, keywords, contact information, and your shoe size and birth date, if you feel they're important. You can have as many `<meta>` elements in the `<head>` of your document as you want, but you can't nest them. In other words, `<meta>` elements can't have any child elements.

```
ch0503.smi - Notepad                                              _ □ ×
File  Edit  Search  Help
<smil id="fredvideo"
      class="smil-media"
      xml:lang="en-US"
      title="Fred's Video Debut"
      xmlns:smil="http://www.w3.org/SMIL-Boston.dtd"
      xmlns:Fred="http://www.fredvideo.com/Fred-Video.dtd">


  <head id="Fred-Head"
        class="smil-head"
        xml:lang="en"
        title="Freds Video-Meta Data"
        profile="http://www.w3.org/SMIL-Boston.dtd">


  </head>

</smil>
```

Figure 4-2:
The optional
`<head>`
element
attributes
provide
auxiliary
information
about the
source of
the SMIL
document's
content.

Generally, the most important information to record for each presentation includes the author, copyright, description, and keywords. The importance may not necessarily fall in that order for all presentation projects.

✔ **Description:** If you're placing your SMIL presentation on the Internet, the description (and keywords) information is likely your primary concern. Search engines and other services use this information to help people find your presentation. Typically, you want your description to be a one-sentence statement identifying what your presentation is about. For instance, you can use the following description for Fred's Video: "Fred's debut video extravaganza teaches you the intricate details of stacking books for Books Anonymous Inc."

✔ **Keywords:** Keyword (and description) information is your primary concern when placing a presentation on the Internet. Without keywords, search engines can't help folks find your site!

✔ **Copyright:** The copyright information helps secure your presentation's content. Some folks out there want a free lunch. And, although they're still able to use your material, you have something that says they're breaking the law. Changes in copyright law concerning Internet content require the publication of a copyright statement for the protection of your content.

✔ **Author:** On intranets, or internal networks, the author may be the most important piece of information to store with the document. Everyone in the organization is then able to find the person responsible for the great — or not so great — work.

Think about Fred's Video for a moment. If you were to write down the meta information on his video, your list may look like the following:

Title="Fred's Video"

Author="Fred"

Publisher="Dancers Anonymous Inc."

Copyright="Copyright © 2000, Dancers Anonymous Inc and Fred. All rights reserved."

Description="Fred's debut video extravaganza teaches you the intricate details of dancing a variety of traditional Latin dances."

Keywords="dance video, video cartoons, cartoon"

The `<meta>` element itself has three possible attributes (`name`, `http-equiv`, and `content`), each of which is used to provide a specific type of information:

✔ `content`: Provides the detailed information that's associated with either a `name` or `http-equiv` attribute. Typically, if it's associated with a `name` attribute, it's descriptive text; if it's associated with an `http-equiv` attribute, it's an instruction of some type for the SMIL player.

✔ `name`: Marks the identifier for the information provided in the `content` attribute. It provides a name for the type of information that's given.

✔ `http-equiv`: Provides a marker for information that the SMIL player should process.

For the majority of SMIL players, the `name` and `http-equiv` attributes are completely interchangeable. Some samples of `<meta>` elements that can be applied to your SMIL presentation are shown in the following code sample. I describe each of these attributes further in Table 4-2.

```
<meta name="Author"
      content="Heather Williamson">
<meta name="Keywords"
      content="dance video, video cartoons, cartoon">
<meta name="Description"
      content="Fred's dance video, a bucket of laughs!">
<meta name="Expires"
      content="Thu.1 Jan 2010 12:00:00">
<!-- This Refresh tag loads the second version of this
     video 60 seconds after this page loads.-->
<meta http-equiv="Refresh"
      content="60,URL: http://fredvideo.com/FredTake2.smi">
<!-- This Robots meta tag allows search engines to index
     this page, and follow any links it contains.-->
<meta http-equiv="Robots"
      content="index,follow">
```

Table 4-2	name, http-equiv, and content attributes
Attribute	**Description**
name="author"; content= "Heather Williamson"	Provides the name of the document's author — in this case, Heather Williamson.
name="Expires"; content= "Thu.1 Jan 2010 12:00:00"	Provides information for the SMIL player describing when the document expires. In this case, on Thursday the first of January 2010 at noon.
http-equiv="refresh"; content= "60,URL:http://fredvideo.com/ FredTake2.smi"	Provides instructions for the SMIL player; indicates that this document should be automatically replaced in 60 seconds with the contents of the FredTake2.smi presentation.
http-equiv="Robots" content= "index,follow"	Provides instructions for search engines to index this document and to follow all the links contained within the document.

In Figure 4-3, you can see the `<meta>` element information placed within the `<head>` element between its opening and closing tags.

The *<metadata>* element

You can also include `<metadata>` elements in your presentation that provide meta information about the particular pieces of content in the presentation. Just as you use the `<meta>` element to identify information about the overall presentation, you use the `<metadata>` element to identify information about the individual parts of the presentation. Take Fred's dancing video for an

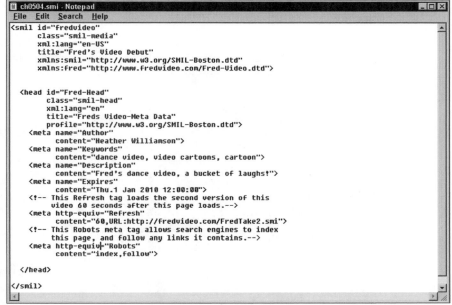

Figure 4-3:
The
`<meta>`
elements
provide
information
for search
engines and
other
document
readers.

example. The meta information in this video includes the video title, author, copyright, description, and keywords for the entire video. It doesn't, however, account for the *individual parts* of the video. If you wanted to define additional information about a particular segment of Fred's Video, then you need to use `<metadata>` elements to do so. Sample metadata regarding a particular segment of Fred's Video may include:

Title="Fred's Training Video - Take 1"

Author="Heather Williamson"

Description="Discover the use of Latin dancing in the dating world."

Keywords="dancing, latin, video, rhumba"

The `<metadata>` elements require the use of *XML Namespaces,* a means of identifying the origin of all the elements in a document, to properly identify each reference and to work in a fashion similar to how `<meta>` tags work. Because of the use of XML Namespaces, `<metadata>` elements can have more than the standard `name`, `http-equiv`, and `content` attributes. These elements can use any of the attribute identifiers that have been made available through the XML Namespace references. `<metadata>` elements, unlike `<meta>` elements, can have child elements. Child elements are just not supported with the `<meta>` element. I discuss XML Namespaces in Appendix C.

A sample of the complexity of a `<metadata>` element is shown in the following code:

```
<metadata id="meta-rdf">
<!-- This code identifies the sources of the XML Namespace
          references used throughout the
    meta data -->
  <rdf:RDF
    xmlns:rdf = "http://www.w3.org/22-rdf-syntax-ns#"
    xmlns:dc = "http://purl.org/metadata/dublin_core#"
    xmlns:smilmetadata = "http://www.w3.org/AudioVideo/
          smil-ns#" >

<!-- Metadata about the SMIL presentation -
      These elements and attributes have been defined
      in the rdf, dc, and smilmetadata documents referenced
      in the above rdf:RDF declaraction -->
  <rdf:Description
        about="http://www.fredvideo.com/FredsFirst.smi"
        dc:Title="Fred's First Video"
        dc:Description="Fred's first attempt at creating
                        multimedia dancing cartoons"
        dc:Publisher="Heather Williamson"
        dc:Date="2005-10-12"
        dc:Rights="Copyright 2005 Heather Williamson"
        dc:Format="text/smil" >
  </rdf:Description>

<!-- Metadata about the video -->
  <rdf:Description
    about="http://www.fredvideo.com/dancer.mpg"
    dc:Title="RDF part one"
    dc:Creator="Fred Funny"
    dc:Subject="Dancing Boogy Men"
    dc:Description="Take a dance on the wild side with
                    these dancing fiends."
    dc:Format="video/mpg"
    dc:Language="en"
    dc:Date="2005-10-12"
    smilmetadata:Duration="60 secs">
  </rdf:Description>
</metadata>
```

That's a long chunk of code that may look like some sort of twisted horror movie if you haven't read the section in Appendix C about XML Namespaces. It's best to tackle it bit by bit. The first line in the code is

```
<metadata id="meta-rdf">
```

This line is the opening tag for all the following information. It has an `id` attribute, giving it a name that can be referenced. Scripts, or other computer programs, can use this name to identify specific `<metadata>` contents within a wide variety of documents.

The next section of the code identifies the sources of the XML Namespace references. The `rdf:RDF` statement identifies a *Resource Description Framework* (RDF). The RDF is a structure that enables organizations or individuals to encode, exchange, and reuse metadata with other organizations and individuals all over the world.

```
<!-- This code identifies the sources of the XML Namespace
          references used throughout the
    meta data -->
  <rdf:RDF
    xmlns:rdf = "http://www.w3.org/22-rdf-syntax-ns#"
    xmlns:dc = "http://purl.org/metadata/dublin_core#"
    xmlns:smilmetadata = "http://www.w3.org/AudioVideo/
          smil-ns#" >
```

Each of the individual `xmlns:` statements reference a particular document that identifies the elements and attributes supported in a particular language. For example, the `xmlns:rdf` statement references the control document for all Resource Description Framework statements, just as the `xmlns:smilmetadata` statement references the control document that identifies all the valid elements and attributes that are available for use in SMIL documents.

The next section of code provides a description of the SMIL presentation. This code uses the `description` element, identified in the `xmlns:rdf` control document, as well as the `description` element's `about` attribute. The other attributes originate from the *Dublin Core document* identified with the `xmlns:dc` statement. The Dublin Core is a document that describes a selection of descriptive elements that are used to format and describe basic text. This document is based on XML, which I discuss in Appendix C. Look at the element's preface to determine the origins of each element and attribute. In other words, because `rdf:Description` starts with the `rdf:` identifier, I know that it's using the `Description` element from the `xmlns:rdf` identified document.

You can find out more information about the Dublin Core set of formatting and descriptive elements at `www.w3.org`.

```
<rdf:Description
      about="http://www.fredvideo.com/FredsFirst.smi"
      dc:Title="Fred's First Video"
      dc:Description="Fred's first attempt at
      creating multimedia dancing cartoons"
      dc:Publisher="Heather Williamson"
      dc:Date="2005-10-12"
      dc:Rights="Copyright 2005, Heather Williamson"
      dc:Format="text/smil" >
  </rdf:Description>
```

The final section of the metadata code mimics the Description code segment above but is used to identify just the video used with the presentation and does not take into consideration any of the text or audio associated with the video.

Although the ⟨metadata⟩ element isn't required to properly display SMIL documents or to make SMIL documents accessible by virtually anyone, it does make the sharing of information between all the multimedia- and XML-focused organizations on the Internet easier. Metadata becomes increasingly important as software improves and uses this information to provide more personalized services for each interaction you have with your computer and the software that runs on it.

Go to the World Wide Web Consortium site located at www.w3.org/TR/smil-boston for more information about the SMIL 2.0 ⟨metadata⟩ element and its attributes.

Sweating yet? You'll be happy to know that after you include the ⟨meta⟩ and ⟨metadata⟩ content in your SMIL presentation, you have a complete ⟨head⟩ element. After that, it's time to start on the ⟨body⟩ of your document.

Getting the ⟨body⟩ Right

The final part of your SMIL presentation's basic document structure is the ⟨body⟩. The ⟨body⟩ contains all the images, text, multimedia, audio instructions, and the timing controls that affect when the presentation displays the information. As with the ⟨head⟩ and ⟨smil⟩ elements, the ⟨body⟩ element supports a few attributes: id, class, title, and xml:lang. Refer to Table 4-1 for the details on these individual attributes.

⟨body⟩ attributes

The attributes of the ⟨body⟩ element (id, class, title, and xml:lang) are optional. Using them, however, provides additional information to the software viewing the presentation. This extra information helps ensure that your information is correctly displayed on the many combinations of operating systems, languages, and SMIL-playing software available. Without these attributes, software may display your information poorly. If you're including JavaScript or other programming code on your document, these attributes identify the content of your SMIL presentation within a single document that includes multiple presentations.

The following sample code, also shown in Figure 4-4, shows the inclusion of the `<body>` attributes (see Table 4-1) within the SMIL presentation that I've discussed throughout this chapter.

```
<body id="Fred-Body"
      class="smil-body"
      xml:lang="en-GB"
      title="Freds Video-The Dancing Cartoon Men">
</body>
```

Figure 4-4:
The `<body>` element provides a structure for including all other timing and media elements within your presentation.

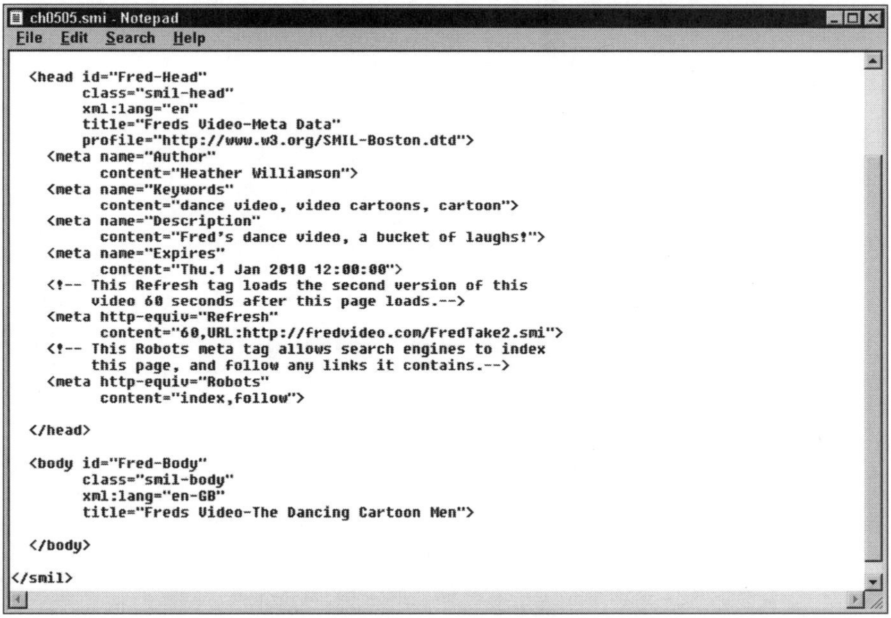

```
ch0505.smi - Notepad
File  Edit  Search  Help

<head id="Fred-Head"
      class="smil-head"
      xml:lang="en"
      title="Freds Video-Meta Data"
      profile="http://www.w3.org/SMIL-Boston.dtd">
  <meta name="Author"
        content="Heather Williamson">
  <meta name="Keywords"
        content="dance video, video cartoons, cartoon">
  <meta name="Description"
        content="Fred's dance video, a bucket of laughs!">
  <meta name="Expires"
        content="Thu.1 Jan 2010 12:00:00">
  <!-- This Refresh tag loads the second version of this
       video 60 seconds after this page loads.-->
  <meta http-equiv="Refresh"
        content="60,URL:http://fredvideo.com/FredTake2.smi">
  <!-- This Robots meta tag allows search engines to index
       this page, and follow any links it contains.-->
  <meta http-equiv="Robots"
        content="index,follow">

</head>

<body id="Fred-Body"
      class="smil-body"
      xml:lang="en-GB"
      title="Freds Video-The Dancing Cartoon Men">

</body>

</smil>
```

<body> child elements

In the `<body>`, you find all the content, timing controls, link controls, animation effects, and transitions that are taking place within your presentation. To control each of these aspects of your content, the `<body>` uses other SMIL elements. See Table 4-3 for the specific task each of these elements performs in your presentation; this table is not all inclusive. The `<body>` contains other elements of your document, but in Table 4-3, I list the primary elements used in almost all SMIL presentations. Table 4-3 also shows what chapter you can consult for more information on these elements. You can see some of these elements at work in the following sample SMIL code, which creates a presentation that enables you to link to different segments of a video file by clicking your mouse in one of four different areas on a still image:

```
<smil>
<head>
  <layout>
    <root-layout width="800" height="600" />
    <region id="buttons_region"
            width="760" height="50"
            top="730" left="20" />
    <region id="video_region"
            width="760" height="500"
            top="20" left="20" />
  </layout>
</head>
<body>
  <par>
    <video src="cat_video.rm"
           region="video_region" />
    <excl>
      <img src="nav_bar.jpg"
           region="buttons_region">
        <area shape="rect"
              coords="0,0,50,35"
              nohref
              begin="0s"
              dur="360s"
              title="watch full video"
              target="video_region />
        <area shape="rect"
              coords="50,0,100,35"
              nohref
              begin="0s"
              dur="60s"
              title="watch birth section"
              target="video_region />
        <area shape="rect"
              coords="100,0,150,35"
              nohref
              begin="60s"
              dur="180s"
              title="watch midlife section"
              target="video_region />
        <area shape="rect"
              coords="150,0,200,35"
              nohref
              begin="240s"
              dur="120s"
              title="watch end of life section"
              target="video_region />
      </img>
    </excl>
  </par>
</body>
</smil>
```

Table 4-3	<body> Child Elements	
Element	*What It Does*	*Chapter*
<a>	Provides a link to another document from the current object, which can be text, images, or animations. It works much the same as its partner <a> element in HTML documents. As with its HTML counterpart, the <a> element provides a link only from a complete image or animation object.	Chapter 12
<animation>	Includes an animation file within your SMIL presentation.	Chapter 2
<area>	Like its HTML counterpart, enables you to create a link from a specific portion of an image or animation object. This enables you to link individual spatial coordinates of an image to particular audio recordings, images, or to another document.	Chapter 12
<audio>	Includes audio files within your presentation.	Chapter 2
<excl>	Plays its child elements in a random order. You can use this for displaying a series of short random video or audio segments that don't need to appear in any particular order.	Chapter 9
<img>	Identifies a flat image used in your presentation.	Chapter 2
<par>	Plays its child elements simultaneously, in parallel. This enables you to display content or simultaneously play video and audio, or video and text, or text and audio.	Chapter 10
<ref>	When you're not sure what media type (animation, audio, image, text, textstream, or video) you're adding, use the <ref> element. Otherwise, use the specific media type element to enhance the readability of your SMIL document and to increase the speed at which the software reads and displays your document.	Chapter 2
<seq>	Plays its child elements one after another in their order of appearance, in their implied sequence. This element enables you to complete the first portion of your presentation before continuing to the next segment. You must place the pieces of your presentation in the order of their intended appearance within the boundaries of this element.	Chapter 9

(continued)

Table 4-3 *(continued)*

Element	What It Does	Chapter
\<switch>	This element enables your presentation player to choose between various alternative elements when displaying your presentation. For example, you can enable a selection of an English, French, or German version of your audio track depending on the software's language selection.	Chapter 5
\<text>	Inserts text in your document. You can format it however you want using the available text attributes.	Chapter 2
\<textstream>	Inserts streaming text, such as a marquee or a banner, into your SMIL presentation.	Chapter 2
\<video>	Inserts video files of all types (mpegs, RealPlayer files, or Apple QuickTime movies) into your document.	Chapter 2

As you add these elements, your SMIL presentation starts to take shape. If you have a well thought-out plan for your multimedia presentation (see Chapter 3), your SMIL presentation flows together from this point without any worries. At least until you start testing your completed results. . . .

Chapter 5

Displaying the Right Information

● ●

In This Chapter

▶ Customizing your presentation with the `<switch>` elements

▶ Creating alternatives for your presentation

▶ Loading what your presentation needs

● ●

*Y*our brother, who uses his computer at work, has a dedicated T1 line to browse the Internet with and can download your presentation pretty fast. Your sister, who lives in the mountains and has only a 33.6K phone connection to her local Internet service provider (ISP), can't download your presentation as quickly as your brother can. But you don't care because you have SMIL. SMIL can adjust to work with either situation.

Using the `<switch>` tag, SMIL has the power to set up for almost any possible viewing situation. One of your visitors is using a 640 x 480 screen resolution? No problem. Another visitor speaks Mandarin Chinese? Not to worry. No matter what presentation your viewers are using or how their computers are set up, you can use a `<switch>` tag to help your visitors' computers decide which set of documents and settings to use. This chapter shows you how to use the `<switch>` element.

Using <switch> for a Better Presentation

The `<switch>` element is the mechanism that enables your visitor's computer to make informed decisions about presentation information. No, it can't tell that your 16-year-old son is using the computer and keep him out of X-rated sites. It can, however, tell how fast your computer's connection to the Internet is, as well as what screen resolution your computer is using. Basically, the `<switch>` element enables you to specify a set of alternative presentation elements that a computer can use when a certain set of criteria is met. For example, you can have one movie file that people with T1 Internet connections can watch and a smaller file that can be more quickly downloaded for people who depend on a modem for their Internet access.

Understanding <switch> criteria

If you're familiar with the logic of a programming case statement, you can understand the use of the SMIL <switch> element. The code contains a series of criteria that's compared to the viewing computer's current setup and configuration. The criteria must be completely satisfied for an action to take place. That means that if you have a series of matching criteria, all the criteria for the element has to match with the user's computer. It also means that the child elements, or those objects that are found within the opening and closing tag of an element, are allowed within a <switch> element.

Your visitor's SMIL player selects an element from a set of <switch> options by doing the following:

1. The SMIL player looks at all the elements contained within the <switch> element in the order that they occur within the document.

2. The SMIL player selects the first element that matches all the testing criteria to the current SMIL player.

Performing a test

If you look at the following example, you can see how to perform a test. This test for bandwidth (*systemBitrate* — the speed at which the system can exchange information with other computers on the Internet) enables you to control what information is played as a part of your SMIL presentation based on the speed of a visitor's connection.

```
...
<par>
  <text.../>
  <switch>
    <par systemBitrate="56000">
      ...
    </par>
    <par systemBitrate="24000">
      ...
    </par>
    <par systemBitrate="9600">
      ...
    </par>
  </switch>
</par>
...
```

In this example, someone using a moderately fast connection, a 56K modem or faster, meets the requirements of the first `<par>` tag within the `<switch>` element. Anyone with a slower connection moves down to one of the other statements and potentially sees a less detailed video, text in a different format, smaller images, or any of a number of other changes, so that the overall presentation continues to play smoothly for everyone.

Because the SMIL players go through the file in a top-down fashion, you must place the most important, or most preferred, settings at the top of the `<switch>` tests. In other words, the most difficult-to-satisfy criteria should come first. If your code starts off with the easiest criteria to satisfy, all viewers will satisfy the very first criteria, and everyone will see the most basic version of your presentation.

Take a look at the previous example code. If you mix up the top and bottom `<par>` elements, the `systemBitrate` attribute that's looking for connections of 9600 bps — likely the bottom of the Internet-connection speed barrel — would have been activated the first time through. The SMIL player wouldn't have continued through the rest of the options because it would have already found one option that satisfies all its requirements.

You may be wondering what happens if none of your `<switch>` tests are matched. What happens? Nothing. If none of the `<switch>` tests are matched, the SMIL player is instructed to do nothing but continue with the remainder of the SMIL file. For instance, you set up a test for a set of languages: English, French, and German. If someone who's using a Hebrew version of software comes upon your presentation, that visitor doesn't see any of the content contained within the `<switch>` element. Perhaps you want this to happen. On the other hand, maybe you want some type of message to appear no matter what type of language visitors are using. Unless you want the user to see none of the `<switch>` element's content, you *must* set up at least one statement that is universally fail-safe.

If your SMIL player supports HTTP (HyperText Transfer Protocol) or RTSP (Real Time Streaming Protocol), you may be able to use the server commands for these servers for negotiating content rather than using the `<switch>` element. You can find more information about HTTP from the World Wide Web Consortium at `www.w3.org`. Go to `www.realnetworks.com/devzone/library/rtsp/` for more information about RTSP.

The `<switch>` skipContent attribute

The `<switch>` element has one attribute contained within it: `skipContent`. (`<switch>` also uses a series of *test attributes,* applied to the elements that play *if* the test criteria are met. I cover these test attributes later in this chapter.) `skipContent` controls whether your visitors' computers should read and evaluate the content of your elements or skip over the contents when interpreting the document. You may be asking yourself why you would want to skip the processing of an element you painstakingly incorporated into your document. The answer isn't simple.

Here is how, and why, skipContent is necessary. Basically, the skipContent attribute is designed to help out future versions of SMIL. Imagine for a moment that a new element (say, for example, the showWidget element) is introduced in SMIL 9.0. (We're currently using SMIL 2.0, which has no showWidget element.) If showWidget enabled you to use a script, or series of scripts, previously not allowed for use with SMIL elements and attributes as part of the showWidget content, the skipContent attribute would force your SMIL player to ignore the contents of the showWidget element. This also works if a previously empty element contains content in a future version of SMIL. Think for a moment of the <img> element. In SMIL 1.0, <img> was always an empty element: <img />. In SMIL 2.0, you can add animation effects and area links within that image: <img> <animate /> </img>. Without a skipContent attribute, SMIL 1.0 players can create errors with content that they were never designed to handle, such as animate elements within an image. This could result in something as simple as a syntax error, or even mishandled images, video, and audio on your SMIL pages.

The skipContent attribute has two values: true and false. If the skipContent is set to true, the SMIL player ignores the content of the element it doesn't support, in this example the showWidget element. If the value of skipContent is false, the content of the element is processed. What does this mean?

Suppose that you have an <img> element that currently has no content other than the image address and name specified in the attributes of the element. Suddenly, version 10 of SMIL is released and now you can have <img> elements that contain *text* content also, as shown in the following code example. In this case, the skipContent attribute enables version 1.0 SMIL players to skip over the text content of the <img> element and treat it as if the text content isn't there, thereby *not* creating any errors. It still shows the image specified by the <img> element because that element is still supported by the SMIL player.

```
<switch skipContent="true">
<img src="image.gif">
     This is a test </img>
</switch>
```

This example displays the image in both SMIL 1 and 2 players but skips the text content of the image element in SMIL 1 players, while the SMIL 2 players display it.

<switch> test attributes

The <switch> element uses a variety of attributes to perform tests on the current setup and configuration of your viewer's SMIL player. I discuss these test attributes throughout the following sections. To properly use the <switch> element, you must use these attributes properly; you do so by attaching the test attributes to the elements for which they're performing the test.

In other words, if you're deciding whether or not to load a specific <video> element based on the available baud rate of your viewer's current Internet connection, you would place the systemBitrate test attribute within the <video> element itself. All these test attributes have the value of either true or false. If the value that you're testing for is true, the SMIL player selects the element associated with that test attribute and uses it in the presentation. Conversely, if the value that you're testing for is false, according to the test attribute of the element that you're currently loading, the SMIL player continues with the remaining elements in the <switch> tag.

Note: In the following sections, I've provided the SMIL 1.0 syntax for those attributes that were available in 1.0. In SMIL 2.0, hyphens are no longer used in the syntax for these attributes, so you may need to adjust your test attributes when your viewers upgrade to SMIL 2.0-compatible players.

systemBitrate

Value: Any integer greater than 0

Syntax: systemBitrate="<integer>"

Syntax (1.0): system-bitrate="<integer>"

Use this test attribute to specify the approximate bandwidth (in bits per second) that's available to the system for sharing information with other computers on the Internet. This test, considered true of the current available bandwidth of the system, is greater than or equal to the given test value. In other words, if you have a statement such as systemBitrate="9600", anyone with a connection of 9600 bps or better would evaluate it as true. If the test is systemBitrate="48000", the SMIL player has to connect to the Internet, or a network, with a bandwidth greater than what's possible with a 33.6K modem. If the value of the test is greater than the current available system bitrate, the test is false and the SMIL player continues down the list until it finds a test that's true.

If you want to find out more about implementing the systemBitrate test attribute, see the section, "Choosing by systemBitrate," later in this chapter.

When you're setting values for the `systemBitrate` test attribute, remember that the standard values that modem users are seeing include 14400, 28800, 33600, and 56000 bits per second. Of course, your modem doesn't *actually* match these speeds. Most 28.8K modems only connect at around 26.4K and most 56K modems connect somewhere between 37K and 45K. If your modem isn't actually connecting at its full speed, then your switch test drops to the next slowest baud that it does meet in the test. For instance, a 56K modem connecting at 45K actually tests `true` for the 33600 test — because the bitrate that's actually achieved is greater than 33.6K, although less than the 56K that's originally tested for.

systemCaptions

Value: on | off

Syntax: `systemCaptions="[ on | off ]"`

Syntax (1.0): `system-captions="[ on | off ]"`

The `systemCaptions` test attribute enables you, the SMIL presentation developer, to specify a text caption to appear in conjunction with an audio file. Using this test attribute, you can create the effect of readily available text for folks who are just learning to read (as in the case of a reading primer presentation), for those who learn better by reading, or for the hearing impaired. If you set `systemCaptions="on"` and the visitor's SMIL player's user preferences indicate that she wants to see text captions for audio files, the text plays. If you set `systemCaptions="off"` and the visitor's SMIL player's user preferences indicate that she doesn't want to see text captions in conjunction with audio files, the text doesn't play. If the value of the `systemCaptions` setting in your visitor's SMIL player's preferences match the setting you select in the test, the test is `true`; otherwise, it's `false`. In other words, if you set `systemCaptions="on"` and the viewer's SMIL player says she doesn't want to see text captions, the text does not play.

If you want to find out more about implementing the `systemCaptions` test attribute, see the section, "Distinguishing captions from ticker tape," later in this chapter.

systemLanguage

Value: A list of language names separated by commas

Syntax: `systemLangauge="<languagecode>"`

Syntax (1.0): `system-language="<languagecode>"`

Use the `systemLanguage` test attribute to test the SMIL player's primary language(s). You'll find this test valuable because you can use it to display English content to English speakers, Spanish content to Spanish speakers, and so on. Table 5-1 shows the list of available language codes. You can use as many of these language codes in your test as you want. For example, you can have a single test for all the Germanic languages (English, Danish, and German) and another test for all the Semitic languages (Arabic, Amharic, and Hebrew).

If you want to find out more about implementing the `systemLanguage` test attribute, see the section, "Using languages to choose," later in this chapter.

Table 5-1	systemLanguage Codes	
Language	*Language Code*	*Language Family*
Abkhazian	ab	Ibero-Caucasian
Afan (Oromo)	om	Hamitic
Afar	aa	Hamitic
Afrikaans	Af	Germanic
Albanian	sq	Indo-European (Other)
Amharic	am	Semitic
Arabic	Ar	Semitic
Armenian	hy	Indo-European (Other)
Assamese	as	Indian
Aymara	ay	Amerindian
Azerbaijani	az	Turkic/Altaic
Bashkir	ba	Turkic/Altaic
Basque	eu	Basque
Bengali, Bangla	bn	Indian
Bhutani	dz	Asian
Bihari	bh	Indian
Bislama	bi	[Not Given]
Breton	br	Celtic
Bulgarian	bg	Slavic
Burmese	my	Asian
Byelorussian	be	Slavic

(continued)

Table 5-1 *(continued)*

Language	Language Code	Language Family
Cambodian	km	Asian
Catalan	ca	Romance
Chinese	zh	Asian
Corsican	co	Romance
Croatian	hr	Slavic
Czech	cs	Slavic
Danish	da	Germanic
Dutch	nl	Germanic
English	en	Germanic
Esperanto	eo	International Aux.
Estonian	et	Finno-Ugric
Faroese	fo	Germanic
Fiji	fj	Oceanic/Indonesian
Finnish	fi	Finno-Ugric
French	fr	Romance
Frisian	fy	Germanic
Galician	gl	Romance
Georgian	ka	Ibero-Caucasian
German	de	Germanic
Greek	el	Latin/Greek
Greenlandic	kl	Eskimo
Guarani	gn	Amerindian
Gujarati	gu	Indian
Hausa	ha	Negro-African
Hebrew	he	Semitic
Hindi	hi	Indian
Hungarian	hu	Finno-Ugric
Icelandic	is	Germanic

Language	Language Code	Language Family
Indonesian	id	Oceanic/Indonesian
Interlingua	ia	International Aux.
Interlingue	ie	International Aux.
Inuktitut	iu	[Not Given]
Inupiak	ik	Eskimo
Irish	ga	Celtic
Italian	it	Romance
Japanese	ja	Asian
Javanese	Jv	Oceanic/Indonesian
Kannada	kn	Dravidian
Kashmiri	ks	Indian
Kazakh	kk	Turkic/Altaic
Kinyarwanda	rw	Negro-African
Kirghiz	ky	Turkic/Altaic
Kurundi	rn	Negro-African
Korean	ko	Asian
Kurdish	ku	Iranian
Laothian	lo	Asian
Latin	la	Latin/Greek
Latvian, Lettish	lv	Baltic
Lingala	ln	Negro-African
Lithuanian	lt	Baltic
Macedonian	mk	Slavic
Malagasy	mg	Oceanic/Indonesian
Malay	ms	Oceanic/Indonesian
Malayalam	ml	Dravidian
Maltese	mt	Semitic
Maori	mi	Oceanic/Indonesian

(continued)

Table 5-1 *(continued)*

Language	Language Code	Language Family
Marathi	mr	Indian
Moldavian	mo	Romance
Mongolian	mn	[Not Given]
Nauru	na	[Not Given]
Nepali	ne	Indian
Norwegian	no	Germanic
Occitan	oc	Romance
Oriya	or	Indian
Pashto, Pushto	ps	Iranian
Persian (Farsi)	fa	Iranian
Polish	pl	Slavic
Portuguese	pt	Romance
Punjabi	pa	Indian
Quechua	qu	Amerindian
Rhaeto-Romance	rm	Romance
Romanian	ro	Romance
Russian	ru	Slavic
Samoan	sm	Oceanic/Indonesian
Sangho	sg	Negro-African
Sanskrit	sa	Indian
Scots Gaelic	gd	Celtic
Serbian	sr	Slavic
Serbo-Croatian	sh	Slavic
Sesotho	st	Negro-African
Setswana	tn	Negro-African
Shona	sn	Negro-African
Sindhi	sd	Indian
Singhalese	si	Indian

Language	*Language Code*	*Language Family*
Siswati	ss	Negro-African
Slovak	sk	Slavic
Slovenian	sl	Slavic
Somali	so	Hamitic
Spanish	es	Romance
Sundanese	su	Oceanic/Indonesian
Swahili	sw	Negro-African
Swedish	sv	Germanic
Tagalog	tl	Oceanic/Indonesian
Tajik	tg	Iranian
Tamil	ta	Dravidian
Tatar	tt	Turkic/Altaic
Telugu	te	Dravidian
Thai	th	Asian
Tibetan	bo	Asian
Tigrinya	ti	Semitic
Tonga	to	Oceanic/Indonesian
Tsonga	ts	Negro-African
Turkish	tr	Turkic/Altaic
Turkmen	tk	Turkic/Altaic
Twi	tw	Negro-African
Uigur	ug	[Not Given]
Ukrainian	uk	Slavic
Urdu	ur	Indian
Uzbek	uz	Turkic/Altaic
Vietnamese	vi	Asian
Volapuk	vo	International Aux.
Welsh	cy	Celtic

(continued)

Table 5-1 *(continued)*

Language	Language Code	Language Family
Wolof	wo	Negro-African
Xhosa	xh	Negro-African
Yiddish	yi	Germanic
Yoruba	yo	Negro-African
Zhuang	za	[Not Given]
Zulu	zu	Negro-African

You can use multiple languages in a single test if you want the content to appear the same for multiple audiences. For example, if you want to show information simultaneously or want to have just one single presentation for all visitors, you can list a variety of languages together. For example, you can show the original *Star Trek* episode in both Klingon and English:

```
<audio src="startrek.rm" systemLanguage="x-Klingon, en"/>
```

Enabling your visitors to read and understand at least a part of your presentation is important, even if it's only the instructions for finding a copy of the presentation that's in their language. You must be careful that you don't leave out a large portion of your audience by specifying languages. If you need to specify languages for your presentation, include a catchall choice at the end of your `<switch>` element. This can be a statement totally unrelated to the language question. For example, the catchall choice can be a simple test of `systemBitrate` to ensure that everyone gets to see and hear something from the presentation.

This may sound like an odd setup, but if you think about it, no single catchall language exists. So, in order for each of your visitors to see or hear *something,* you need to have a basic test — such as a minimal 9600 bitrate test at the end of a selection of your language test to provide everyone with something to see — even if it's only an English or French message that says, `I'm sorry but this presentation isn't available in your language.`

systemRequired
Value: Any valid XML namespace prefix

Syntax: `systemRequired="<namespaceprefix>"`

Syntax (1.0): `system-required="<namespaceprefix>"`

A bit more complicated than others, the `systemRequired` test attribute compares the name of the XML Namespace to those that are supported by the SMIL player. If the namespace is valid, the test is `true`. If the namespace can't be supported, the results of the test are `false`. You can find more information on XML Namespaces in Appendix C.

You can find out more about XML and XML Namespaces in *XML For Dummies,* 2nd Edition, by Ed Tittel and Frank Boumphrey (published by IDG Books Worldwide, Inc.).

systemScreenSize

Value: Integers, in pixels, representing the size of the screen

Syntax: `systemScreenSize="heightXwidth"`

Syntax (1.0): `system-screen-size="heightXwidth"`

The `systemScreenSize` test attribute tests the size of the visitor's screen and looks at the resolution of the visitor's monitor, comparing it to the available options. You can test for as many screen sizes as you want, but be sure to include the most common resolutions:

```
systemScreenSize="640X480"
systemScreenSize="800X600"
systemScreenSize="1024X768"
```

If the SMIL player is capable of handling the presentation at the given size, this test is `true`. If the SMIL player can only display smaller images, the test is `false`.

All the `<switch>` test attributes have a `true` or `false` value. In a series of tests, the first test that evaluates as `true` is used. So you need to place the most common, or catchall test, at the end of your list. In the case of `systemScreenSize`, this is the 640 x 480 test of its equivalent on various hardware platforms, such as WebTV and Palm devices.

If you want to find out more about implementing the `systemScreenSize` test attribute, see the section, "Selecting by screen size and color depth," later in this chapter.

systemScreenDepth

Value: Any integer greater than 0

Syntax: `systemScreenDepth=" [1 | 4 | 8 | 24 | 32 | <integer> ]"`

Syntax (1.0): `system-screen-depth=" [1 | 4 | 8 | 24 | 32 | <integer> ]"`

You can use the `systemScreenDepth` test attribute to test the number of colors on the screen's color palette based on the number of bits that are required for displaying the data on-screen. Although typical values for setting screen color palettes exist, you don't have to use these values in your tests. If the SMIL player is capable of dealing with images and video of the color depth that you're testing, the test is `true`. If the SMIL player can't display that many colors, the test becomes `false`.

If you want to find out more about implementing the `systemScreenDepth` test attribute, see the section, "Selecting by screen size and color depth," later in this chapter.

systemOverdubOrSubtitle

Value: overdub | subtitle

Syntax: `systemOverdubOrSubtitle="[ overdub | subtitle ]"`

When you're testing the SMIL player's preferences for receiving over-dubbing, which is the change of a soundtrack so that it replaces the original soundtrack, or subtitles with your audio tracks, you need to use the `systemOverdubOrSubtitle` test attribute. If a SMIL player requests over-dubbing, the current audio file is replaced with one from the SMIL player's designated primary language. If the SMIL player instead selects subtitle, your presentation displays text in a language that the visitor can hopefully read.

For this test to evaluate as `true`, the `systemOverdubOrSubtitle` test attribute value has to match the SMIL player's preferences; any other setting results in a `false` value.

If you want to find out more about implementing the `systemOverdubOrSubtitle`, see the section, "Using overdub and subtitles," later in this chapter.

systemAudioDesc

Value: on | off

Syntax: `systemAudioDesc="[ on | off ]"`

When you're testing for whether or not to display closed audio descriptions, you need to use the `systemAudioDesc` test attribute. This test, companion to the `systemCaptions` attribute that displays text for hearing-impaired computer users, plays audio files for visitors who are sight-impaired. When the SMIL player has this setting *on,* the visitor can hear an audio description of what he would otherwise be seeing. When the SMIL player has this setting *off,* the audio file isn't played.

The test attribute value and the SMIL player's preferences have to match in order for this test to be `true`; any other setting results in a `false` value.

systemOperatingSystem

Value: One of the XML-accepted operating system codes shown in Table 5-2

Syntax: `systemOperatingSystem="<os-code>"`

Use the `systemOperatingSystem` test attribute to perform the test that determines which operating system a presentation visitor is using, such as Windows or Macintosh. Table 5-2 lists the available operating system codes.

Table 5-2	XML-Accepted Operating System Codes
OS Code	**Description**
AIX	UNIX operating system developed by IBM.
BeOS	The BeOS operating system for personal computers and handheld devices.
BSDI	The BSDI Unix-based commercial operating system.
DGUX	One of the many flavors of Unix.
FreeBSD	A free version of Unix, similar to Linux, that is a common Web server platform.
HPUX	Hewlett Packard's version of Unix.
IRIX	A Unix-like operating system developed by Silicon Graphics.
Linux	A free, or low-cost, operating system that is successfully used in many network environments and on standalone PCs. This operating system is one of the common alternatives to Windows and Macintosh OS.
MacOS	The Macintosh Operating System.
NCR	A networking systems operating system similar to Unix, developed by NCR Software.
NEC	A server operating system, similar to Unix.
NetBSD	A version of the BSD Unix operating system that is being distributed free over the Internet and is a collaborative effort of volunteers.
NextStep	A Unix-based graphical operating system.
NTO	A Unix-based operating system.
OpenBSD	A free, multiple-platform operating system based on BSD Unix.
OpenVMS	A Unix-based operating system often used on IBM mainframes.
OS2	IBM's OS2 operating system that has a relatively small but vocal support group.

(continued)

Table 5-2 *(continued)*

OS Code	Description
OSF	The Open Software Foundation's version of Unix.
PalmOS	The operating system used on most Palm devices.
QNS	Another Unix-like operating system.
Rhapsody	A pre-release version of the Macintosh Operating System.
SCO	A version of Unix developed by the Santa Cruz Operation, Inc.
Sinix	This is the Siemens Nixdorf Informationssysteme AG derivative of AT&T's UNIX System.
Solaris	A sophisticated version of Unix that is used as a relatively high-end base for a Web server.
SunOS	A version of Unix developed by Sun, Inc., for use on servers.
UnixWare	Another of the many flavors of Unix.
Win16	A 16-bit Windows based operating system, such as Windows 3.1 or Windows for Work Groups 3.11.
Win32	A 32-bit Windows-based operating system, such as Windows 95, Windows 98, Windows NT, or Windows Me.
Win9x	Support for both Windows 95 and Windows 98 operating systems.
WinCE	A Windows-based operating system for handheld devices.
WinNT	The Window NT operating system.
Unknown	(A setting that's provided for privacy.)

The test attribute value and the SMIL player's preferences have to match in order for this test to be true; any other setting results in a false value. The values of this test aren't case-sensitive — so WINNT, Winnt, WinNT, and winnt are all the same test values.

systemCPU

Value: One of the XML-accepted CPU codes listed in Table 5-3

Syntax: systemCPU="cpu-code"

Use the systemCPU attribute to perform the test that determines which type of CPU a presentation visitor is using, an RS6000 or an x86 microcomputer chip, for instance. I've listed the available codes in Table 5-3.

Table 5-3	CPU System Codes
System Code	**Description**
ALPHA	A CPU designed to work with high-end mainframes.
ARM	A processor designed in the U.K. and used frequently with Linux and Unix computer systems.
ARM32	A processor developed by Digital, based upon ARM, which is used for Linux and Unix systems.
HPPA1.1	A processor used with GNU-based operating systems.
M68K	The CPU typically used with Macintosh computer hardware.
MIPS	A RISC processor used in many different devices from computers to handheld devices.
PPC	A Motorolla chip used in many of the newer model Macintosh G3 and G4 systems.
RS6000	An advanced processor developed by IBM for use in RISC-based servers.
VAX	A standard hardware configuration for Unix servers.
X86	An Intel chip-based system, such as a standard desktop PC running the Windows operating system.
UNKNOWN	(Provided for privacy purposes.)

The test attribute value and the SMIL player's preferences have to match in order for this test to be true; any other setting results in a false value. The values of this test are not case-sensitive.

systemComponent

Value: String of text characters

Syntax: systemComponent="<string>"

The systemComponent test attribute enables you to test the various components of a visitor's SMIL player. For instance, you can test to see what code a player is using or whether the player supports the use of JavaScript. The exact string values that you need to use depend on the SMIL players that your visitors are using. For instance, if you were using RealPlayer, you might use a statement such as systemComponent="Javascript" and get a false value, while the GRiNS SMIL 2.0 Player may return a true value.

If the SMIL player supports the system component that you've described, the test is true; otherwise, it's false.

Implementing Test Attributes

It doesn't do you any good to have a lot of information tossed in your lap with no idea how to use it. All the <switch> test attributes that I throw at you in the previous section of this chapter have very hard and fast uses. I provide the following examples to show you how you can use the test attributes in your own SMIL presentations.

Choosing by systemBitrate

The systemBitrate test attribute is one of the most common uses for a <switch> test. Because of the huge disparity between the speed of network connections and modem connections, you can't often expect a modem user to wait an hour to see your presentation, even if the network users can download the presentation within about five minutes. In the following code, a series of <par> elements are being tested using the systemBitrate test attribute. If the connection speed of the visitor's computer is greater than 50K, the first <par> element and its contents load; otherwise, one of the others loads.

```
<smil>
<head>
....
<head>
<body>
  <par>
    <text .../>
    <switch>
      <par systemBitrate="50000">
        ...
      </par>
      <par systemBitrate="24000">
        ...
      </par>
      <par systemBitrate="2400">
        ...
      </par>
    </switch>
  </par>
  ...
</body>
</smil>
```

In addition to the generic selection of sets of information — which you perform by using a <par> element for testing (based on the bitrate of your system) — you can sort through individual media files, such as audio, image, and video, by applying the systemBitrate test attribute directly to the media element. In this example (see bolded lines in following code), the audio file "hiqual" is loaded for systems with bitrates over 30,000 bps, while the "lowqual" file is loaded for all the rest of the systems, provided they're connected by at least 9000 bps.

```
<smil>
<body>
  ...
  <switch>
    <audio src="hiqual" systemBitrate="30000" />
    <audio src="lowqual" systemBitrate="9000" />
  </switch>
  ...
  <switch>
    <img src="testingBig.jpg" systemBitrate="24000" />
    <img src="testingSm.jpg" systemBitrate="10000" />
  </switch>
</body>
</smil>
```

Using languages to choose

When you need to play a different audio or video file or display a different text file based on the language of your audience, you need to use the systemLanguage test attribute. In the following code, the systemLanguage test attribute is bring applied to a series of audio, text, and video files. With each test, either a German, English, or Spanish audio, text, or video file is played.

```
<smil>
<body>
  ...
  <switch>
    <audio src="German-sound" systemLanguage="de"/>
    <audio src="English-sound" systemLanguage="en"/>
    <audio src="Spanish-sound" systemLanguage="es" />
  </switch>
  ...
  <switch>
    <text src="German-text" systemLanguage="de"/>
    <text src="English-text" systemLanguage="en"/>
    <text src="Spanish-text" systemLanguage="es" />
  </switch>
  ...
  <switch>
    <video src="German-video" systemLanguage="de"/>
    <video src="English-video" systemLanguage="en"/>
    <video src="Spanish-video" systemLanguage="es " />
  </switch>
  ...
</body>
</smil>
```

Selecting by screen size and color depth

Often, you may worry about how large your presentation can be and how many colors your visitors' computers use to display it. For example, a presentation with a lot of photographs looks downright awful on a 16-color monitor. You can test your visitors' systems to discover their settings. Then, you can use images with few colors and smaller sizes on those screens that only display 16 colors at a 640 x 480 resolution. Photographic images typically have 16 million colors within them, so when you reduce those to the 16 colors available on a 16-color monitor, your image looks pale, blotchy, and may be completely discolored. On screens with higher resolutions and larger color palettes, you can use images with more colors and larger dimensions. The following code uses both the systemScreenSize test attribute and the systemScreenDepth test attribute to find the best match for your visitors' computer setups. It tests for screen resolution first and then for the number of bits in the color palette.

```
<smil>
<body>
  ...
  <par>
    <text .../>
    <switch>
      <par systemScreenSize="1024X768"
           systemScreenDepth="8">
        ...
      </par>
      <par systemScreenSize="800X600"
           systemScreenDepth="32">
        ...
      </par>
      <par systemScreenSize="640X480"
           systemScreenDepth="32">
        ...
      </par>
    </switch>
  </par>
  ...
</body>
</smil>
```

Using overdub and subtitles

Have you ever watched a French movie, listening to the lovely lilting tones of the language in which you can tell someone he's a blooming idiot with no redeeming characteristics and make it sound as though you were telling him every reason you loved him? Well, no matter what soft, sweet tones you use, if you add subtitles or overdub to your movie, the real meaning comes across for anyone in any language.

In the following code example, I show the French movie with English, Spanish, and Italian overdubs or subtitle tracks based on the options available with the visitor's presentation preferences.

```
<smil>
<body>
  ...
  <par>
    <switch>
      <audio src="vr-audio-en.rm" systemLanguage="en"
        systemOverdubOrSubtitle="overdub"/>
      <audio src="vr-audio-es.rm" systemLanguage="es"
        systemOverdubOrSubtitle="overdub"/>
      <audio src="vr-audio-it.rm" systemLanguage="it"
        systemOverdubOrSubtitle="overdub"/>
      <!-- If none of the above languages are found,
          French is used -->
      <audio src="vr-audio-fr.rm"/>
    </switch>
    <video src="vr-video.rm"/>
    <switch>
      <textstream src="vr-subtitles-en.rt"
                  systemLanguage="en"
                  systemOverdubOrSubtitle="subtitle"/>
      <textstream src="vr-subtitles-es.rt"
                  systemLanguage="es"
                  systemOverdubOrSubtitle="subtitle"/>
      <textstream src="vr-subtitles-it.rt"
                  systemLanguage="it"
                  systemOverdubOrSubtitle="subtitle"/>
      <!-- Now show French captions for those
          who want them as well -->
      <textstream src="vr-captionss-fr.rt"
                  systemCaptions="on"/>
    </switch>
  </par>
  ...
</body>
</smil>
```

Distinguishing captions from ticker tape

In the following example, I use the `systemCaptions="on"` test attribute to display captions if the visitors' software is set to accept them. If the visitors' software isn't set to accept captions, the SMIL player only displays the contents of the ticker tape. You create ticker tape effects by using the `<textstream>` element, which I discuss in Chapter 2.

```
<smil>
<body>
  <seq>
    <par>
      <audio src="vr-audio.rm"/>
      <video src="vr-video.rm"/>
      <textstream src="tickertape.rt"/>
      <textstream src="captions.rt"
                  systemCaptions="on"/>
    </par>
  </seq>
  ...
</body>
</smil>
```

Getting What You Need with <prefetch>

You may be thinking that performing all these tests adds precious time to
your presentation download. You can avoid this potential problem by loading
your images, video, animations — anything that takes a while to load —
before the presentation is played with the <prefetch> element. By preloading large parts of the presentation, you can achieve an instantaneous appearance of new information as your visitors interact with your presentation. Use
preloading to make your presentation run more smoothly.

SMIL players can ignore the <prefetch> element when they don't recognize
it or when it's included within a <switch> test that wasn't met. If they do
ignore it, the replay of your presentation may be temporarily interrupted
when the presentation needs the object you were attempting to preload.
Essentially, the playing of your presentation is slowed to a normal pace,
before the use of the <prefetch> element.

The <prefetch> element enables you, the presentation developer, to control
when and how a SMIL player retrieves your presentation's media elements.
You can time your media retrieval to points where your resource usage is low
in the playing of the presentation. For example, if you're at a holding point in
the presentation while the visitors are reading text, you can download the
video and images used in the next few portions of the presentation. You base
the actual scheduling of the <prefetch> element on its order within the document or on actual timing codes. (See Chapter 8 for more on timing codes.)
So, if you place all your <prefetch> elements before the loading of your first
screen, you have all your resources loaded prior to ever needing them. Keep
in mind, however, that doing so slows the initial loading of your presentation
to the point where you may lose impatient visitors.

<prefetch> attributes

The `<prefetch>` element uses the same attributes that you find with all the media elements, which I discuss in Chapter 2, including:

- `id` — Sets the identifier of the `<prefetch>` element.
- `src` — Identifies the address of the file to be fetched.
- `begin` — Sets the begin time that the fetching process should start.
- `end` — Sets the time at which the prefetch process should stop.
- `dur` — Sets the duration of the prefetch process.
- `clipBegin` — Sets the time, within the intrinsic duration of the fetching process, that the fetch should actually start.
- `clipEnd` — Sets the time, within the intrinsic duration of the fetching process, that the fetch should stop.

The `id` and `src` attributes are exactly the same as those that you use with the media elements (see Chapter 2), with `id` providing the name for the element and `src` providing the address of the resource being fetched. The `begin`, `end`, `dur`, `clipBegin`, and `clipEnd` attributes are only available if you've incorporated timing into your use of the `<prefetch>` element.

The `begin`, `dur`, and `end` attributes define the time period during which the fetching operation can take place. For example, if the element fetching process was started 30 seconds into the presentation and it had a `dur` (duration) of 30 seconds, as much of the media element that was able to be fetched would be ready to use after the presentation had played for one full minute. It would then not resume loading until the element itself was called to start playing. You can use the `clipBegin` and `clipEnd` attributes to identify the specific portion of the media element to load, so that you don't have to download the entire element. This is especially useful if you have a limited amount of time to perform the fetching operation.

The `<prefetch>` element has three more attributes that it doesn't share with any other element. To find out more about these unique attributes, read on.

mediaSize

Value: bytes-value | percent-value

Syntax: `mediaSize="[ bytes-value | percent-value ]"`

Use the `mediaSize` attribute to specify the exact number of bytes of a media file that should be fetched. You can specify a percentage of the file, such as 25%, 12%, or 100% if you want to load the entire file. Percentages work best if you don't know the file size, but do know roughly what percentage of the file size you want. If you know the exact file size and the exact number of bytes that make up the portion you're using, you can specify the number of bytes that you want to download. The default setting for this attribute is 100%. Any attribute with a value of 0% is ignored and treated as if the attribute wasn't specified.

mediaTime

Value: clock-value | percent-value

Syntax: mediaTime="[clock-value (hh:mm:ss) | percent-value]"

Use the mediaTime attribute to specify the exact amount of the playing time of the file that you want to fetch. You can specify a percentage of the file, such as 25%, 12%, or 100%, if you want to load the entire file. Percentages work best if you don't know the actual playing time of the file but know roughly what percentage of the file's duration comprises the portion that you want. You can specify a selection of the file's duration if you know exactly how long the file plays. The default setting for this attribute is 100%. Any attribute with a value of 0% is ignored and treated as if the attribute wasn't specified.

If you're using the mediaTime attribute for non-time based media, such as a text file or a non-animated image, this attribute forces the entire file to download, no matter what you set the attribute's value to.

If you specify both mediaSize and mediaTime, the SMIL player uses mediaSize and ignores mediaTime.

bandwidth

Value: bitrate-value | percent-value

Syntax: bandwidth="[bitrate-value | percent-value]"

You can use the bandwidth attribute to define how much of the network bandwidth (or Internet connection bandwidth) the SMIL player needs to use to fetch the media element. If you want to use all the available bandwidth, set this attribute to 100% (the default setting). Any attribute with a value of 0% is ignored and treated as if the attribute wasn't specified.

Implementing <prefetch>

To effectively use these elements and attributes all together, you need to see the pieces in action. Luckily, <prefetch> is just as simple to use as the media elements, such as <img> and <textstream>, which I discuss in Chapter 2.

In the following example, an image is pre-fetched so that it can be displayed as soon as the current video file has finished running. This example doesn't use any timing attributes to control when the prefetch happens or when the video starts. The `<prefetch>` element fetches a single image that is used directly following the video presentation. The first text field displays the contents of the `wait.htm` file. This file is displayed while the closing image is loaded. As soon as that's complete, the main video starts.

```
<smil>
  <body>
    <seq>
      <par>
        <prefetch id="closimg"
          src="http://www.catsback.com/cbclogo.gif"/>
        <text id="intermission"
              src="http://www.catsback.org/wait.htm"
              fill="freeze"/>
      </par>
      <video id="main-vid"
             src="rtsp://www.catsback.com/vr.mpg"/>
      <image
            src="http://www.catsback.com/cbclogo.gif"
            fill="freeze"/>
    </seq>
  </body>
</smil>
```

You can exercise a lot of control over your media elements. By using the `<switch>` element and the `<prefetch>` element in combination, you can control how your video loads and the order in which it loads, which fills any holes that the SMIL 1.0 document control department may have left.

Part III
A Time and Place for Everything

"No, Thomas Jefferson never did 'the Grind.'; however, this does show how animation can be used to illustrate American history on the Web."

In this part . . .

The chapters in this part take you deeper into SMIL. Here you can read about the options for positioning objects within the SMIL player's window. Discover how to position objects relatively or absolutely, set up containment regions for setting specific areas of your presention for different media, and even delve into the vast issue of timing so that you can join audio and video, and audio and text. You can control when and how to use your images, videos, animations, text, and audio files on your presentation.

So, read on! Explore the various methods that you can use to link your current SMIL presentation with other documents, and dare to bring new content into the presentation based on the interactions of your presentation's viewers.

Chapter 6

Positioning Your Media

Making plans is human nature for some and as alien as living on Pluto to others. But when you're creating a SMIL document, you need to think carefully about that planning stage. In Chapter 3, I describe one plan of attack for designing your SMIL presentation. If you refer to that chapter, you can see exactly where everything goes on your presentation. After you know where you want things, you simply have to know how to position your presentation objects. In this chapter, I discuss doing just that and using the `<layout>` and `<root-layout>` SMIL elements to place your objects.

Positioning Elements

Have you ever thought about your position in the world? Not your personal position but the position of your house, for instance? My house is located just off the 45th parallel at 117 degrees longitude. There's no way my house is going to move, barring a landslide or a major earthquake. This permanent fixed position is an *absolute* position. No matter where in the world I am, my house will always be in that one location. An absolute address is one that doesn't move no matter what's happening around it.

On the other hand, I am always in a *relative* position. I may be positioned 5 feet from the doorway or 18 inches from my computer screen. Because I move and flow with events and circumstances, I'm never in an absolute position. By using relative positioning, you can keep your objects a set distance from another object, even though they're always affected by the positioning of other elements around them.

SMIL primarily uses absolute positioning to place the objects on your presentation, but it can use relative positioning through *Cascading Style Sheets.* Cascading Style Sheets (CSS) provide a way to control the position of your objects and their appearance. When you're doing advanced development in SMIL, HTML, XHTML, or XML, an understanding of CSS practically becomes a necessity.

A full discussion of Cascading Style Sheets (CSS) is a book in and of itself. To find out more about CSS, pick up a copy of *Dreamweaver 3 For Dummies* by Janine Warner and Paul Vachier or *Dynamic HTML For Dummies* by Michael Hyman (both published by IDG Books Worldwide, Inc.).

For more in-depth coverage of the CSS properties, check out *HTML Master Reference,* by yours truly (published by IDG Books Worldwide, Inc.).

Using absolute positioning

Absolute positioning is a rigid, although convenient, way to format your presentation. An absolutely positioned element is one that's fixed within the space of your presentation screen. For example, if you position a picture 100 pixels down and over from the top of your presentation document, that image is always exactly 100 pixels from the top-left corner of your presentation document, no matter how big or small the presentation area is. This picture scrolls up and down with the rest of the document, maintaining its relationship to the top of the document itself, not to the document window.

Whenever you place an image, or other object, in an absolute position, you always know exactly where it's located. But you may have problems with the other information on your page, if that information isn't also absolutely positioned. Absolutely positioned elements are outside the natural flow of your SMIL page and can, therefore, sometimes obscure the information in the regular flow of your page.

Imagine for a moment a large rock in the middle of a river. The water flows around the rock, right? If that rock is positioned absolutely, the rock isn't carried in the flow of the river at all. It's embedded in a stationary spot, and the river flows along around it like the rock wasn't even there. If you were to look straight down on the rock from above, it would hide the river's water from view. Absolutely positioned elements on your SMIL pages do the same thing. They don't impede the flow of information in the river of your presentation, but they may obscure it from view because the flow of information continues on behind the absolutely positioned elements.

You can also embed other absolutely positioned objects within an absolutely positioned object, and they can contain their own flow of information. If the river rock analogy isn't clear, you may want to think of an absolutely positioned object as a separate document within a primary document; just imagine the absolutely positioned document floating above the primary document.

As odd as absolute positioning may sound at the outset, it is actually the easiest way to format documents using desktop-publishing-like effects. Without using absolute positioning, you can't control where images are placed — at least not exactly. Absolute positioning gives you control over the location of your information and how that information interacts with other objects on-screen. When you're creating a presentation, so much of the presentation's effect is in the actual layout of information that any other type of positioning actually inhibits your ability to make the presentation appear exactly as you want it to.

Fixed positioning is a variation on the absolute positioning scheme. With fixed positioning, you don't position your object in relation to the presentation document, you position it in relation to the SMIL presentation window. Thus, instead of scrolling with the rest of the document, the information contained within a fixed positioned object always appears at the bottom, top, or middle of the presentation window without regard to what the rest of the presentation is doing. This enables you to create a constant footer at the bottom of your screen or a constant header at the top of your screen.

The only way to create a fixed-position object on a SMIL presentation is to use Cascading Style Sheets. If you're interested in creating this type of effect in your presentation, go to the World Wide Web Consortium's Web site at www.w3.org/Style/CSS and look up the position property.

In the following sample code (see Figure 6-1 for the results), the 100 x 100 pixel region object named Region1 is absolutely positioned 40 pixels inside and down from the top of the SMIL document.

```
<smil>
   <head>
      <layout>
         <root-layout height="140" width="139"/>
         <region id="Region1"
                 left="40"
                 top="40"
                 height="100"
                 width="100"
                 backgroundColor="Red"
                 z-index="0" />
      </layout>
   </head>
   <body>
      <seq>
         <textstream id="playnext"
                 src="playnext.rt"
                 region="Region1"
                 system-language="en"
                 system-bitrate="2121"/>
      </seq>
   </body>
</smil>
```

Figure 6-1:
This
presentation
draws a
100- x- 100 -
pixel red
box inside
the black
background.

Red box   Black background

Using relative positioning

Relative positioning isn't typically done within a SMIL presentation's overall layout because the default type of positioning used is absolute. But you can create relatively positioned elements within individual regions of the document. Think of a leaf floating in a river. It doesn't get in front of or behind anything else floating in the river unless it's a stationary object, such as a rock — or a heavier object like a log, but we don't want to get that technical here! That leaf keeps its position relative to all the other leaves around it. This is how a relatively positioned object works. It just places itself in the flow of your document and goes along with all the rest of the objects as they work around images, videos, and other blocky objects.

By using relative positioning within your regions, which I discuss in Chapter 7, you can create the same effect within your SMIL presentation that you see in most Web sites. By using relative positioning for objects within your regions, you can more easily allow for different screen sizes that adjust the flow of your text around images and other objects.

The only way to relatively position a `<region>` is by using a Cascading Style Sheet (CSS) attached to your SMIL presentation.

Defining that Gal-darned <layout>

The `<layout>` element is primarily a container that defines how the individual regions of your SMIL presentation are positioned within your document. In other words, the `<layout>` element is like the stage of a play that's used to contain all the scenes, actors, and props. This element contains all the individual region identifiers, which, to use the stage analogy, are areas like stage right, stage left, back stage, and so on. I give you all the details on setting up regions in Chapter 7.

Just as you must build your play's stage before any of the scenes can take place on it, you have to specify the `<layout>` element before you can create any regions in your SMIL presentation.

The `<layout>` element must be contained within the `<head>` of the SMIL presentation, as shown in bold text in the following example. You can read more about the `<head>` element in Chapter 2. I discuss the `<root-layout>` and `<region>` in the section, "Setting Up the <root-layout>," later in this chapter.

```
<smil>
<head>
   <layout>
      <root-layout... />
      <region... />
      <region... />
   </layout>
</head>
<body>
   <!-- Body Information and content go here -->
</body>
</smil>
```

As you know, people don't run their computers in the same way. Some people have monitors set to a large resolution, while others have monitors set to very fine resolutions. In order to create a presentation that looks the same and that's completely visible on everyone's screen, you need to provide an alternative document layout for each screen setting that a visitor may use. You also want to keep in mind the various connection speeds that different users may have.

You can create this alternative layout by using a `<switch>` element within your presentation's `<head>`. In the following code, you can see a `<switch>` element that loads one of a series of layouts dependent on the baud rates that are available for downloading the document. Within each of the `<layout>` elements is the `systemBitrate` test attribute that accompanies the `<switch>` element that's used to perform the text. The `systemBitrate` test attribute is only valid when the `<layout>` element is included within a `<switch>`. See Chapter 5 for more information on the `<switch>` element.

```
<smil>
<head>
   <switch>
      <layout systemBitrate="50000">
         <switch>
            <root-layout systemScreenSize="640X480"... />
            <root-layout systemScreenSize="800X600"... />
```

```
            <root-layout systemScreenSize="1024X768"... />
          ...
        </switch>
      </layout>
      <layout systemBitrate="24000">
        <switch>
          <root-layout systemScreenSize="640X480"... />
          <root-layout systemScreenSize="800X600"... />
          <root-layout systemScreenSize="1024X768"... />
          ...
        </switch>
      </layout>
      <layout systemBitrate="2400">
        <switch>
          <root-layout systemScreenSize="640X480"... />
          <root-layout systemScreenSize="800X600"... />
          <root-layout systemScreenSize="1024X768"... />
          ...
        </switch>
      </layout>
    </switch>
  </head>
  <body>
    <!-- Body Information and content go here -->
  </body>
</smil>
```

Only one attribute is used with the <layout> element: type. This attribute specifies which version of the SMIL language is to be used to lay out the elements. The default value is text/smil-basic-layout, which informs the SMIL presentation player that you're using a version of SMIL that's compatible with the SMIL 1.0 and SMIL Layout Level 0 (from SMIL 2.0) syntax.

```
<layout type="text/smil-basic-layout">
```

If the SMIL presentation software that you're using doesn't recognize the SMIL language specified within the type attribute, all the elements contained within the <layout> element are ignored until the closing </layout> element is encountered.

The <layout> element can contain three other elements: <root-layout>, <viewport>, and <region>. I discuss <root-layout> and <viewport> later in this chapter, and in Chapter 7, I cover <region> in detail.

Setting Up the <root-layout>

You need some way to dictate how your primary software window is going to look. Now, you can't control how RealPlayer or QuickTime show off your presentation, but you can control what appears in the background of your presentation window. This is the job of the <root-layout> element.

The <root-layout> element has one job — controlling the visual appearance of your presentation screen. The <root-layout> element uses the width, height, backgroundColor, and title attributes to control the appearance of your SMIL presentation-playing window. Because you can only have one background for your presentation, you can only have one <root-layout> element within <layout>. If you were to add more than one <root-layout> element for any presentation, you create an error, and most SMIL players then won't display your presentation.

The <root-layout> element is an *empty element,* which means that it doesn't have any children (it doesn't contain other elements within itself). For example, the <layout> element can have both <root-layout> and <region> elements within its opening and closing tags. The <root-layout> element, like the HTML <img> element, doesn't have a closing tag; all the information pertinent to use with the <root-layout> element is contained within the element by using attributes.

The <root-layout> element controls the display of your information through the use of a variety of attributes. For instance, the backgroundColor attribute controls the visible color of the background behind the other objects you place in your presentation. The attributes of <root-layout> include backgroundColor, height, region, and width.

The <root-layout> backgroundColor attribute

All windows have a background, so the first attribute you need to look at is the backgroundColor attribute. This attribute was called background-color in SMIL 1.0. In the growth to SMIL 2.0, its spelling was changed to follow the standard naming practice used with Cascading Style Sheets. If you're familiar with Cascading Style Sheets, you're familiar with the use and function of the backgroundColor attribute with SMIL. The sole function of this attribute is to define what color should be used as a background behind the various text, image, and video objects that you place on your SMIL presentation.

SMIL software can support either the SMIL 1.0 background-color, or the SMIL 2.0 backgroundColor attributes, or both. If neither of these attributes is present, the background color of your window is transparent, showing the default background color of the particular SMIL software that's displaying the information.

In Figure 6-1, the default background of the RealPlayer is black. The following sample code changes the background color of your presentation to yellow with a red square in the middle, as shown in Figure 6-2.

```
<smil>
   <head>
      <layout>
         <root-layout backgroundColor="#FFFF00"
                      height="180"
                      width="180"/>
         <region id="Region1"
                 left="41"
                 top="40"
                 height="100"
                 width="100"
                 z-index="1"
                 backgroundColor="#FF0000"/>
         <region id="Region2"
                 left="0"
                 top="0"
                 height="180"
                 width="180"
                 z-index="0"/>
      </layout>
   </head>
   <body>
      <seq>
         <img id="0202"
              src=" /junkfolder/0202.gif"
              region="Region1"
              system-bitrate="12000"/>
      </seq>
   </body>
</smil>
```

Figure 6-2:
This presentation uses the back-ground-Color attribute to switch the background to yellow, rather than the default black.

Red box   Yellow background

The <root-layout> height attribute

All objects have dimension. You control the height dimension with the height attribute of the <root-layout> element. This attribute sets the vertical size of the box that the entire presentation must be included within. You can set the values of this attribute to almost any measurement value. In other words, you can say that the height of the presentation is 10 cm, 100 mm, or 1000 pixels. If you have a number that doesn't have a measurement designation assigned to it, it's treated as a measurement of pixels, as shown in the following example:

```
<root-layout backgroundColor="#FFFF00"
          height="180"
          width="180"/>
```

The <root-layout> width attribute

In the <root-layout> element, you control the width of the presentation with the width attribute of the <root-layout> element. You use this attribute to set the horizontal size of the box that your entire presentation must be included within. You can set the values of this attribute to any measurement value, so you can say that the width of the presentation is 12 cm, 120 mm, or 200 pixels. If you have a number that doesn't have a measurement designation assigned to it, it's treated as a measurement of pixels, as shown in the following example:

```
<root-layout backgroundColor="#FFFF00"
          height="180"
          width="180"/>
```

The <root-layout> title attribute

The title attribute provides some additional information about the presentation background area. Some SMIL players use the contents of the title attribute to provide additional information to the viewer. In other cases, the SMIL player ignores this attribute. The title attribute is completely optional. The following code applies the title "Fred's Dance Presentation" to the <root-layout> element of the presentation.

```
<root-layout backgroundColor="#FFFF00"
          height="180"
          width="180"
          title="Fred's Dance Presentation" />
```

Laying Out Your <viewport>

In most presentations, you set up your document and configure the size and color of the presentation's background based on the assumption that only a single window is showing your presentation. But with the advent of the SMIL 2.0 specification and its additional layout elements, you can now have multiple presentation windows. Confusing, huh? As if one presentation window just wasn't enough to worry about!

When you have multiple presentation windows, the original window — the source of the primary SMIL document — is called the *root window*. This is the window that was first created, and it serves as the creator of the other windows. When you create multiple windows by using the `<viewport>` element in your original presentation window, each window shows a different portion of the presentation.

The new `<viewport>` element provides you with a method of defining multiple layout windows within a single presentation. This isn't like HTML frames. The `<viewport>` element actually opens multiple copies of your SMIL player, each showing a different part of your presentation. The ability to define information for multiple windows with a single presentation enables you to create a table of contents in one window that can interact with the actual content of a book presentation in a second window.

You have to be careful about using the `<viewport>` element because it isn't currently supported in very many pieces of SMIL software. Support for the use of `<viewport>` is currently in the hands of the software developers, and all the SMIL gurus have to wait patiently for it to happen.

When you're working with multiple windows within a single presentation, they're termed *top-level* windows — a term that's applied to each instance of your SMIL player that's open. The idea of a single presentation window affected by the `<root-layout>` element no longer exists.

Just as with the `<root-layout>` element, you can control the size and placement of each of these top-level windows. Of course, you can use as many `<viewport>` elements as you need to create your presentation's top-level windows, as shown in the following sample code, which creates two windows. The first is called `TOC` and represents the Table of Contents of an online book. The second window, called `contents`, contains the individual pages of the book being viewed.

```
<layout>
    <!-- Open  the first window (100 x 250), call it TOC,
        give it the title Table of Contents which
        should appear in the SMIL Player's title
        bar if the title attribute is supported. -->
    <viewport id="TOC"
            title="Table of Contents"
            width="100"
            height="250"/>
        <!-- Draw in the region that will contain the actual
            Table of Contents entries. This region takes
            Up 100% of the Viewport window. -->
        <region id="TOC_Entries"
            title="Contents Entries"
            height="100%"
            fit="meet"/>
    </viewport>
    <!-- Open  the second window (600 x 250), call it
        contents, give it the title Book Contents which
        should appear in the SMIL Player's title
        bar if the title attribute is supported. -->
    <viewport id="contents"
            title="Book Contents"
            width="600"
            height="250">
        <!-- Draw in the region that will contain the actual
            book pages. This region takes
            Up 90% of the Viewport window. -->
    <region id="pages"
                title="page text"
                top="90%"
                fit="meet"/>
    </viewport>
</layout>
```

Within the first window, the table of contents is created within the
"TOC_Entries" region. In the second window, the contents of the book
are displayed within the "pages" region.

At the time of this writing, none of the current SMIL players support this
aspect of SMIL 2.0 — although the GRiNS SMIL Player 2.0 should support
the <viewport> element when it's released.

All the windows that you create using the <viewport> element are opened
simultaneously as soon as your presentation is started. In the case of our
book example, this means that both the TOC and the contents windows
appear at the same time, loaded with the requested content appearing at the
start of the presentation. If you close one of your windows, the timeline of the
presentation continues without interruption.

Timing and top-level windows

This combination of top-level windows can still be controlled with one timeline. It doesn't create multiple timelines, which I discuss in detail in Chapter 8. One of the beauties of SMIL is its ability to control the appearance, motion, movement, and disappearance of information on-screen. When you create a presentation with multiple top-level windows by using the `<viewport>` element, you don't create multiple timelines. You still have one timeline with which to control the appearance or disappearance, starting or stopping, and action of all your SMIL presentation objects. This enables you to synchronize the actions taking place within multiple windows. In other words, you can click a button on one window, and have it open a new file in a second window, and have it start playing a video and audio file in a third window just 5 seconds after you clicked the original button.

It may be worthwhile to program your presentation to open any top-level windows that may have been closed during part of a presentation, as soon as that window is needed again. In some SMIL players, this action can create errors in the display of your presentation or simply shut down the presentation entirely.

When you're using the `<viewport>` element to organize your regions, you need to be aware that each region can only be assigned to one window at a time. This means that you can't have `"region1"` assigned to both a `"TOC"` and a `"contents"` window. You need to create separate regions for each top-level window — which means that, yes, you must have unique names for all your regions.

Chapter 7

Setting Up Regions

● ●

In This Chapter

▶ Identifying regions that store information in your presentation

▶ Positioning regions correctly

▶ Matching your presentation regions with your presentation objects

● ●

*I*n Chapter 6, I show you how to set up your SMIL document using the `<layout>` and `<root-layout>`, or `<layout>` and `<viewport>` elements. After you decide whether to use a single window (`<root-layout>`) or multiple windows (`<viewport>`) to display your information, you need to set up *regions*. A region is basically a box that you set aside for storing information: text, images, video, or audio. I mention regions in Chapter 6, but you really need to understand all their nitty-gritty options — I help you do that in this chapter.

Identifying Regions

You use the `<region>` element to control the location of all the information inside a SMIL presentation. You can have as many different regions on your document as you want, and each of these regions can contain multiple objects.

Take a look at the following sample code. In this code, the `<layout>` and `<root-layout>` elements define the working area of the presentation. The `<region>` element defines an area that has text displayed within it. The `<text>` element found within the body of the SMIL document identifies the name of the region that the text will be placed in. You can read more about linking regions to objects, such as text areas, in the section, "Matching Regions and Objects," later in this chapter.

```
<smil>
   <head>
      <layout>
         <root-layout width="300"
                      height="300" />
         <region id="text_region"
                 top="5"  left ="5"
                 height="290" width="290"/>
      </layout>
   </head>
   <body>
      <text region="text_region"
            src="new_text.html"
            dur="10s" />
   </body>
</smil>
```

This code specifically creates a 300 by 300 presentation screen using the `<root-layout>` element with a single region in it that starts 5 pixels down (`top`) and 5 pixels in (`left`) from the top-left corner of the presentation area. It defines the size of the region as 290 pixels tall (`height`) and 290 pixels wide (`width`), so the region is framed by the presentation area with 5 pixels of space on either side (300 [`total`] – 290 [`region`] – 5 [`left` and `top`] = 5 [`right` and `bottom`]).

All `<region>` elements are placed relative to their position and size of their parent element, which in SMIL documents is the `<layout>` element. Because the size and position of the `<layout>` element are defined using the `<root-layout>` element, the `<region>` elements are then positioned relative to the dimensions specified in the `<root-layout>` element, rather than `<layout>`. You can think of this as a big brother letting the little brother know what the parents said to do.

The `<region>` element has attributes that define its position and appearance. Each of these attributes controls one specific portion of the region's setup process. For example, the `top` and `left` attributes control the location of the top and left edges of the region but have nothing to say about how far the region extends down and to the right. These dimensions are controlled by other attributes. In the next few sections, I examine these attributes.

The backgroundColor attribute

Because all windows have a background, `<region>` has to have an attribute to control its background color — the `backgroundColor` attribute. This attribute was called `background-color` in SMIL 1.0, but in the growth to SMIL 2.0, the element was altered to follow the standard naming practice used with Cascading Style Sheets. (To find out more about Cascading Style Sheets, see Chapter 6.)

If you're familiar with Cascading Style Sheets, you already know how the backgroundColor attribute works with SMIL. The sole function of this attribute is to define what color is used as a background behind the various text, image, and video objects placed on your SMIL presentation's region.

SMIL software can support either the SMIL 1.0 background-color, or the SMIL 2.0 backgroundColor attributes, or both. If neither of these attributes is present, the background color of your window is transparent, showing the background color specified with the <root-layout> element or of the SMIL software that's displaying the presentation.

You can see the background color in action in Figure 7-1, which uses the following sample code to change the background color of your region to a red square over the top of a yellow background window. Without the <root-layout> element setting the background color to yellow, the red square is shown over a black background, the default background color in RealPlayer.

Figure 7-1:
A yellow
block with a
red region
in its
center must
supersede
the
RealPlayer
default
black
background.

Red square   Yellow background

Throughout the code in this chapter, I've bolded the sections that specifically relate to the <region> element to make it easier for you to find what I'm discussing in the text.

```
<smil>
   <head>
      <layout>
         <root-layout backgroundColor="#FFFF00"
                      height="180"
                      width="180"/>
         <region id="Region1"
                 left="41"
                 top="40"
                 height="100"
```

```
                    width="100"
                    z-index="1"
                    backgroundColor="#FF0000"/>
        </layout>
    </head>
    <body>
        <seq>
            <img id="0202"
                src=" /junkfolder/0202.gif"
                region="Region1"
                system-bitrate="12000"/>
        </seq>
    </body>
</smil>
```

This presentation uses the backgroundColor attribute to switch the background color of the <region> to red so that it shows up against the yellow background specified in the <root-layout> element.

The bottom attribute

The bottom attribute is used to identify the location of the bottom edge of the region. This attribute uses either an absolute length (in pixels) or a relative percentage to specify the amount of space between the bottom edge of the region and the bottom edge of the area specified by the <root-layout> element.

Unlike the Cascading Style Sheets bottom property, SMIL doesn't require you to specify the pixel (px) unit designator in your value. The value is treated as a measurement of pixels automatically. If you don't provide these values when creating your region, they default to auto and take up the entire area of the <root-layout> box.

```
<region regionName="Region1"
        backgroundColor="#FF0000"
        top="10"
        left="10"
        bottom="10"
        right="10"/>
<region regionName="Region2"
        backgroundColor="#FF00FF"
        top="5%"
        left="5%"
        bottom="5%"
        right="5%"/>
```

The fit attribute

The `fit` attribute in SMIL has no direct relationship to any other property in Cascading Style Sheets or HTML, so this is new for everyone. This attribute controls what happens if the contents of a `<region>` are bigger than the region's dimensions. For example, if your presentation has a region that's only 100 pixels by 100 pixels but contains an animated GIF image that's 150 pixels by 100 pixels, `fit` controls how the region is adjusted for the larger contents.

This attribute can have a variety of values, as follows, which all have different effects:

🖛 `fill`: This value forces the contents of the region to be stretched or shrunk so the object exactly fits the size of the region. This stretching or shrinking doesn't take an object's height or width into consideration, so most objects are no longer proportionate when they're fit to a region, as shown in Figure 7-2.

Original image

Figure 7-2: The `fill` value stretches the image to fit the region, without regard to the proportions of the image.

Region area

Filled image

✔ hidden: This value has one of two effects, depending on the size of the object within your region:

- If the object (an image, for example) is smaller than the region, it fills up as much of the region as it naturally takes, starting in the upper-left corner. The background color of the region shows around the image wherever the image doesn't meet the edge of the region.

- If the image is larger than the region, it fills up the entire region and any portions of the image outside the region are cropped. If the image is smaller than the region, it's shown in its entirety (see Figure 7-3).

hidden is the default value for the fit attribute.

Visible smaller image

Figure 7-3: The hidden value crops off the image where it extends past the boundaries of the region.

Region area

Hidden larger image

✔ meet: This setting scales the object until one of its dimensions, either height or width, matches that of the region. The rest of the region is shown with the background color visible. For example, if you take an image that's 150 pixels wide by 100 pixels tall and place it in a region that's 300 pixels wide by 300 pixels tall, the image appears 300 x 200 because its width is stretched to the width of the region. Figure 7-4 shows you what this looks like.

Original image   Image stretched to meet region edge

Figure 7-4:
The meet value stretches the image proportionately until an edge of the image matches the edge of the region.

Region area

> ✔ scroll: Adds scroll bars to the edges of the region if the contents of the region extend past the region's boundaries. Scroll bars enable a visitor to view the entire image. An example of this effect is shown in Figure 7-5.

Figure 7-5:
The scroll value adds scroll bars to the image.

Scroll bars added to image

> ✔ slice: This setting scales the object so that it maintains its proportions but extends itself so only one edge of the image is cropped. In other words, if the image is wider than the region but not taller, the image is stretched until the height matches and the width is cropped. If you use this setting in your presentation, only one edge of the image, either bottom or right, is clipped.

The height attribute

All objects have a dimension to them. The vertical length of a region is controlled by the `height` attribute. This attribute sets the vertical size of the box that creates the region. You can set the values of this attribute to either an absolute length value in pixels, such as 1000 px (pixels), or a relative percentage length, such as 100 or 75 percent.

If you have a number that doesn't have a measurement designation assigned to it, as shown in the first region in the following example, it is treated as a measurement of pixels. If you don't provide these values when creating your region, they default to `auto` and take up the entire area of the `<root-layout>` box.

```
<region regionName="Region1"
        backgroundColor="#FF0000"
        top="10"
        left="10"
        height="180px"
        width="180px"/>
<region regionName="Region2"
        backgroundColor="#FF00FF"
        top="10px"
        left="10px"
        height="80%"
        width="60%"/>
```

The left attribute

The `left` attribute is used to identify the location of the left edge of the region as either an absolute length (in pixels) or a relative percentage of the entire horizontal dimensions of the area specified by the `<root-layout>` element.

Unlike Cascading Style Sheets, SMIL doesn't require you to specify the pixel (px) unit designator in your value. The value is treated as a measurement of pixels automatically. If you don't provide these values when creating your region, they default to `auto` and take up the entire area of the `<root-layout>` box.

```
<region regionName="Region1"
        backgroundColor="#FF0000"
        top="10"
        left="10"
        bottom="10"
        right="10"/>
<region regionName="Region2"
        backgroundColor="#FF00FF"
        top="5%"
```

```
         left="5%"
         bottom="5%"
         right="5%"/>
```

The regionName attribute

Every region must have a name, and you use the `regionName` attribute to provide it. Because objects must be placed in regions, the easiest way to specify their location is by linking them to the region by its name. Later in this chapter, in the section "Matching Regions and Objects," I discuss how to link the two together, but for now you simply need to understand how to name your regions.

You may be thinking that region names must be unique, but they don't have to be. You can name multiple regions with the same name, although when you're first learning SMIL, I suggest avoiding this practice and using unique names. By creating multiple regions with the same name, however, you can place the same media elements within multiple regions simultaneously. Letters, numbers, and underscores can comprise the names of your regions. You can't have a space in your region name, so use the underscore instead (_). The following sample code shows some possibilities for names of regions.

```
<region regionName="PlanetPic">
<region regionName="Planet_Pic">
<region regionName="Planet_00_Pic">
<region regionName="planetpic">
<region regionName="Planet00">
```

The right attribute

The `right` attribute is used to identify the location of the right edge of the region as either an absolute length (in pixels) or a relative percentage of the entire horizontal dimensions of the `<root-layout>` element.

Unlike Cascading Style Sheets, SMIL doesn't require you to specify the pixel (px) unit designator in your value. The value is treated as a measurement of pixels automatically. If you don't provide these values when creating your region, they default to `auto` and take up the entire area of the `<root-layout>` box.

```
<region regionName="Region1"
        backgroundColor="#FF0000"
        top="10"
        left="10"
        bottom="10"
        right="10"/>
```

```
<region regionName="Region2"
        backgroundColor="#FF00FF"
        top="5%"
        left="5%"
        bottom="5%"
        right="5%"/>
```

The showBackground attribute

You need to define whether the background color of your presentation is shown, even if no media elements are drawn into the region. The showBackground attribute is responsible for controlling this phenomenon. The two possible settings for the showBackground attribute are as follows:

- ✔ always: If the value of showBackground is always, the background color, set by the backgroundColor attribute, is always shown — whether a media object is assigned to that region or not. always is the default value.

- ✔ whenActive: If the value of the showBackground attribute is set to whenActive, the background color of the region is only visible when some type of media object is currently active within the region — whether image, video, or text.

The top attribute

The top attribute is used to identify the location of the upper edge of the <region> as either an absolute length (in pixels) or a relative percentage of the total height of the <root-layout> box. This amount sets the space between the top edge of the region and the top edge of the <root-layout> area.

SMIL doesn't require you to specify the pixel (px) unit designator in your value. The value is treated as a measurement of pixels automatically. If you don't provide these values when creating your region, they default to auto and take up the entire area of the <root-layout> box.

```
<region regionName="Region1"
        backgroundColor="#FF0000"
        top="10"
        left="10"
        bottom="10"
        right="10"/>
<region regionName="Region2"
        backgroundColor="#FF00FF"
        top="5%"
```

```
         left="5%"
         bottom="5%"
         right="5%"/>
```

The width attribute

The horizontal measurement of a region is controlled by the `width` attribute. This attribute sets the horizontal size of the box that creates the region. You can set the values of this attribute to either an absolute length value, such as 1,000 px, or a relative percentage length, for example 100 or 75 percent.

If you have a number that doesn't have a measurement designation assigned to it, as shown in the following example, it's treated as a measurement of pixels. If you don't provide these values when creating your region, they default to `auto` and take up the entire area of the `<root-layout>` box.

```
<region regionName="Region1"
        backgroundColor="#FF0000"
        height="180"
        width="180"/>
<region regionName="Region2"
        backgroundColor="#FF00FF"
        height="80%"
        width="60%"/>
```

The z-index attribute

The `z-index` attribute is a simple notation that keeps the vertical stacking order of regions sorted, or stacked, in the correct order on-screen. If your presentation has several regions that overlap, you can use the `z-index` attribute to indicate which appears on top and which ones are hidden or partially hidden. For instance, imagine that you have several transparencies that you want to display for your company's annual board member meeting. What happens if you drop them on the ground? They scatter, right? If you have them all numbered, you can easily put them back in order. For a SMIL presentation, the `z-index` attribute keeps the parts of your presentation in order.

If you're familiar with Cascading Style Sheets, you're probably experiencing déjà vu right about now. Yes, the `z-index` attribute in SMIL works the same as the `z-index` CSS property with one exception: the timing element involved in SMIL. If you have two boxes that have the same stacking level (`z-index` value) but box 1 is played after box 2, box 1 is placed on top of box two — because that's their temporal order. In other words, SMIL stacks items not only by their `z-index` value but also by their position in the timeline of the playing presentation.

The following sample code shows the use of the z-index attribute for two regions: Region1 and Region2. These regions create two boxes 100 x 100 pixels. Region1 is placed 40 pixels down and over from the top-left corner of the presentation, and Region2 is placed 80 pixels down and over from the top-left corner of the presentation. Which do you think appears over the top of the other? Region2, because it has a stacking value of 2, versus Region1's z-index value of 1. The higher the number, the closer to the top of the stack the object appears.

```
<layout>
    <root-layout backgroundColor="#FFFF00"
                 height="180"
                 width="180"/>
    <region id="Region1"
            left="40"
            top="40"
            height="100"
            width="100"
            z-index="1"
            backgroundColor="#FF0000"/>
    <region id="Region2"
            left="80"
            top="60"
            height="100"
            width="100"
            z-index="2"
            backgroundColor="#FF00FF"/>
</layout>
```

Positioning the Region

SMIL defines dimensions of a region in the following two ways:

- ✔ Using the top, left, width, and height attributes
- ✔ Using the top, left, bottom, and right attributes

But what happens when you use a top, left, right, bottom, width, *and* height attribute on your region?

Actually nothing, *if* the settings correspond correctly. For instance, no problem occurs if the presentation area is 100 pixels square, and the top, left, right, and bottom attributes are all set to 5 with the width and height attributes set to 90. This works perfectly because no disparity exists between the various attributes. The problem arises when the bottom, right, width, and height values collide.

In this case, SMIL follows the rules of Cascading Style Sheets: The values specified for the `bottom` and `right` attributes are used instead of the `width` and `height` attributes. This means that your object can be cropped, as specified in the `fit` attribute of the `<region>` element.

Matching Regions and Objects

With all your regions defined, you have to specify the content that goes into them. In Chapter 2, you can read about all the various media objects and media types that you can place within your SMIL document. These various objects are placed within specified regions in order to control their location, actions, timing, and so on.

Take a look at the following media elements (which I describe in Chapter 2):

```
<img src = "url"
     alt = "information for reader"
     author = "author name"
     longdesc = "long description"
     region = "Region1"
     title = "title of image"
     type = "MIME type">
<text src = "http://www.mydomain.com/smiltext.txt"
     id = "TextName"
     region = "Region2"
     title = "TextTitle"
     type = "text/plain">
<textarea src = "http://www.mydomain.com/smil.html"
     region = "Region3"
     type = "text/html">
<video src = "http://www.mydomain.com/smillogo.qt"
     id = "VideoName"
     region = "Region4"
     title = "VideoTitle"
     type = "video/quicktime">
<audio src = "http://www.mydomain.com/smilsong.au"
     id = "AudioName"
     region = "Region5"
     title = "AudioTitle"
     type = "audio/basic">
<ref src = "http://www.mydomain.com/smilsong.au"
     id = "MediaName"
     region = "Region6"
     title = "MediaTitle"
     type = "text/html">
```

Each of these media elements uses a region attribute to identify the name of the region that that particular piece of media should be placed in. The region attribute doesn't necessarily have to be provided: If it is *not* provided, the information is placed on the root layout of the SMIL presentation screen and not in any regions. Some SMIL players don't display or play any information that isn't included in a region. The best way to control the placement of your image, however, is to place it within a region and format that region to work with the media content that you've placed within it.

As you can see in the following sample code, six regions have been defined within the <layout> element as well as <root-layout>.

```
<smil>
    <head>
    <layout>
        <root-layout backgroundColor="#FFFF00"
                height="400"
                width="400"/>
        <region id="Region1"
                left="40"
                top="40"
                height="100"
                width="100"
                z-index="1"
                backgroundColor="#FF0000"/>
        <region id="Region2"
                left="80"
                top="60"
                height="100"
                width="100"
                z-index="2"
                backgroundColor="#FF00FF"/>
        <region id="Region3"
                left="10%"
                top="5%"
                height="100"
                width="100"
                z-index="3"
                backgroundColor="#FF00FF"/>
        <region id="Region4"
                left="80"
                top="60"
                height="100"
                width="100"
                z-index="4"
                backgroundColor="#FF00FF"/>
        <region id="Region5"
                left="380"
                top="380"
```

```
                height="10"
                width="10"
                z-index="5" />
        <region id="Region6"
                left="80"
                top="60"
                height="10"
                width="100"
                z-index="6"
                backgroundColor="#FF00FF"/>
    </layout>
    </head>
    <body>
        <img src = "url"
             alt = "information for reader"
             author = "author name"
             longdesc = "long description"
             region = "Region1"
             title = "title of image"
             type = "MIME type">
        <text src = "http://www.mydomain.com/text.txt"
              id = "TextName"
              region = "Region2"
              title = "TextTitle"
              type = "text/plain">
        <textarea src = "http://www.mydomain.com/smil.html"
              region = "Region3"
              type = "text/html">
        <video src = "http://www.mydomain.com/logo.qt"
               id = "VideoName"
               region = "Region4"
               title = "VideoTitle"
               type = "video/quicktime">
        <audio src = "http://www.mydomain.com/song.au"
               id = "AudioName"
               region = "Region5"
               title = "AudioTitle"
               type = "audio/basic">
        <ref src = "http://www.mydomain.com/smil.htm"
             id = "MediaName"
             region = "Region6"
             title = "MediaTitle"
             type = "text/html">
    </body>
</smil>
```

For each of these regions, a media type that references it has been defined. This provides a predefined region that's set to contain the various images, text files, videos, and what-have-you that you're including in your presentation.

Chapter 8

Timing Is Everything

*T*iming is truly everything. You met your one true love because you were in the right place at the right time. You got your job because you had the right thing to say to the right person, at the right interview. And according to the astrologists, even our personalities are a result of the exact alignment of the stars and moons at the exact second of our births. Although the timing of a SMIL presentation may not be as radically important as the moment of your birth or that first look into your true love's eyes, it may help to keep that perfect job that you found, or at least keep your employer looking on you with favor.

SMIL documents are concerned with the exact timing that's taking place within your presentation. When creating SMIL documents, you have to make sure that everything happens at just the "right" time. This means that you have to understand time — and timing — and that you also have to be conscious of how long it takes each object to complete its playing period and how to control that duration of play.

Measuring Time in SMIL

SMIL timing is broken into categories, much like the real world. SMIL's categories of time are *global time* and *local time*. Global timing is also called *document time* because you use it to control all the overall timing issues within your SMIL presentation. You use local timing to control the individual objects that are playing within your presentation.

Global time is much like the everyday happenings of the world: The crash of an airplane may not directly affect your life at the exact second that it happens, but it may affect your neighbor in a very personal way, which, ultimately, may come back to affect you. Global time affects everything in your presentation. For instance, the start of the presentation is a global time setting. This time affects all the individual objects within the presentation because they can't start until the presentation starts.

Local time works something like your own personal schedule. You get up, drink your coffee, drive to work, park your car, get to your desk, and begin the day's tasks. Local time provides a way of measuring an object's individual time. For instance, you can start a video playing in your presentation without affecting any other objects in that presentation, unless those other objects — a text file for instance — are directly looking for the start of that video to start their own local time processes.

Within the concept of local time are three more categories of time:

- **Active time:** The measurement of the element's or object's active duration. Active time begins to be measured whenever an object, such as a video, starts to play and ends when that video stops playing.

- **Simple time:** A measurement that's relative to the start of the playing of an object. This time measurement serves as an offset to the playing of a video, for example. You can use simple time to express that an event should occur 5 seconds after a particular video has started to play.

- **Media time:** A measurement of the intrinsic duration of a particular type of media. For example, the intrinsic, or built-in, duration of a video can be anywhere from a few seconds to minutes or even hours. You can then use attributes, such as `clipBegin` and `clipEnd` (which I discuss in Chapter 9), to mark just the portion of the media that you want to actually display.

All the elements placed within your SMIL presentation support elements and attributes that define the time at which they begin playing, the duration of that playing time, and the number of times the object replays. (See Chapter 10.)

Linear versus nonlinear media

Linear media is continuous media that can't be played back in a random manner. Most streaming video and audio files available on the Internet are linear. *Nonlinear media* can be played in a random fashion. You can start playing from the middle of the file, or just play every 5 seconds of the video without regard to what's happening between your video clips.

The capability of a particular type of media to be either linear or nonlinear isn't a function of the media type; it's more a function of the software that's playing the media back to you. For example, you can have a linear media type, such as a RealAudio file, that can be played randomly, *if* the player supports that function for the audio file.

Setting the Duration

Attributes that can be used to control an element's timing behavior are built into the SMIL timing modules. These attributes, such as dur, clipBegin, and clipEnd, control the duration and starting point of the individual media elements. Because all elements must have a beginning and a simple duration when part of the timing module, you must use these attributes to specify how a video or other object should play and for how long.

An element can be started in a variety of ways and played for many different lengths of time. For example, you can start an element at a specific time on the global timeline, base the beginning of the element's playback on when another element begins or ends, or base it entirely on when someone viewing your presentation clicks his or her mouse on a specific picture or piece of text. You can also base the end of an element on another element's beginning or end or on the click of a visitor's mouse. You can also begin or end an element in relation to the start of the presentation or to a clock time. I discuss all the options for controlling the values of your begin and end attributes in the sidebar, "Controlling begin and end events," elsewhere in this chapter. No matter how the element starts, you can use the dur attribute to control how long the element plays. The value of the dur attribute can be preempted by an end attribute.

The dur attribute

One simple attribute, when applied to a media or sequencing element, provides you with the power to set up the length of time for which a particular object is displayed. Specifying a length of time is the only job of the dur attribute.

You can apply three types of values to the dur attribute:

- A value of the clock (10s, for example, where *s* stands for seconds): The clock value must be a positive number greater than zero. If you place a negative or zero value within your SMIL presentation, it's most likely ignored or found as an error within the SMIL player. You can specify partial seconds by using decimal places, such as .5s for one-half second. You must specify minutes as seconds also, so a 3-minute presentation is 180s.
- The intrinsic duration of the media element itself (media): For example, this is the length of time that a video runs without interruption from start to finish.

✔ Indefinite (`indefinite`): You can use the indefinite setting to make the duration of an element last forever. This helps when you want a background image to last until a presentation is over or when you want text to appear until a visitor forces it to close by using the mouse or keyboard.

Take a look at the syntax that controls the `dur` attribute:

```
<elementName dur="value" ... />
```

The element name can either be one of the recognized media types (`<img>`, `<audio>`, `<video>`, `<text>`, `<textarea>`, `<rev>`, and so on) or one of the timing syntax controls, such as `<seq>`, `<excl>`, and `<par>`. (For detailed information on `<seq>` and `<excl>`, see Chapter 9. You can find more on `<par>` in Chapter 10.) You can see sample durations in the following sample code:

```
<video dur="10s" ...>
<audio dur="media" ...>
<textarea dur="indefinite" ...>
<par dur="100s" ...>
```

In addition to defining how the element starts playing, you can also use the `dur` attribute to control the number of times it repeats itself. Consider the example in the following code. If you give a 30-second video clip a duration of one minute, the video repeats two times, as shown in Figure 8-1. The *simple duration* of the video is 30 seconds (the intrinsic length of the video itself), whereas the *active duration* (`dur`) of the video is 60 seconds — the amount of time that the video actually plays, including any repetition or frozen frames. No matter how many times the element repeats itself, it remains active. As soon as all its repetitions have completed, you have the option of removing the element or freezing it on its last frame (using the `fill=freeze` attribute) to avoid empty areas in the presentation. I've bolded the `dur` attributes to help you find them easier.

```
<par begin="0s" dur="60s">
    <video begin="1s"
           dur="30s"
           repeatCount="2"
           fill="freeze" />
</par>
```

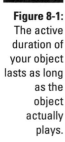

Figure 8-1:
The active
duration of
your object
lasts as long
as the
object
actually
plays.

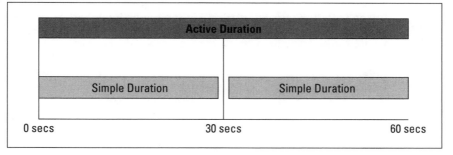

Using dur with the <par>, <seq>, and <excl> elements

As you can see from the previous code, not only are the begin, end, and dur attributes applied to the media elements but they can also be applied to the various elements, such as <par>, <seq>, and <excl>, that actually hold the media element and control the sequence (timing) by which they are played. The <par> element allows you to play media simultaneously, <seq> plays media in sequence, and <excl> plays media exclusively of each other, but in no particular order. By placing the dur attribute directly within one of these timing elements, you can control the duration of a whole series of media objects at once. I discuss <seq> and <excl> in further detail in Chapter 9, while you can find more detail on <par> in Chapter 10.

If you use the dur attribute to specify a time for the parent of the media objects, the timing setting on the parent object is used — if no timing is provided with the child media. For example, if you were to set up a <par> element for 10 seconds but its child <audio> element contained an audio file that lasted for 30 seconds, the presentation stops at the 10-second mark, leaving the audio file stopping in mid-sentence or mid-song, whichever the case may be. If the audio file only lasted 5 seconds, the audio file completes itself, but the <par> element continues until its 10-second duration is reached.

But what about those times when a duration of an image is specified that's longer than the intrinsic duration of the image element itself? The answer comes in two parts. *Discrete media* (media without its own built-in duration, such as text or a still image), when contained within a <par>, <seq>, or <excl>, is shown for the total amount of time that's specified by the container element, when that element is a <par>element. If discrete media is contained within a sequence (<seq>) or an exclusive time list (<excl>), then the image, if it doesn't include its own dur attribute, appears and disappears in a flash, because it doesn't have an intrinsic duration.

To keep the image visible for a longer length of time, you have to provide that image with its own dur attribute. If the media itself had its own duration, as would a video file, the last frame of the video continues showing until the end of the time specified by the container element. Audio files work a bit differently. Because you don't want to hold on to a single sound for a potentially indefinite period of time, audio files stop and are simply silent until the duration ends.

There are a few changes to these rules that occur to the contents of <seq>, <par>, and <excl> scheduling elements. Because media often contain their own durations, whether intrinsic or forced through the use of the dur attribute, a sequence of media sometimes ends before the time applied to the entire sequence ends. Because the media are in a <seq> element, the media plays in order, lasting for their own intrinsic or implied durations. If all the media have completed their own durations before the duration assigned to a <seq> element, the last child is frozen until the end of the specified duration, but this only happens if the media element itself has a freeze or hold value associated with its fill attribute (which I discuss in Chapter 5). Fill controls how the area taken up by a specific media element is dealt with when that media has reached its conclusion. If the media elements are children of a <par> or a <excl> scheduling element, all the children freeze — if the children's individual fill attributes are set to freeze or hold. If the fill attributes aren't set, the media types just end without freezing.

Indefinite and explicit duration

If an element doesn't have a valid duration specified, the intrinsic, or built-in, duration of the media type is used. That means that your text and non-animated images immediately appear and then disappear because they have intrinsic duration; they have no built-in time dimension. If you're working with a lot of text headings, you want to be sure to set your duration (dur) for the headings to indefinite (dur=indefinite) so that they maintain their appearance for the length of the presentation or until they're closed by the presentation viewer, as shown in the following examples.

```
<img src="somefile.gif" dur="indefinite" />
<text src=somefile.htm" dur="indefinite" />
```

If you know exactly how long your text or images need to appear, you can time them along with the remainder of your presentation, using explicit duration statements, showing the length of time that a media element should run.

```
<img src="somefile.gif" dur="100s" />
<text src=somefile.htm" dur="60s" />
```

dur attribute errors

One of the nice things about SMIL is that if an error occurs in the `dur` attribute, the SMIL player is instructed to ignore it, as if it weren't there at all. This works out well for those times when you're just testing a script or trying to find the balance between a stationary, nonanimated object and a region of streaming video.

Putting it all together with dur

Look at the following SMIL code. It creates a series of three regions: The first contains text, the second contains video, and the third contains a non-animated image. Each of these objects appears within their own designated region and is viewed in sequence by the SMIL player. You can see the final outcome of this presentation in Figure 8-2.

In this example, three regions are created to contain text, video, and image files. The text, video, and image are contained within a `<seq>` element forcing them to play in sequence. The entire sequence should last 30 seconds, with the majority of that time taken up by the playing of the video. The text appears immediately and remains frozen on-screen for the duration of the `<seq>`. The video then plays, and its last frame remains visible as soon as it's completed. At that point, the image appears and stays visible until the end of the `<seq>` element.

```
<smil>
   <head>
     <layout>
       <root-layout width="305"
                    height="300"
                    background="#FF0000"/>
       <region id="text_region"
               top="5"  left ="5"
               height="290" width="95"/>
       <region id="video_region"
               top="5"  left ="105"
               height="290" width="95"/>
       <region id="image_region"
               top="5"  left ="205"
               height="290" width="95"/>
     </layout>
   </head>
   <body>
     <seq dur="30s">
       <text region="text_region"
             src="new_text.txt"
             fill="freeze" />
```

```
      <!-- This video ships with Sausage Software's
           SMIL Composer as a demo. -->
      <video src="composer.rm"
             region="video_region"
             fill="freeze" />
      <img src="0801.gif"
             region="image_region"
             fill="freeze" />
    </seq>
  </body>
</smil>
```

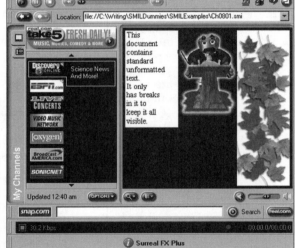

Figure 8-2:
All three
regions are
frozen at
their last
frame
until the
presentation
ends.

Setting the Delay

Sometimes you just don't want everything to happen at once. When presentations aren't timed properly, things look like they were done at the last minute and don't impress anyone, let alone your employer. Because SMIL is nice enough to let you work out your own timing of events, you can decide when your information is displayed, or played. You can set an event to occur relative to another object, when a visitor clicks the mouse, a certain number of seconds after a page has been loaded, or after another timing-based object has started. The power is in your hands to control the timing of your presentation.

You use the `begin` attribute to specify the beginning of an object's playing time. You can specify this attribute as a reference to the starting time of another object or as a reaction to a click by a presentation viewer.

In the following code, you can see one example of offset timing — the start of the video file is dependent on the presence of other objects. In this case, the `<video>` element is started exactly 5 seconds (`begin="5s"`) after the `<par>` element has loaded.

```
<smil>
    <head>
        <layout>
            <!-- regions go here -->
        </layout>
    </head>
    <body>
        <par>
            <video id="video1"
                   src="video.rm"
                   begin="5s"/>
        </par>
    </body>
</smil>
```

In the next example code, the playing of an audio file controls the display of an image. In this case, the `begin` attribute of the audio file works just like the video file in the previous example. It starts playing the audio file exactly 5 seconds after the `<par>` element has been loaded (`begin="5s"`). The additional twist on this example is that the `begin` attribute of the image (`<img>`) loads the image exactly 3 seconds after the audio file has started playing (`begin="audio1.begin+3s"`). `audio1` in the `begin` attribute of the `<img>` element references the name of the audio file. The presentation then waits 3 seconds (`+3s`) before displaying the image. For more information on audio and video media, see Chapter 2.

```
<smil>
    <head>
        <layout>
            <!-- regions go here -->
        </layout>
    </head>
    <body>
        <par>
            <audio id="audio1"
                   src="audio.ra"
                   begin="5s"/>
            <img id="image1"
                 src="showme.gif"
                 begin="audio1.begin+3s"/>
        </par>
    </body>
</smil>
```

The following example is a bit different from the previous two. It uses the click of a visitor's mouse to start the playing of the audio file. Whenever a visitor clicks the image, named `image1`, the audio file starts playing.

```
<smil>
   <head>
     <layout>
        <!-- regions go here -->
     </layout>
   </head>
   <body>
     <par>
        <img id="image1"
             src="showme.gif" />
        <audio id="audio1"
               src="audio.ra"
               begin="image1.click"/>
     </par>
   </body>
</smil>
```

Ending an Object's Playing Time

You specify the end of an object's playing time by using the end attribute, unless it's superseded by the dur attribute. Think of it this way: If you have a CD in your player and you hit the stop button, the CD stops playing. It stops whether the CD was done playing the entire song or not. This is how the end attribute works. It stops the playing of an object even if the object doesn't think it's done yet, according to the duration specified by the dur attribute.

In the following code, you can see one example of offset timing, where the end of the video file is dependent on the existence of other objects. In this case, the <video> element ends exactly 5 seconds (end="15s") after the <par> element has been loaded.

```
<smil>
   <head>
     <layout>
        <!-- regions go here -->
     </layout>
   </head>
   <body>
     <par>
        <video id="video1"
               src="video.rm"
               end="15s"/>
     </par>
   </body>
</smil>
```

In the following example, the playing of an audio file controls the display of an image. In this case, the end attribute of the audio file works just like the video file in the previous example. The presentation starts to play the audio file exactly 5 seconds after the <par> element has been loaded (begin="5s"). The big difference in this example is that the end attribute of the <img> element closes and removes the image 3 seconds after the audio file has started playing (end="audio1.begin+3s"). audio1 in the end attribute of the <img> element is the name of the audio file entry. The end attribute then waits 3 seconds (+3s) after the audio has begun playing and then closes the image.

```
<smil>
   <head>
    <layout>
        <!-- regions go here -->
    </layout>
   </head>
   <body>
    <par>
       <img id="image1"
            src="showme.gif"
            end="audio1.begin+3s"/>
       <audio id="audio1"
              src="audio.ra"
              begin="5s"/>
    </par>
   </body>
</smil>
```

The following example differs from the previous two: In this example, the click of a visitor's mouse stops the playing of the audio file. When a visitor clicks image1, the audio file stops playing.

```
<smil>
   <head>
    <layout>
        <!-- regions go here -->
    </layout>
   </head>
   <body>
    <par>
       <img id="image1"
            src="showme.gif" />
       <audio id="audio1"
              src="audio.ra"
              end="image1.click"/>
    </par>
   </body>
</smil>
```

Controlling begin and end events

SMIL provides many ways to control the beginning and ending of the playback of a media object. You can use a multitude of constructs to calculate a variety of settings for these attributes. I discuss each of these in the following list:

✔ **Synchbase:** This control enables you to synchronize the beginning or ending of your media object with the beginning or ending of another media object.

```
begin="mediaobjectname.begin +
    5s"
begin="mediaobjectname.end +
    1s"
end="mediaobjectname.begin +
    30s"
end="mediaobjectname.end + 15s"
```

✔ **Offset Value:** This uses a displacement of time, either positive (after) or negative (before), to control the start or end of the playback of your media object.

```
begin="+3s"
begin="-5s"
end="+60s"
end="-2s"
```

✔ **SyncToPrev:** Synchronizes your current object in relation to its media object listed previously in the document structure.

```
begin="prev.begin"
begin="prev.begin + 3s"
end="prev.begin + 10s"
end="prev.end"
```

✔ **Event Value:** Synchronizes the event to actions by a viewer. The names of the events are matched to the events used in HTML and Cascading Style Sheets and include such motions as onMouseOver, onMouseOut, onMouseDown, and so on.

```
begin="mediaobjectname.click"
end="mediaobjectname.dblclick"
```

✔ **Repeat Value:** This ends or begins a media element's playback when another object has repeated itself the specified number of times.

```
begin="mediaobjectname.
    repeat(1)"
begin="mediaobjectname.
    repeat(10)"
end="mediaobjectname.repeat(4)"
end="mediaobjectname.repeat(2)"
```

✔ **Access Key Value:** Synchronizes the element to the press of a specific key character by the presentation viewer.

```
begin="accessKey(A)"
    <!-- Begins when 'A' is
    pressed -->
begin="accessKey(Z)"
    <!-- Begins when 'Z' is
    pressed -->
end="accessKey(^M)"
    <!-- Begins when 'Ctrl+M'
    is pressed -->
end="accessKey(Alt+M)"
    <!-- Begins when 'Alt+M'
    is pressed -->
```

✔ **Wallclock Synchronization:** Synchronizes your site to a real-world clock.

```
begin="wallclock(13:01:00)"
end="wallclock(19:55:00)"
```

✔ **Indefinite:** This setting forces the element to play constantly until it's either ended by the end of the presentation or ended through a presentation viewer's interaction.

```
begin="indefinite"
end="indefinite"
```

You can find out more information on these methods at the World Wide Web Consortium Web site located at www.w3.org.

Because of the many ways that you can end the playing of your audio files, I could create a hundred different examples to show you how to use these values in as many different situations. Hopefully, these few examples help you see how to use the combination of the `being`, `dur`, and `end` attributes to find a timing solution to all your presentation needs.

Chapter 9

Setting a Sequence

● ●

In This Chapter

▶ Synchronizing your presentation

▶ Controlling the order in which your objects appear

▶ Understanding how the dur and delay attributes affect an object's appearances

● ●

*C*ontrolling the synchronization of information is a long, arduous task that you must deal with when you want your SMIL presentation to look professional. In this chapter, I discuss some methods that you can use to control the timing and synchronization of your presentation. You find out how to control when your objects appear in your presentation and how long they stay visible. As you'll discover, by using a series of synchronization elements, you can create a wide variety of effects within your presentations.

The Basics of Synchronization

In addition to controlling all the various timing mechanisms that take place within a SMIL document, you have to think about synchronizing the information that's appearing within the presentation. Think about how difficult it is to watch a movie with subtitles if those subtitles are a scene behind the picture you're seeing. Imagine watching a karate fight but not seeing the "pow," "bang," and "bop" subtitles until after the hero walks off the battlefield, victorious? Subtitles are annoying anyway, but they'd be unbearable if they were out of sync with the rest of the picture.

SMIL enables you to use two types of synchronization:

✔ **Hard sync:** This is the more restrictive of the synchronization methods. It requires that the entire presentation be constrained to a single time-line that must be strictly followed by all the SMIL viewing software used to view the presentation. In a hard sync system, factors, such as network congestions and slow connections, affect the playback of the entire document. The SMIL player stops playing the entire document while the SMIL software waits for more information to load.

✔ **Soft sync:** This method is easier on your SMIL player. It allows a looser implementation of the timing system by the SMIL player itself. This means that in a soft sync document only that one element is slowed down by the interruptions caused by slow connections and congested networks.

With the release of SMIL 2.0, you can define which of your SMIL elements must remain within a hard sync relationship and which of them can use a soft sync, or *slip,* relationship. By mixing both hard and soft sync elements, you can force elements that follow each other to maintain their strict order, but it also allows you the time to download all the required elements for a presentation without having to view a choppy presentation.

SMIL defines elements and attributes that are used to control and coordinate the timing and synchronization of your presentation's media elements, including still images, text, and vector-based graphics, as well as intrinsically time-based media, such as videos, audio tracks, and animation files. You use the following three elements to control synchronization:

✔ `<seq>`: Plays its child elements one after another in a sequence.

✔ `<excl>`: Plays one child element at a time, but without imposing any specific order.

✔ `<par>`: Plays the child elements as a group in parallel. I discuss this element further in Chapter 10.

Each of these elements works as a *time container,* which enables you to group your media elements in a coordinated timeline.

Setting the Order of Appearance

The `<seq>` element enables you to force an order of appearance of your presentation media. This element identifies the sequence of elements that play, one after another, within its area of the presentation. This element uses the order of the media elements, as found within the SMIL document, to control the playback order of the elements contained within the presentation. Imagine a presentation with a video, text block, and an audio file. If, for example, such a presentation were created with the following SMIL code, the video (`<video>`) plays, the image (`<img>`) appears, and finally the text (`<text>`) content appears. Hopefully, you can see how this works from Figure 9-1.

```
<seq>
   <video id="vid1".../>
   <img id="img1".../>
   <text id="txt1".../>
</seq>
```

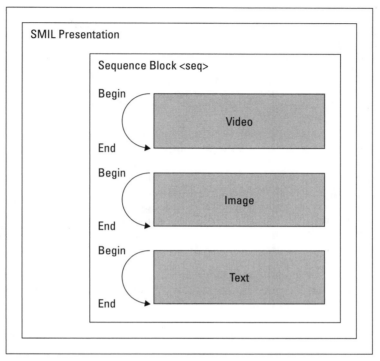

Figure 9-1:
Each media element of a `<seq>` event must run one after another.

Using the `<seq>` element, each of your media types starts as soon as the previous media finishes. In other words, as soon as the `<video>` element stops playing, the `<img>` element appears. As soon as the `<image>` element disappears, the `<text>` element appears. The `<video>` element itself uses the `<seq>` element as its begin marker. As soon as the `<seq>` element is loaded, the `<video>` element loads and begins playing. The sequence itself lasts as long as the length of its combined media children. This means that if one of its media child elements has an indefinite duration, the sequence itself is indefinite.

Elements that are contained within a `<seq>` element have all the same attributes and values that I discuss in Chapter 8, including `dur`, `begin`, and `end`. The behavior of the duration attribute (`dur`) and the `end` attribute aren't affected by the `<seq>` element, but the `begin` attribute works a bit differently. In Chapter 8, you can read about the various values that you can use to synchronize your media to different events, along with other media that you're using in your presentation. None of these events, other than a standard non-negative offset value, such as 3s (3 seconds), can be used with a `<seq>`. You *cannot* use a `begin` attribute with any of the following values within a `<seq>` element:

```
begin="MyImage.begin + 5s"
begin="-5s"
begin="prev.begin + 3s"
begin=" MyImage.click"
begin=" MyImage.repeat(10)"
begin="accessKey(A)"      <!-- Begins when 'A' is pressed -->
begin="wallclock(13:01:00)"
begin="indefinite"
```

Although the begin attribute is limited for the media elements contained *within* a <seq> element, only one value of the begin attribute is limited when it's applied to the sequence *itself*. This limitation prohibits the use of the endsync value, which is only valid for use with the <par> and <excl> elements and is used to control the inherited duration of the timing containers, as a function of their media child elements. You can use the endsync value as a way of stopping the playing of one element simultaneously with another element. By the nature of the <seq> element, this is impossible because each media element plays in sequence — not simultaneously.

Take a look at the following segments of code, which both play indefinitely. This code uses the dur attribute as a way of controlling the length of the media elements without using the begin and end attributes.

The following code shows a sequence that plays indefinitely because the dur (duration) attribute of the <seq> element itself is set to indefinite:

```
<seq dur="indefinite">
    <video id="vid1".../>
    <img id="img1".../>
    <text id="txt1".../>
</seq>
```

And this code shows a sequence that plays indefinitely because the dur attribute of the <img> element is set to display indefinitely:

```
<seq>
    <video id="vid1".../>
    <img id="img1" dur="indefinite".../>
    <text id="txt1".../>
</seq>
```

Who Cares About Order?

Okay, at times you're really worried about everything taking place in its proper order, but what about those other times? If you don't care about your media elements occurring in a specific order but only want them to occur one at a time, you can use the <excl> element, which plays all its media children in any order ordained by the individual media element's `begin` attributes but only one at a time (*exclusively*).

Only one element can play at a time: If the `begin` attributes of two or more elements direct them to play at the same time, one element plays and all others pause. The pausing, or stopping, behavior of each `<excl>` child element is controlled by that element's place in the list of media elements contained by the `<excl>` element. Suppose that you have a series of three elements that are all contained within an `<excl>` element. The three elements will run in order — as long as they have the same beginning time.

In the following sample code, the `<text>` element, which has a duration of 10 seconds, starts playing as soon as the `<excl>` element is reached. But just 3 seconds after the `<excl>` element is started, the `<video>` element is set to start (while the text is still visible). The hitch is that the `<excl>` element only plays one media element at a time. This means that because the beginning of the video element interrupts the displaying of a `<text>` element, the `<text>` is either paused or stopped until the `<video>` element is done playing. Two seconds after the video ends (`video.end +2s`), the image is displayed for 15 seconds.

```
<excl>
    <video id="vid1" begin="+3s".../>
    <img id="img1" begin="video.end+2s" dur="15s".../>
    <text id="txt1" dur="10s".../>
</excl>
```

The `<excl>` element works much the same as the `<par>` element, which I discuss in Chapter 10. Each element enables you to play a series of media types with each element's `begin` attribute determining the order.

Prioritizing your media

When you use the `<excl>` element, you can categorize your media elements into *classes*. Each class, or category, can be set to pause or stop whenever one of those media elements are superseded by another piece of media that's playing. The `<excl>` element's media objects must still follow their exclusive playing rules, but you can control an entire class of elements by using the `<priorityClass>` element introduced in SMIL 2.0, the current SMIL standard at the time of this writing.

The `<priorityClass>` element sets the hierarchy of the `<excl>` element's children. It works kind of like a nanny for a group of kids. If the oldest kids, those with more social clout, want to talk, the little kids have to be quiet. When using this element, you group all your media by how they react to the playing of another media element. The `<priorityClass>` element identifies whether the media included in that group pauses or stops when another media element begins playing.

The `<priorityClass>` element uses the `peers` attribute to control how its child elements interact. The `peers` attribute can have one of four values:

- ✔ `stop`: If one child element begins while another is currently playing, the currently playing element is stopped. This is the default value for the `peers` attribute.

- ✔ `pause`: If one child element begins while another is currently playing, the currently playing element is paused. It restarts as soon as the interrupting element is complete.

- ✔ `defer`: If one child element begins while another is currently playing, the interrupting element is deferred, or postponed, until the currently playing element is complete.

- ✔ `never`: If one child element begins while another is currently playing, the interrupting element is ignored and doesn't play at all.

The following sample code uses the pause value of the `peers` attribute, shown in the bolded text, to pause the video currently playing when another video starts playing.

```
<excl>
    <priorityClass id="subads"
                   peers="pause">
       <video id="ad1" .../>
       <video id="ad2" .../>
       <video id="ad3" .../>
       <video id="ad4" .../>
    </priorityClass>
</excl>
```

I don't discuss a lot of other attributes that the `<priorityClass>` element supports, but some of these attributes may come in handy when you get more comfortable with SMIL. You can read more about all the attributes that affect this element at the World Wide Web Consortium Web site at `www.w3.org/AudioVideo/`. This address points to the primary SMIL page on which you can access the specification containing the attribute descriptions, tutorials, and software that works with SMIL. If you only want to see the actual SMIL specification, go to `www.w3.org/TR/smil20/`.

There is one catch to this interruption behavior control, however. If you use groupings of elements to control their interruption behavior, you have to group *all* your elements. You can't leave some of them outside of a `<priorityClass>` identified group. For instance, the following segment of code defines two advertising videos that are outside of a `<priorityClass>` element when all of the other videos are contained within it. This code creates an error in your SMIL-playing software.

```
<excl dur="indefinite">
   <video id="ad1" .../>
   <video id="ad2" .../>
   <priorityClass id="subads"
                  peers="stop">
      <video id="ad3" .../>
      <video id="ad4" .../>
      <video id="ad5" .../>
      <video id="ad6" .../>
   </priorityClass>
</excl>
```

All your media elements must be contained within `<priorityClass>` elements, as shown in the following example code:

```
<excl dur="indefinite">
   <priorityClass id="topads"
                  peers="defer">
      <video id="ad1" .../>
      <video id="ad2" .../>
   </priorityClass>
   <priorityClass id="subads"
                  peers="stop">
      <video id="ad3" .../>
      <video id="ad4" .../>
      <video id="ad5" .../>
      <video id="ad6" .../>
   </priorityClass>
</excl>
```

Putting <excl> to work

By combining the `<excl>` and the `<priorityClass>` elements, you can create time containers that provide much of the functionality commonly seen on Web sites that feature alternating images triggered by a visitor moving the mouse over a button or selecting some other menu option. For instance, you can create an interactive play list that enables you to select from a series of music videos or a selection of various subtitle languages to go with your video.

An interactive play list

A *play list* is a simple list of songs or videos that can be played one after another. To make a play list interactive, you can use the SMIL `<excl>` element with the `<priorityClass>` element to control how you want your songs to interact when different selections are made. This example creates a document that plays a series of audio tracks and displays information about each song, when the button representing this track is pressed.

When a viewer clicks a track button, the `<par>` element, which monitors the activity of that button, starts playing. Because each series of songs is contained within the `<excl>` element, the songs run exclusive of each other but parallel with their text information. That's because the `<par>` element is contained within the `<excl>` element, and each song is contained within the `<par>` element. When the `<par>` sequence starts, both the audio track and the text are displayed. If a track is selected during the playing of one track, the original track stops playing, as instructed by the `peers="stop"` attribute of the `<priorityClass>` element.

```
<excl>
 <priorityClass peers="stop">
  <par begin="track1Btn.click">
    <audio id="track1s" src="mysong.ra" />
    <text id="track1t" src="mysong.txt" />
  </par>
            <par begin="track2Btn.click">
    <audio id="track2" src="hissong.ra" />
    <text id="track2t" src="hissong.txt" />
  </par>
  <par begin="track3Btn.click">
    <audio id="track3" src="hersong.ra" />
    <text id="track3t" src="hersong.txt" />
  </par>
  <par begin="track4Btn.click">
    <audio id="track4" src="theirsong.ra" />
    <text id="track4t" src="theirsong.txt" />
  </par>
 </priorityClass>
</excl>
```

Subtitles for a video

You can use a series of `<par>` events, containing objects to be displayed in parallel, within an `<excl>` element that makes each `<par>` run independently of each other. This type of setup can be used to identify the specific subtitles that you want to see with a movie. Think back to that last great French romance flick that you watched. Now, if your high school French is as rusty as mine, you may understand when they were heading to the library, bathroom, or maybe even opening a door, but not much else. You need subtitles, dang it! But you need them in a language that you can read. I remember one time traveling to Mexico and watching the 1980s classic movie *Terminator*. I'd seen it a dozen times: I practically had all the lines memorized. Problem is, Schwarzenegger doesn't sound like Schwarzenegger when "I'll be back!" comes out as "Regresare!" Add to that the great Japanese subtitles, and I was really ready to enjoy the movie. (Not!)

If I'd watched that movie on a SMIL player, I'd had the option of seeing sub-titles in a language that I can understand. The following SMIL code does just that:

```
<par>
    <video id="vid1" .../>
    <excl>
        <par begin="englishBtn.click" >
            <text begin="vid1.begin" src="english.ra" />
        </par>
        <par begin="frenchBtn.click" >
            <text begin="vid1.begin" src="french.ra" />
        </par>
        <par begin="spanishBtn.click" >
            <text begin="vid1.begin" src="spanish.ra" />
        </par>
    </excl>
</par>
```

The <par> element runs the video and the subtitles, when they're selected, at the same time. The <excl> element allows only one set of subtitles to be shown at once. The <par> elements within the <excl> element select the subtitles to use based on the language button that the viewer clicks. For instance, if a viewer presses the button with the id "englishBtn", the English subtitles appear.

Chapter 10

Timing: It's All Relative . . . Unless It's Parallel

As exciting as it may be to run everything in your presentation in a sequence, or even just one element at a time, you'll eventually want more than one thing happening at once. Just as you want your dessert to come after your dinner and your drink to come with your dinner, you will, at times, want parts of your presentation to only occur after another event has occurred or while another event is occurring. The element that you use to run media elements simultaneously in your presentation is the <par> element, which I discuss in this chapter. You'll see how to use this element to create effects with multiple objects, each running for a different length of time and starting at a different moment.

Playing Elements at the Same Time

The only element that allows parallel playing of your media types is the <par> element. This element identifies a series of elements that play together, based on the values of their begin, end, and dur attributes, within its area of the presentation. The order of the media elements within the SMIL document has no effect on the playback order of the elements. With the <par> element, the playback order can be simultaneous or widely varied over time, depending on the value of each element's begin attribute. Imagine a presentation with a video, text block, and an audio file. If, for example, you created it with the following SMIL code, the video, image, and textarea content appear simultaneously.

```
<par>
    <video id="vid1".../>
    <img id="img1".../>
    <textarea id="txt1".../>
</par>
```

With the <par> element, each of your media types starts as soon as
the <par> block is started. In other words, the image element appears
without waiting for the video to stop playing. The <video>, <image>, and
<textarea> elements all use the <par> element as their begin marker. As
soon as the <par> element is loaded, all the media located between the opening and closing <par> tags load and begin playing. The <par> element has a
duration as long as the length of its longest media child. For example, if one
of its media child elements has an indefinite duration, the <par> element
itself is indefinite.

Elements that are contained within a <par> element have all the same attributes and values that I discuss in Chapter 8, including dur, begin, and end. In
Chapter 8, you can also read about the various values that you can use to
synchronize your media to different events and other media also being used
on your presentation. All of these events and rules can be used with the
<par> element. This means that a begin or end attribute with any of the fol-
lowing values is effective and valid within the elements contained within your
<par> block.

Although you can't use any of the following begin value examples, other than
begin="2s" within a <seq> element directly, as I discuss in Chapter 9, you
can use them within a <par> element that's a child of a <seq> element.

```
begin="MyImage.begin + 2s"
begin="2s"
begin="-2s"
begin="prev.begin + 2s"
begin="MyImage.click"
begin="MyImage.repeat(2)"
begin="accessKey(Z)" <!--Begins when 'Z' is pressed-->
begin="wallclock(11:01:00)"
begin="indefinite"
```

Also, unlike the <seq> element, the <par> element doesn't limit basing a
begin or end attribute's value on another object or a mouse click when
applied to the <par> element's begin or end attributes directly.

In the following example, the video, image, and textarea files all appear
simultaneously (see Figure 10-1), but the image is the only element that
stays visible indefinitely. This also keeps the <par> element open indefinitely.
The video itself plays for the length of its recording time — whether that's
10 seconds or 10 minutes — and then stops. Because the text file's duration
is set to 30 seconds (30s), it appears for 30 seconds before disappearing.
For example, the video starts at the same time as the image but disappears

whenever the video's intrinsic time runs out. The textarea quickly displays the contents of its associated file and disappears because it has neither a fill attribute nor a dur attribute that forces it to stick around longer.

```
<par>
    <video id="vid1".../>
    <img id="img1" dur="indefinite".../>
    <text id="txt1" dur="30s".../>
</par>
```

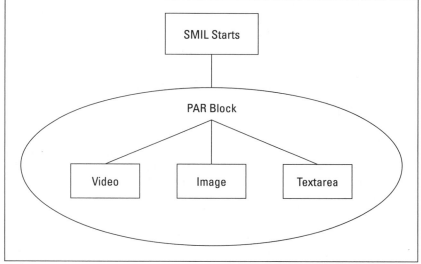

Figure 10-1:
All the elements in a <par> block run simultaneously.

Understanding Duration and Delay

Have you ever been late for work? Was it perhaps because only one person can use the bathroom at a time? Or was it because everyone was trying to use the bathroom at the same time, and no one had any room to complete his or her own morning ritual? Just as you and your family may have worked out a bathroom schedule, SMIL enables you to work out a display schedule for your presentation. The display schedule is based on a lot of different factors, but the top three are dur, begin, and end.

Duration: As long as it takes

In Chapter 9, I show you how you can use the dur attribute with the <seq> and the <excl> elements to control how long information is available and how the start of other media elements affects those elements and their media children. Media elements found within a `<par>` block work a little differently than either of those options.

Just as with the `<seq>` and `<excl>` elements, you can use the `<par>` element to run a series of images indefinitely by setting the `dur` attribute of the `<par>` element to indefinite. In this example, `<par>` forces the video, image, and text to display indefinitely:

```
<par dur="indefinite">
    <video id="vid1".../>
    <img id="img1".../>
    <textarea id="txt1".../>
</par>
```

Time always has a beginning: Starting play

In addition to controlling the duration of the media element, you can set both its `begin` and `end` time, while the element is contained within a `<par>` block. You can use the `begin` attribute as a delay device. By default, all the elements contained within a `<par>` element begin at the same time. The `begin` attribute of each media element can be modified so that you can have multiple media elements running simultaneously but with different starting times.

For instance, suppose that you want to play a video but want to display another image at steady intervals, as shown in Figure 10-2. The following code begins a *freeze* that lasts for a period of 4 seconds every 15 seconds on a series of images. The `begin` attributes of each image specify that image's start time. If you look through the code, you see that the `begin` times for each image are 15 seconds apart. In addition, the `dur` attribute of each image is 4 seconds. That means that you see an image for 4 seconds that's replaced by another image 11 seconds later. The video plays continually throughout the image rotation process. I discuss the `fill="freeze"` media attribute values in Chapter 5.

```
<par>
    <video id="vid1" src="video1" .../>
    <img id="img1" src="img1.gif"
        dur="4s"  begin="15s" fill="freeze"... />
    <img id="img2" src="img2.gif"
        dur="4s"  begin="30s" fill="freeze" ... />
    <img id="img3" src="img3.gif"
        dur="4s"  begin="45s" fill="freeze" ... />
    <img id="img4" src="img4.gif"
        dur="4s"  begin="60s" fill="freeze" ... />
    <img id="img5" src="img5.gif"
        dur="4s"  begin="75s" fill="freeze" ... />
</par>
```

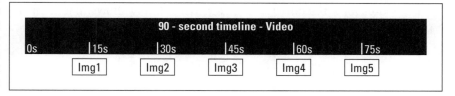

All these images can run simultaneously, but they don't — simply because of their dur and begin attributes. You can add additional control to the display of your parallel elements by using the end attribute.

Nothing lasts forever: Ending play

At times, you may want to run media elements simultaneously but have control over the duration or end time of the media without depending on its intrinsic time duration. Because you can use the end attribute to control the active duration of a media element, you can control the duration of a media element even when its built-in duration may be indefinite.

As you know, some media types, such as videos and animations, have an intrinsic duration. They have a built-in length that can't be changed without modifying the file itself. But you can use the end attribute to put a stop to the playing of a file at the point that you no longer want to display it — in this case, after 10 seconds.

```
<anim src="infinitely_repeating_animation.gif"
     end="10s"... />
```

You can also force a video to appear longer than its intrinsic duration by setting the end time past the point at which the video naturally stops. In this case, the video ends 30 seconds into the presentation, but the end attribute specifies that the video should last for 45 seconds. The last frame of the video is, therefore, held open for another 15 seconds.

```
<video src="30_second_video.mpg"
     end="45s".../>
```

You can also specify that the media play for its full implicit duration by using the *media* value of the dur attribute but allow a presentation viewer to stop the playing of the video by clicking a mouse.

When the dur attribute is set to media, the presentation uses the intrinsic length of that media as the total duration of the element. If the video is 3 minutes long, the dur="media" attribute simply allows that media to end at its natural time.

```
<video dur="media"
       src="movie.mpg"
       end="click".../>
```

You can also allow your visitors to stop the playing of your presentation by pressing a key, as shown in the following code:

```
<video dur="media"
       src="movie.mpg"
       end="accessKey(Z)".../>
```

Sometimes you can't exactly time your media or you may want one media element to shut off whenever another media element ends. You can do this by using the *synchronization rules* that I discuss in Chapter 8 and summarize in Table 10-1. Confusing, isn't it? Think about it in terms of this real-life example. Suppose that you're creating the intermission entertainment for your drama group's Winter Festival. You have to play the same song, over and over, until the next act starts. In SMIL, you can simply set up an audio file that repeats itself indefinitely until the next section of the presentation begins.

Table 10-1	Synchronization Rules	
Rule	*Example*	*Description*
Synchbase	begin="*objectname*.begin"	Starts playing the current object when the specified object is started.
Offset Value	begin="+3s"	Starts the current object 3 seconds after the close of the previous object in the document.
SyncToPrev	begin="prev.begin"	Synchronizes your current object's start to the start of the previous element in the document.
Event Value	begin="objectname.click"	Synchronizes the start of the object's playing time to a mouse click on the specified object.
Repeat Value	end="objectname.repeat(4)"	This ends the element's playing time, when the other object has repeated four times.

Rule	Example	Description
Access Key Values	end="accessKey(A)"	Synchronizes the start of the element to the press of a key character by the presentation viewer.
Wallclock Synchronization	end="wallclock(19:55:00)"	Ends the object in time to a real-world clock.
Indefinite	begin="indefinite"	Forces the object to play indefinitely, unless shut down by a script.

In the following example, the audio file (intermission.au) is started when act1 ends and ends when act2 begins. You know the intermission lasts no more than 10 minutes. So, you set the repeatDur attribute to your 10-minute limit (600 seconds). You know that the music you're playing is only 1 minute long, so you set the dur attribute to 60 seconds. This forces the song to repeat itself as many times as it takes, in this case 10, until the total amount of time specified by the repeatDur attribute is reached, or act2 begins.

```
<audio src="intermission.au"
    begin="act1.end+5s"
    end="act2.begin"
    repeatDur="600s"
    dur="60s"
    .../>
```

In this case, as soon as the first act ends, the audio file waits 5 seconds and starts playing. It repeats the intermission song for up to 10 minutes or until act2 begins. In this way, you don't have to worry about having your intermission music playing while the other portion of the presentation is starting.

You can achieve this effect of playing an intermission for an unknown amount of time by putting your intermission and acts in an exclusive (<excl>) block, which I discuss in Chapter 9.

Beginning an Event on Time

See . . . timing is everything. SMIL uses timing to make sure that everything runs at the point that it's supposed to. Throughout this chapter, I discuss the dur, begin, end, min, and max attributes. You use these attributes to control the timing of your elements: when they start and how long they last. Look at some of the examples in the following sections to better familiarize yourself with how to use timing in your SMIL documents.

Setting minimums and maximums

Two more attributes, min and max, give you some additional control over your media element's durations. These attributes do just what they imply: They enable you to set a *minimum* and a *maximum* amount of time that the media element can play. For instance, if you have an element that uses the click of the user's mouse to end its play time, you may want to ensure that the click can't stop the playback before important information, such as licensing agreements, have been played back fully. You may also want to set a maximum time limit so that your users don't have music playing steadily on their computer and annoying their cat while they run off to have a coffee break.

The min attribute can be specified as either a positive clock value such as 3s (3 seconds) or media. If set to a clock value, the media, such as a video, must play for at least the specified number of seconds. If set to media, the element has to play its complete intrinsic duration. The default value of min is 0, which doesn't constrain the active duration at all and enables it to play until it has ended or until its intrinsic duration is reached.

In the following example, the min attribute forces users to at least pretend to read the licensing agreement until it scrolls completely by. They can't get out of it by clicking the GoOn button, which is identifed as the end event by the end attribute. Of course, after the media has played once, in this case the full 30 seconds of the license agreement, they can click GoOn and skip watching the license agreement repeat itself.

```
<textarea src="license.txt"
          dur="30s"
          repeatDur="90s"
          min="media"
          end="GoOnBtn.click"
    .../>
```

The max attribute specifies the maximum value of the active duration of the attribute and can be a clock value, media, or indefininte. If set to a clock value, the media, such as a video, must play for at least the specified number of seconds. If set to media, the element has to play its complete intrinsic duration. If set to indefinite, no constraint limits the length of time that the media can play, and it must be ended by either the end attribute or by a set active duration. The default value of max is indefinite, which doesn't constrain the active duration at all, and enables it to play until it has ended or until its intrinsic duration is reached.

In the following example, the video plays for a maximum of 15 seconds, even though it's actually 30 seconds long.

```
<video id="vid1"
       max="15s"
       src="30s_video.rm"
    .../>
```

Comment on what's happening

Have you ever sat and watched MTV or VH1? If you spend any time at all watching music videos, you see the latest trends in popping up on-screen information about the artist's life, habits, songs, history, lovers, and ancestors. You can create the same technique using SMIL.

Imagine for a moment a simple SMIL document that plays three videos, with an introduction interview between each video. Add a series of three comments on each of the videos and you have SMIL code that looks something like the following:

```
<smil>
  <head>
    <!-- This is the layout for the entire screen.
         It sets up a root screen of 300 x 300 pixels
         with two regions for video and comments. The
         video region is 296 x 296 pixels and set in
         the root area so that it has a 2 pixel border
         around the entire video. The comment region
         is set in the lower 15% of the video region,
         and appears over the video as seen in its
         z-index value, and is 276 x 36 pixels -->
    <layout>
      <root-layout top="0" left="0"
                    width="300" height="300" />
      <region id="video_region"
              top="2" left="2"
              width="296" height="296"
              z-index="0" />
      <region id="comment_region"
              top="252" left="12"
              width="276" height="36"
              z-index="1" />
    </layout>
  </head>
  <body>
    <!-- The running of each set of videos must be in a set
         sequence -->
    <seq>

      <!-- Within each video the comments must appear
           simultaneously with the video itself. -->
      <par>

        <!-- The rap video begins 1 second after the par
             loads and runs for the minimum duration (160s)
             of the video. -->
        <video id="rap_vid"
               src="rapvid.rm"
               region="video_region"
               dur="160s"
               min="media"
               begin="1s" />

        <!-- The following code identifies the text that
             will appear on the screen during the video.
             Each text comment is displayed for 5
             seconds at regular intervals throughout
             the duration of the video. -->
```

```
        <text id="rap_txt1"
              src="raphist.txt"
              region="comment_region"
              dur="5s"
              min="2s"
              begin="10s" />
        <text id="rap_txt2"
              src="rapart.txt"
              region="comment_region"
              dur="5s"
              min="2s"
              begin="60s" />
        <text id="rap_txt3"
              src="rapcourt.txt"
              region="comment_region"
              dur="5s"
              min="2s"
              begin="90s" />
</par>

    <!-- Play Commercial 1 -->
<video id="comm1"
       src="commercial1.rm"
       region="video_region"
       dur="10s" />

<par>

    <!-- The country video begins 1 second after the par
         loads and runs for the minimum duration (120s)
         of the video -->
    <video id="country_vid"
           src="countryvid.rm"
           region="video_region"
           dur="120s"
           min="media"
           begin="1s" />

    <!-- Each text comment is displayed for 5
         seconds at regular intervals throughout
         the duration of the video. -->
    <textarea id="country_txt1"
              src="countryhist.txt"
              region="comment_region"
              dur="5s"
              min="2s"
              begin="10s" />
    <textarea id="country_txt2"
              src="countryart.txt"
              region="comment_region"
              dur="5s"
              min="2s"
```

```
                   begin="60s" />
        <textarea id="country_txt3"
              src="countrycourt.txt"
              region="comment_region"
              dur="5s"
              min="2s"
              begin="90s" />
    </par>

        <!-- Play Commercial 2 -->
    <video id="comm2"
          src="commercial2.rm"
          region="video_region"
          dur="10s" />

    <par>

      <!-- The jazz video begins 1 second after the par
            loads and runs for the minimum duration (180s)
            of the entire length of the video -->
      <video id="jazz_vid"
            src="jazzvid.rm"
            region="video_region"
            dur="180s"
            min="media"
            begin="1s" />

      <!-- Each text comment is displayed for 5
            seconds at regular intervals throughout
            the duration of the video. -->
      <textarea id="jazz_txt1"
            src="jazzhist.txt"
            region="comment_region"
            dur="5s"
            min="2s"
            begin="10s" />
      <textarea id="jazz_txt2"
            src="jazzart.txt"
            region="comment_region"
            dur="5s"
            min="2s"
            begin="60s" />
      <textarea id="jazz_txt3"
            src="jazzcourt.txt"
            region="comment_region"
            dur="5s"
            min="2s"
            begin="90s" />
    </par>
  </excl>
 </body>
</smil>
```

You can find this presentation on the CD. Just look for the file `comments.smi` in the `Examples/Chapter10` directory.

Use your users

If you never allow your presentation viewers to interact with your presentation, you're overlooking a lot of the capabilities of SMIL. You can use the click of your user's mouse as the key to start or stop any number of media elements, as I discuss throughout this chapter and in Chapters 8 and 9.

Imagine for a moment that you're creating online training material for your company's new employees. The following code uses one video, in this case an employee training video, that can be started and stopped by the use of the play and stop buttons created with the `<img>` elements.

You can find this presentation on the CD. Just look for the file `training.smi` in the `Examples/Chapter10` directory.

```
<smil>
<head>
    <!-- This is the layout for the entire screen.
         It sets up a root screen of 300 x 300 pixels
         with three regions. The first is for video
         and text instruction. The other 2 are for the
         control buttons. The video region is 275 x
         275 pixels and set in the root area so that
         it has a 2 pixel border around the top and
         sides of the video or text. The other regions
         appear in the lower portion of the screen,
         and display the Play and Stop buttons. -->
    <layout>
    <root-layout top="0" left="0"
                 width="300" height="300" />
    <region id="class_region"
            top="2" left="2"
            width="296" height="275"
            z-index="0" />
    <region id="play_region"
            top="280" left="15"
            width="123" height="18"
            z-index="1" />
    <region id="stop_region"
            top="280" left="153"
            width="123" height="18"
            z-index="1" />
    </layout>
</head>
<body>
```

```
<!-- Title Screen for Training is Shown First.
     It is shown indefinitely, or until the user
     clicks  the play button. -->
<text id="title_screen"
      src="title.txt"
      region="class_region"
      dur="indefinite"
      end="play.click" />

<!-- Identifies the video to play that will
     provide their training information.
     This video is started by the click of the
     Play button, and ended by the click of the
     Stop button. Otherwise it plays for 1500
     seconds (25 minutes)-->
<video id="training_vid"
       src="training.rm"
       region="class_region"
       dur="1500s"
       begin="play.click"
       end="stop.click" />

<!-- Identifies the play button. It is visible at
     all times. The play button is used to start
     the playing of the video, and close the text
     title information. -->
<img id="play"
     src="play.gif"
     region="play_region"
     dur="indefinite" />

<!-- Identifies the stop button. It only becomes
     visible (begins) when the title screen has been
     closed and the video has been started. -->
<img id="stop"
     src="stop.gif"
     region="stop_region"
     dur="indefinite"
     begin="title_screen.end" />
   </body>
</smil>
```

You can also use the same event to toggle the start and stop of an event, as shown in the following code. In this example, the click of the same button (toggle) starts and stops the display of the image. The restart attribute specifies that the image should restart whenever it isn't active, thus allowing the begin event to occur.

```
<img id="foo"
     begin="toggle.click"
     end="toggle.click"
     restart="whenNotActive" ... />
```

You can't have an element that begins itself. For instance, if you have a begin="click" attribute and value, the attribute is never visible. The attribute can't appear until it has begun, and it can't begin until a viewer clicks it; viewers can't click it unless they can see it. For instance, the following code is *invalid.* A visitor can't click the image if it hasn't become visible yet.

```
<img id="badimage"
     begin="click" ... >
```

Watching Other Events

Just as you can use the click of a user's mouse to start the display of information on-screen, you can use the playing of one piece of media to start the display of another.

Imagine a slide show presentation. When you're sitting at that family reunion watching the slides of your grandparents' latest trip to Kenya, you see each image for just long enough to see it clearly, hear a bit of information about it, and then go on to see the next slide. You can create the same effect using SMIL: You can either automate the advancing of the slides or you can use a Next button to scroll through them at the user's own pace.

In this easy example, you can just automate the advance of each slide with a slight pause between the display of each new slide.

```
<smil>
<head>
    <!-- This is the layout for the entire screen.
         It sets up a root screen of 300 x 300 pixels
         with one region which shows each slide. -->
    <layout>
      <root-layout top="0" left="0"
                   width="300" height="300" />
      <region id="slide_region"
              top="2" left="2"
              width="296" height="296"
              z-index="0" />
    </layout>
  </head>
  <body>
    <!-- Title Screen for Slideshow is Shown First -->
    <text id="title_screen"
          src="title.txt"
```

```
                region="slide_region"
                dur="10s" />

    <!-- Identifies the first slide to display.
         It loads for 10 seconds and starts when
         the title screen ends.-->

    <video id="slide1"
           src="slide1.jpg"
           region="slide_region"
           dur="10s"
           begin="title_screen.end" />

    <!-- Identifies the second slide display.
         It loads for 10 seconds and starts
         when slide 1 ends.-->
    <video id="slide2"
           src="slide2.jpg"
           region="slide_region"
           dur="10s"
           begin="slide1.end" />

    <!-- Identifies the third slide display.
         It loads for 10 seconds and starts
         when slide 2 ends.-->

    <video id="slide3"
           src="slide3.jpg"
           region="slide_region"
           dur="10s"
           begin="slide2.end" />

    <!-- Identifies the fourth slide display.
         It loads for 10 seconds and starts
         when slide 3 ends.-->

    <video id="slide4"
           src="slide4.jpg"
           region="slide_region"
           dur="10s"
           begin="slide3.end" />

    <!-- Identifies the fifth slide display.
         It loads for 10 seconds and starts when
         slide 4 ends.-->
    <video id="slide5"
           src="slide5.jpg"
           region="slide_region"
           dur="10s"
           begin="slide4.end" />

  </body>
</smil>
```

You can put all these effects together so that you have images that automatically advance or that advance until a viewer clicks a button. Practically no limit restricts what you can do with the loading of your presentation objects.

Chapter 11

Customizing Your Presentation

*I*n Chapter 5, I talk about the `<switch>` element, which enables your visitor's computer to make informed decisions about the information to be shown during a presentation. This is sort of like you walking into a mechanics shop, and the mechanic recognizes right away that your Honda has a problem with the oil pan that only costs fifty cents to fix. SMIL can't tell what make and problems you have in your car, but it can tell a lot about your computer. That information about your computer enables you to specify a set of alternative presentation elements that can be used when a specific selection of criteria is met. This works just as well on controlling your presentation timing as it does on any other type of information.

Identifying Which Tests to Perform

The first step to customizing your presentation is to identify the areas of your presentation that you want to alter. After you've identified these areas of concern, you need to decide how to alter your presentation and timing properly for each situation.

As I point out in Chapter 5, the `<switch>` element uses the following selection rules to decide which element to display in your visitor's document:

1. **The SMIL player looks at all the elements contained within the `<switch>` in the order that they occur in the document.**

2. **The first element to match all the testing criteria to the current SMIL player is selected.**

The basic types of switch test attributes that you can use to perform are shown here in Table 11-1. *Switch test attributes* are used to identify the current settings on your visitor's computer and the SMIL player's settings. For more detail, see Chapter 5.

Table 11-1	Switch Tests	
Test	*Syntax*	*Description*
systemBitrate	systemBitrate= "*integer*"	Specifies the approximate bandwidth, in bits per second, that's available for the presentation on the current connection.
systemCaptions	systemCaptions= "[on | off]"	Specifies a text caption to appear in conjunction with an audio file.
systemLanguage	systemLanguage= "*languagecode*"	Specifies one of the supported primary language codes, such as "en," that are listed in Table 5-1 in Chapter 5.
systemRequired	systemRequired= "*namespaceprefix*"	Compares the name of the XML Namespace to those namespaces supported by the SMIL player. (See Appendix C for more information.)
systemScreenSize	systemScreenSize= "*height X width*"	Tests the resolution of the visitor's monitor and compares it to the available screen dimensions.
systemScreenDepth	systemScreenDepth= " [1 | 4 | 8 | 24 | 32 | *integer*]"	Tests the number of colors that are supported by the screen's color palette, based on the number of bits that are required for displaying

the presentation
on-screen.

Test	Syntax	Description
systemOverdubOrSubtitle	systemOverdubOrSubtitle= "[overdub | subtitle]"	Tests the SMIL player's preference settings for receiving overdubbing or subtitles with the audio and video tracks.
systemAudioDesc	systemAudioDesc= "[on | off]"	Tests for the SMIL player's preference settings for displaying closed audio descriptions, or audio captions for visually challenged individuals, for your presentations.
systemOperatingSystem	systemOperatingSystem= *"os-code"*	Determines the operating system currently used by the presentation visitor. In Chapter 5, I list valid operating systems; some of the primary systems are BeOS, Linux, MacOS, OS2, PalmOS, UnixWare, Win16, Win32, Win9x, WinNT, and WinCE.
systemCPU	systemCPU= *"cpu-code"*	Determines the type of CPU in use by the visitor's computer. In Chapter 5, I include a list of valid CPU codes, which include such systems as M68K, RS6000, VAX, and X86.
systemComponent	systemComponent= *"string"*	This is an open-ended test that enables you to test the various components of a SMIL player. You can use this test to see if the SMIL player tests for JavaScript or Java, for instance. The exact string that you need to use varies depending on the SMIL player that your visitor is using.

Testing for Operating System

Now, one of the first steps you may want to take toward tailoring your presentation to visitors' needs is to use the `systemOperatingSystem` test attribute to match up your presentation with the computer that's used to view it. You may ask, "Why is knowing the operating system important?" One reason is to provide images that are optimized for each operating system. Images created on a Macintosh appear too dark on a Windows machine because the Macintosh hardware and standard Windows PC hardware use different gamma corrections for their monitors. (I could spend a lot of time telling you what a gamma correction is, but all you really need to know is that Mac images look dark on a PC.) This also means that any image that's created on standard PC hardware appears slightly washed out when viewed on a Macintosh.

The following snippet of code tests each operating system, from most to least popular, and then loads the correct image, text, video, or whatever, into the presentation. In this example, if viewers aren't using one of these three operating systems, they don't see any of the presentation that's included inside the `<switch>` element. Because you don't want your visitors to see nothing, you need to be sure to include an option for all operating systems, or close your `<switch>` statement with a universal minimum, such as a `systemBitrate="9600"` test (even though that test is unrelated to the operating system). You can then put the most basic text, and flat images, in within that section of the `<switch>` element so that all your visitors see something — even if it's a message that says: `Because you aren't using a Windows, MacIntosh, or Linux machine, you aren't seeing the whole presentation`. You can see a flowchart explaining this section of code in Figure 11-1.

```
<switch>
   <par systemOperatingSystem="Win32">
      <!-- SMIL media elements here -->
   </par>
   <par systemOperatingSystem="MacOS">
      <!-- SMIL media elements here -->
   </par>
   <par systemOperatingSystem="Linux">
      <!-- SMIL media elements here -->
   </par>
</switch>
```

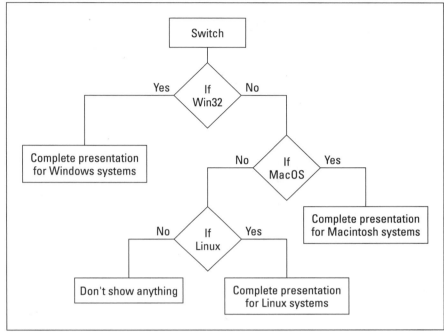

Figure 11-1:
As your
SMIL player
progresses
through the
`<switch>`
element,
your
computer is
checked to
see if it
matches
one of the
specified
operating
systems.

Testing for screen size

If you've ever developed a Web page, you know exactly how frustrating it is to design your presentation window for several different screen sizes. You no longer have the comfort of creating a design that permanently goes on an 8.5 x 11-inch piece of paper. When you're designing your presentation for use on the Internet, or even your company network, you have to take into account that you're dealing with a wide variety of screen sizes. The following example checks for each of the primary screen sizes. If they're found, it creates a region of the appropriate size, which can then be filled with appropriately sized text, images, video, and animation files. The worst case scenario situation is the last test. This is the test that should be met unless someone is using a small PDA (personal digital assistant) device. This last test allows for the display of the presentation on a screen size as small as 100 x 100. Figure 11-2 shows a flowchart explaining this section of code.

```
<switch>
    <region systemScreenSize="1280x1024"
            width="800"
            height="800"
            name="region1"... />
```

```
<region systemScreenSize ="1024x768"
        width="600"
        height="600"
        name="region2"... />
<region systemScreenSize ="800x600"
        width="450"
        height="450"
        name="region3"... />
<region systemScreenSize ="640x480"
        width="300"
        height="300"
        name="region4"...  />
<region systemScreenSize ="100x100"
        width="300"
        height="300"
        name="region4"...  />

</switch>
```

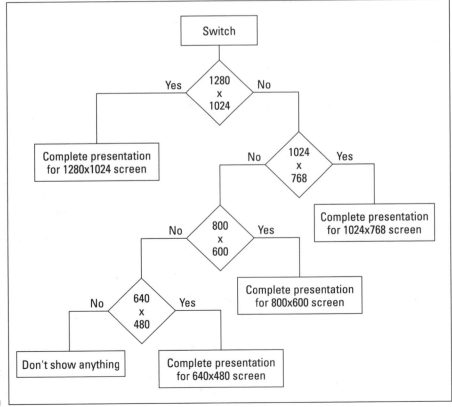

Figure 11-2:
As you progress through the `<switch>` element and your screen resolution is reached, your presentation displays the media elements listed in that area.

Testing for color

As you've cruised about the Internet, I'm sure that you've seen a variety of different images, some of which look fabulous and some that look downright nasty. Have you ever seen those images that look like they were poured from an oil slick with just a few colors in them? This happens when you're looking at an image that has a lot more colors in it than your current monitor can display. You can prevent visitors from having this problem by using the systemScreenDepth test attribute to load images with the appropriate color depth for their current monitor settings. This test attribute tests for the number of bits in a color. For instance, if you're displaying 256 colors, then you have an 8-bit color display because it takes 8 bits in order to identify 256 separate colors. If you're using a monitor with 16 million colors, you're using a 24-bit display. It takes at least a 4-bit display to show 16 colors and a 1-bit display to show a black and white screen.

In the following code, the tests are performed from the most to the least number of colors, so that visitors have the opportunity to see as many colors in your presentation as their monitors support. The worst case scenario is a two-color (1-bit) screen, which is used by some PDA devices. Most desktop computers have at least 16 colors (4-bit) visible.

```
<switch>
    <par systemScreenDepth="32">
        <!-- SMIL media elements here -->
    </par>
    <par systemScreenDepth ="24">
        <!-- SMIL media elements here -->
    </par>
    <par systemScreenDepth ="8">
        <!-- SMIL media elements here -->
    </par>
    <par systemScreenDepth ="4">
        <!-- SMIL media elements here -->
    </par>
    <par systemScreenDepth ="1">
        <!-- SMIL media elements here -->
    </par>
</switch>
```

Setting Up the Switch

To set up your <switch> element, you have to know which of the switch tests are important for your presentation. Do you use a lot of video? Then the systemBitrate test attribute is one of your top concerns. Do you have a lot of visitors who speak a variety of languages? If so, you need to spend some time thinking about the systemLanguage test attribute. For everything that you want to customize, a test attribute is available to help you accomplish your goal. You may have to be very software-specific and use the `systemComponent` test attributes to find every single piece of information about the specific software that's used to view the presentation, but you can do it.

You'd have it easy if you knew exactly which language, software, operating system, and connection speed all your presentation's viewers are using. Sadly, all we know about the users of the Internet is that they cover the entire gambit of possible software, operating systems, connection speeds, and languages. So when creating your SMIL presentation, be aware of how the information you're distributing is available to people who don't speak your primary language or don't have access to the level of equipment that you do.

The following SMIL document uses the `systemLanguage` and `systemBitrate` test attributes to test for both the natural language of the reader and connection speed. First, the presentation regions are created using the `<layout>`, `<root-layout>`, and `<region>` elements that I discuss in Chapters 6 and 7. After each of the regions has been defined, a test is performed to discover which language the visitor's computer is set for. When the language is known, the appropriate audio file is selected. After the audio is selected, the video is selected based upon the amount of bandwidth (bitrate) that's available on the computer's current connection. If the user's connection is too slow to support a video, an alternative still image is used.

```
<smil>
  <head>
    <!-- This is the layout for the entire screen.
         It sets up a root screen of 300 x 300 pixels
         with two regions for video and comments. The
         video region is 296 x 296 pixels and set in
         the root area so that it has a 2 pixel border
         around the entire video. -->
    <layout>
      <root-layout top="0" left="0"
                   width="300" height="300" />
      <region id="video_region"
              top="2" left="2"
              width="296" height="296"
              z-index="0" />
      <region id="audio_region"
              top="10" left="10"
              width="10" height="10"
              z-index="1" />
    </layout>
  </head>
  <body>
    <!-- The running of each video must be in a set
         sequence -->
    <seq>
```

```
<!-- Within each video the audio must appear
     simultaneously with the video itself. -->
<par>

   <!-- This switch statement decides whether to
        load the English (en) or Spanish (sp)
        version of the audio file that is
        available to play with the video. -->
   <switch>
     <audio src="en_rap.au"
            region="audio_region"
            dur="160s"
            min="media"
            begin="1s"
            systemLanguage="en" />
     <audio src="sp_rap.au"
            region="audio_region"
            dur="160s"
            min="media"
            begin="1s"
            systemLanguage="sp" />
   </switch>

   <!-- The video begins 1 second after the par
        loads and runs for the minimum duration
        of the entire length of the video. If the
        video is too large to run in the available
        bandwidth (requiring a 56K connection),
        then the image will display -->
   <switch>
     <video id="rap_vid"
            src="rapvid.rm"
            region="video_region"
            dur="160s"
            min="media"
            begin="1s"
            systemBitrate="56000" />
     <img src="rap_vid.jpg"
            region="video_region"
            dur="160s"
            fill="freeze"
            begin="1s"
            systemBitrate="24000" />
   </switch>
</par>

     <!-- Play Commercial 1 -->
<video id="comm1"
       src="commercial1.rm"
       region="video_region"
       dur="10s" />
```

```
<par>

   <!-- This switch statement decides whether to
        load the English (en) or Spanish (sp)
        version of the audio file that is
        available to play with the video. -->
   <switch>
     <audio src="en_cntry.au"
            region="audio_region"
            dur="120s"
            min="media"
            begin="1s"
            systemLanguage="en" />
     <audio src="sp_cntry.au"
            region="audio_region"
            dur="120s"
            min="media"
            begin="1s"
            systemLanguage="sp" />
   </switch>

   <switch>
   <!-- The video begins 1 second after the par
        loads and runs for the minimum duration
        of the entire length of the video. If the
        video is too large to run in the available
        bandwidth (requiring a 56K connection),
        then the image will display -->
     <video id="country_vid"
            src="countryvid.rm"
            region="video_region"
            dur="120s"
            min="media"
            begin="1s"
            systemBitrate="56000" />
     <img src="country_vid.jpg"
            region="video_region"
            dur="120s"
            fill="freeze"
            begin="1s"
            systemBitrate="24000" />
   </switch>

</par>

     <!-- Play Commercial 2 -->
<video id="comm2"
       src="commercial2.rm"
       region="video_region"
       dur="10s" />
```

```
    <par>

        <!-- This switch statement decides whether to
             load the English (en) or Spanish (sp)
             version of the audio file that is
             available to play with the video. -->
        <switch>
          <audio src="en_jazz.au"
                 region="audio_region"
                 dur="180s"
                 min="media"
                 begin="1s"
                 systemLanguage="en" />
          <audio src="sp_jazz.au"
                 region="audio_region"
                 dur="180s"
                 min="media"
                 begin="1s"
                 systemLanguage="sp" />
        </switch>

        <!-- The video begins 1 second after the par
             loads and runs for the minimum duration
             of the entire length of the video. If the
             video is too large to run in the available
             bandwidth (requiring a 56K connection),
             then the image will display -->
        <switch>
          <video id="jazz_vid"
                 src="jazzvid.rm"
                 region="video_region"
                 dur="180s"
                 min="media"
                 begin="1s"
                 systemBitrate="56000" />
          <img src="jazz_vid.jpg"
                 region="video_region"
                 dur="180s"
                 fill="freeze"
                 begin="1s"
                 systemBitrate="24000" />
        </switch>

    </par>
  </excl>
 </body>
</smil>
```

This sample uses two different tests to identify exactly which parts of the
presentation to use and which to ignore. These tests are repeated each time
but can be stacked together so that you're using multiple levels of switch
tests.

Using Multilevel Switches

In addition to deciding what you want to display for each particular test, you can also *nest* your switch tests (place additional tests within the child elements of other elements containing test attributes) to avoid performing the same tests multiple times, such as when you need to test to see if at 56K this person has 24-bit `systemDepth` or a 4-bit `systemDepth`. By using switch tests within the hierarchy of your code so that you have one test, buried within another, you don't have to go back and repeat a test, nor do you have to set up a multitude of tests within each branch of your presentation. Imagine for a moment that you want to make a sandwich. First you find the bread, then the lunchmeat, then the mayonnaise, mustard, pickles, lettuce, and so on. When you're making your sandwich, you never have to go back and look for the bread after you first find it. Just think what a pain it would be if, every time you wanted a slice of bread, you had to get the bread out of the drawer, take out one slice of bread and then put the loaf back in the drawer. You would then have to get the bread back out, take out your second slice of bread, and return the loaf to the drawer again when you're ready to finish your sandwich. In SMIL, that means you no longer have to go back and run the same test multiple times.

SMIL can work that way, but why do you want it to? Because you can nest your tests, you eliminate any reason to perform the same test multiple times. Of course, some situations may arise that require repeating tests, such as when you need to test for `systemBitrate` for sections of documents at a variety of points within one presentation because of the way the presentation flows or has to be organized.

In this sample, a series of embedded tests each perform one test on the information contained within the presentation so that only the most appropriate media files are shown. This system works by testing first for the operating system. After the operating system is discovered, the presentation then checks the number of available colors on the system.

You can find this file on the CD as `switchtest.smi` in the `Examples/Chapter11` directory.

```
<smil>
  <head>
    <layout>
      <root-layout top="0" left="0"
                   width="300" height="300" />
      <region ... />
      <region ... />
    </layout>
  </head>
  <body>
  <switch>
```

```
<!--The contents of this par test for a Win32
    operating system. If the viewer has Win32
    then the text file is displayed. At that point,
    if the systemScreenDepth is 24 or more bits
    then two images are displayed. If not, the
    SMIL player skips down to the next seq element.
    If the screen is displaying 8-bit colors then the
    next selection of images is displayed. It continues
    through each selection of screen color depth
    until a supported number of colors are matched. -->
<par systemOperatingSystem="Win32">
  <text src="text.txt"
           region="text_region"
           fill="freeze"/>
  <seq systemScreenDepth="24">
    <image src="widescreen.jpg"
           region="region1"
           dur="2s" />
    <image src="widescreen1.jpg"
           region="region1"
           dur="2s" />
  </seq>
  <seq systemScreenDepth ="8">
    <image src="256-screen.gif"
           region="region1"
           dur="2s" />
    <image src="256-screen1.gif"
           region="region1"
           dur="2s" />
  </seq>
  <seq systemScreenDepth ="4">
    <image src="16-screen.gif"
           region="region1"
           dur="2s" />
    <image src="16-screen1.gif"
           region="region1"
           dur="2s" />
  </seq>
  <seq systemScreenDepth ="1">
    <image src=" blackwhite.gif"
           region="region1"
           dur="2s" />
    <image src="blackwhite1.gif"
           region="region1"
           dur="2s" />
  </seq>
</par>

<!--The contents of this par test for a MacOS
    operating system. If the viewer has MacOS
    then the text file is displayed. At that point,
    if the systemScreenDepth is 24 or more bits
```

```
            then 8-bit colors, etc... It continues
            through each selection of screen color depth
            until a supported number of colors are matched. -->

   <par systemOperatingSystem="MacOS">
     <seq systemScreenDepth="24">
      <!-- Contains rotating images from above -->
     </seq>
     <seq systemScreenDepth ="8">
      <!-- Contains rotating images from above -->
     </seq>
     <seq systemScreenDepth ="4">
      <!-- Contains rotating images from above -->
     </seq>
     <seq systemScreenDepth ="1">
      <!-- Contains rotating images from above -->
     </seq>
   </par>

   <!--The contents of this par test for a Linux
       operating system. If the viewer has Linux
       then the text file is displayed. At that point,
       if the systemScreenDepth is 24 or more bits
       then 8-bit colors, etc... It continues
       through each selection of screen color depth
       until a supported number of colors are matched. -->


   <par systemOperatingSystem="Linux">
     <seq systemScreenDepth="24">
      <!-- Contains rotating images from above -->
     </seq>
     <seq systemScreenDepth ="8">
      <!-- Contains rotating images from above -->
     </seq>
     <seq systemScreenDepth ="4">
      <!-- Contains rotating images from above -->
     </seq>
     <seq systemScreenDepth ="1">
      <!-- Contains rotating images from above -->
     </seq>
   </par>
  </switch>
  </body>
</smil>
```

With the ability to test for the right combination of operating system, supported colors, and system speed, you can be sure to provide a presentation customized for the majority of possible computer setups.

Part IV
Linking Up

The 5th Wave   By Rich Tennant

DAD ADDS MULTIMEDIA SOUND AND GRAPHICS TO THE TRADITIONAL CAMPFIRE GHOST STORY.

In this part . . .

I invite you to explore SMIL links in the following chapters. Here I show you how to control the destination of your link, how to use links to control the playing of your presentation, and how to control the opening and closing of the timing and spacing of your presentation — yes, all with links! I even show you how to jump into the middle of a presentation and how to combine the various linking effects into a whole multimedia control board.

Throughout this part, I provide the combined SMIL development of three sample SMIL presentations for your perusal. In each of these presentations, I use the timing, links, region placement, and the images, text, and video that I discuss in the previous sections of this book.

Chapter 12

Linking to the Proper Destination

*H*ave you ever heard it said that networking is the way to get someplace in the business world? Well, guess what? Networking, or *linking* as it's also known, is the primary way of getting places on the Internet also. On the Internet, you can always find someplace to go and someone new to talk to. Now, if you're thinking HTML links, you're in for a surprise. SMIL has incorporated many more controls into its linking system than you can probably imagine.

Using links, you can control not only the destination of your visitors, but, as you can with HTML, you can also control what happens to your existing document, how the new document is loaded, where you arrive within the new document, and how you can view multiple documents altogether. In Chapter 13, I discuss even more things that you can do with the links that you create.

If you aren't sure what a link is, think about a book index. Take the index of this book, for example. You're looking for information on "images" and want to know where the <img> element is discussed in this book. In a book, you have to look up the page number and turn the pages in the book until you find the information that you want. A link, on the other hand, does the page turning for you. By clicking on a link, you're telling your SMIL presentation to find the page that the text is referencing. It's as simple as that. And just like in HTML, your visitors can use the Tab key to tab through all the links on your document.

Controlling Your Destination

When you're creating links between documents, ensuring that you're going to the right location is of primary importance. Of course, you have to use the proper SMIL elements to direct yourself. Within SMIL, just as in HTML, you have two elements that you can use to create links within SMIL documents:

- ✔ `<a>`: Creates a direct link from one source to any part of another document.

- ✔ `<area>`: Creates a direct link from an area of an image, or video, to any part of another document.

`<a>` link

Everyone who's worked with HTML pages is familiar with the anchor `<a>` element, which in SMIL functions similarly to how the `<a>` element functions in HTML. The `<a>` element creates a link. It provides a location in your current presentation (the source) that, when clicked, takes the visitor to another location (the destination), either within the same presentation or in another presentation or document as specified by the anchor's `href` attribute. `href` contains the address of the destination of the link. Using the `<a>` element, you can create a link from your current presentation to any point within another presentation. A variety of rules dictate the use of the `<a>` element to create links within your SMIL presentation. I've outlined these rules in the following list, although these may differ from the HTML `<a>` element rules:

- ✔ The `<a>` element has no effect on the positioning of your media elements.

- ✔ The `<a>` element must have an `href` attribute (which I discuss in more detail in the section, "Setting the destination with href," later in this chapter) to designate the destination of the link.

- ✔ The `<a>` element cannot be nested within other `<a>` elements.

- ✔ The `<a>` element doesn't have any effect on the synchronization of other elements within your SMIL document.

SMIL enables you to specify several ways in which your link can be triggered. For instance:

- ✔ A user can click it with the mouse.

- ✔ An event can activate it at a specific time.

- ✔ The pressing of a keyboard key can activate it.

This all sounds the same as HTML, right? Well, things are about to change.

Because SMIL has a whole variety of timing systems, your links also have to be activated within a specific time. For instance, if your link is a part of a `<text>` element that's only visible for a specific amount of time, your link must be active during the time in which the `<text>` element is visible. If text disappears from the screen, visitors obviously aren't able to activate any links in it. A text file doesn't have any intrinsic time duration. If a visitor must have the option of clicking a particular link at any time during the presentation, that link (and the element it's in) must be visible at all times or at least during the time when the link needs to be accessible. For example, you have to use a `fill="freeze"` attribute with your text objects in addition to a `dur="indefinite"` attribute to force the contents of your text file to stay visible during the entire presentation.

The `<a>` element has a variety of attributes, all of which I discuss in this chapter, that provide the SMIL player with the information that it needs to properly deal with any links it may find within your documents. These attributes are as follows:

- `alt`: Provides alternative text that describes the link.
- `acceskey`: The keyboard character, or character combination, that activates the link when pressed.
- `href`: The address of the link's destination.
- `tabindex`: The numerical value that represents the order of appearance of this link when a visitor uses the Tab key to navigate the presentation.
- `target`: The name of the window, or region, that contains the contents of the destination of the link, after that link is activated.
- `actuate`: Controls whether the link is triggered simply when the media element, to which it's assigned, becomes active, or whether a presentation viewer has to click the link.
- `destinationLevel`: Controls the volume of the destination documents audio elements.
- `destinationPlaystate`: Controls how the destination document is opened, either running or paused.
- `external`: Determines whether the computer controls which software application loads the destination of the link or whether the current SMIL player opens the destination file.
- `show`: Controls how the presentation is opened.
- `sourceLevel`: Controls the volume of the current document's audio elements when a visitor presses the link.
- `sourcePlaystate`: Controls what happens to the source document as far as deciding whether it closes or simply pauses.

The `<a>` element has been deprecated in favor of the `<area>` element, although it's still supported through the SMIL 2.0 specification. If you're developing documents that have a long shelf life, I'd suggest not using this element and instead creating all your links using the `<area>` element that I discuss in the section, "<area> link," just a bit later in this chapter.

Describing your link with alt

You can use the `alt` attribute of the `<a>` element to describe your link and its destination, as well as to provide an additional means of helping some search engines on the Internet to index your site.

```
<a alt="This is my link">
   <text src="mytext.txt"
            region="Text_region"
            dur="indefinite"
            begin="5s"/>
</a>
```

Setting up an accesskey

The `accesskey` attribute creates a keyboard shortcut that enables your pres-entation viewers to activate the link by simply pressing the key on their keyboard. This forces you to be careful when using text files in your SMIL presentation. Because you can add links with `accesskey` attributes within a text tile, which are then referenced and loaded by your SMIL document, the potential exists for multiple links to have the same `accesskey` value.

If you have a keystroke that you've assigned as an `accesskey` for a link, both within the SMIL file and in the text file that makes up a part of your SMIL pres-entation, the keystroke identified within the SMIL file takes precedence. Another possibility is to assign two links in the same SMIL document to the same `accesskey`. In this situation, the link that's assigned to the media element that becomes active first (loaded and played first) is the one that gets activated (the link's destination is loaded) when a viewer presses the access key. If both links become active simultaneously, the link identified within the SMIL document first is used. The following code uses the `accesskey`attribute to load the text file `mytext.txt` whenever a viewer presses the *L* key.

```
<a accesskey="L"
   alt="This is my link">
   <text src="mytext.txt"
            region="Text_region"
            dur="indefinite"
            begin="5s"/>
</a>
```

Setting the destination with href

You use the href attribute, required for <a> elements, with the <a> element to specify the destination document of the link. The <a> element in SMIL can contain as many different media and sequencing elements as you want it to. The following sample code loads the presentation mydestination.smi whenever any of the text in the Text_region is clicked.

```
<a href="mydestination.smi"
   accesskey="L"
   alt="This is my link">

  <text src="mytext.txt"
           region="Text_region"
           dur="indefinite"
           begin="5s"/>
</a>
```

The possibility exists that your presentation has links physically stacked over the top of each other. If this happens, the layering of regions causes the link that resides in the region that's topmost on the stack to activate when you click that link area.

Setting a tab order

Because pressing the Tab key to move through the SMIL presentation accesses the links in the presentation, you need to set a tabbing order for your links. You do this by using the tabindex attribute. If you don't set the tab order for your document, pressing the Tab key simply takes you through the locations of the links in the order that they're designated on the file, which may not have anything to do with their appearance on-screen. Of course, only the currently playing elements are affected by the tabbing order, but you still need to be aware of how your tab takes you through the available links at any given time in your presentation. The following sample code uses the tabindex attribute to set the numerical order of the links. In this case, the second textarea is the destination of the first tab press, and the first textarea is the destination of the second tab press. Without using the tabindex attribute, this example reverses itself, and the Tab key takes you through the document in order of <a> elements.

```
<a tabindex="2"
   href="mydestination.smi"
   accesskey="L"
   alt="This is my link">

  <text src="mytext.txt"
           region="Text_region"
           dur="indefinite"
           begin="5s"/>
```

```
</a>
<a tabindex="1"
   href="otherdestination.smi"
   accesskey="A"
   alt="This is my otherlink">

   <text src="myothertext.txt"
            region="Text_region"
            dur="indefinite"
            begin="5s"/>
</a>
```

Hitting your target

In HTML, you can have a link load information into a specific frame of your site using the `target` attribute, which works the same way in SMIL. But in SMIL, you can also load your information into a SMIL region, an HTML frame, or another named window. This attribute can also create a new display window with a specified name. The value in the `target` attribute should match the name of the destination of the information. For example, if you're using a `target` attribute to load information into a SMIL region, the value of the target attribute needs to be equal to the name of that region.

```
<a target="region_1"
   tabindex="1"
   href="mydestination.smi"
   accesskey="L"
   alt="This is my link">

   <text src="mytext.txt"
            region="Text_region"
            dur="indefinite"
            begin="5s"/>
</a>
```

If the element has both a `show` attribute and a `target` attribute, the `show` attribute is ignored.

Putting it all together — some examples

You can use the `<a>` element to open a new presentation to replace the one that was playing. To do so, simply use `<a>` the same as you use an HTML `<a>` link. For example, the following code enables readers to click a video and open a new document, `somedocument.smi`, in the video's place.

```
<a href="http://myserver.com/somedocument.smi">
   <video src="rtsp://www.myserver.com/video.rm"
            region="region_1"/>
</a>
```

Or, you can create a series of links that load information into a variety of regions. For example, the following code loads the document new.smi into the region identified as toggle_region.

```
<smil>
  <head>
    <layout>
      <region id="toggle_region"
              width="300" height="300"
              top="40" left="5" />
      <region id="text_region"
              width="300" height="30"
              top="5" left="5" />
    </layout>
  </head>
  <body>
    <a href="new.smi"
       target="toggle_region">
    <text src="title_text.txt"
          region="text_region"/>
    </a>
    <ref src="old_doc.smi"
         region="toggle_region" />
  </body>
</smil>
```

Some SMIL players, such as RealPlayer, don't enable you to link to SMIL documents from within your SMIL documents. The SMIL specification allows this, and all SMIL players should support it. They don't, however. At this point, it's only a matter of time before all SMIL players fully support the SMIL 2.0 standard.

<area> link

HTML enables you to create a link from a portion of an image and so does SMIL. The <area> element, which operates much the same as it does in HTML, enables you to associate a link with only a part of a single media object, such as a corner of a video or a specific spot on an image. The <a> element only enables you to create a link from a complete media object.

By using the <area> element, rather then the deprecated <a> element, you can have a single image, such as a mural, and provide links to different parts of your presentation from different aspects of the image. For example, if you had a community presentation with a mural showing a house and some kids walking to school past a post office, you could use the house to give your visitors information about the local residents, the post office to give visitors information about the town, and the school to give information about the local education systems. Using this type of setup, you can provide links to multiple pieces of information all from the same image.

How does the <area> element work? Simple: It enables you to identify the specific spatial coordinates of a media object and to create a map that matches those locations with a destination document. But that isn't all. The <area> element also enables you to link to a specific time within the playing duration of its destination object.

You place the <area> elements within the boundaries of your media element so that, unlike in HTML, they're linked by *element enclosure* rather than by a unique name.

```
<img src="mystreetsigns.gif">
    <area shape="poly"
          coords="0,0,0,100,100,100,100,0,0,0" />
</img>
```

The <area> element is an *empty element* — it can't have any children. It must be enclosed by the media element tags (which I discuss in Chapter 2), which can also be expressed as empty elements, but not when used in conjunction with <area>.

The <area> element has a variety of attributes (alt, accesskey, tabindex, target, and href) that function in the same way for <area> as they do for the <a> element. I describe these attributes in the section, "<a> link," earlier in this chapter. Other attributes that the <area> element supports include the following:

- ✔ coords: The coordinates of each corner of the area drawn on your image.

- ✔ nohref: Allows the area element to not have an address or href attribute.

- ✔ shape: Controls the shape of the area being drawn on the image.

- ✔ actuate: Controls whether the link is triggered when the media element to which it's assigned becomes active or whether a presentation viewer has to click the link.

- ✔ destinationLevel: Controls the volume of the destination file's audio elements.

- ✔ destinationPlaystate: Controls how, and when, the destination file starts playing.

- ✔ external: Controls which software displays the contents of a destination file.

- ✔ show: Controls how the new presentation is shown on-screen when the link is activated.

- ✔ sourceLevel: Controls the volume of the audio files in the source document.

- ✔ sourcePlaystate: Controls the playing or pausing of the current presentation when a viewer presses the link.

Coordinates are the key

Because the `<area>` element works on just a section of a complete media object, you have to specify the coordinates of the area that it affects. Take for example the image shown in Figure 12-1. This is a very simple image showing some of the basic shapes, such as rectangles, octagons, circles, and triangles, in the form of street signs. You can create a map out of this figure by using the `coords` and `shape` attributes.

When specifying the coordinates of this shape, you need to keep in mind a few things about how your coordinates are going to be measured:

- ✔ All of your coordinates are measured from the top-left corner of the image itself, not the region that the image is being placed in.

- ✔ Coordinates are measured in pixels, just as in HTML. Sometimes, the pixel value of the displaying software, which is used by the `<area>` element, is different than the pixel values of the image. This happens a lot when the `fit` attribute for a region is not set to `hidden`, which causes the region to distort the image. For more on the `fit` attribute, see Chapter 7.

- ✔ SMIL's ability to force images to fit within a specific region may cause part of the image to not appear at all. This means that only part of your image may show up. If this happens, the coordinates creating a map of your image for linking purposes still exists, but it's outside the existing image area.

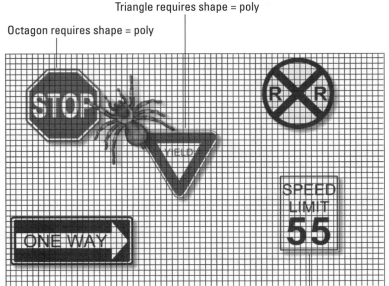

Triangle requires shape = poly

Octagon requires shape = poly

Figure 12-1:
Street signs
make great
shapes to
practice
with when
creating
image maps.

Rectangle requires shape = rect

The number of coordinate pairs that you use depends on the `shape` attribute:

- ✔ If `shape=rect`, use `"x1,y1"` as the coordinates of the upper-left corner of the rectangle and `"x2,y2"` as the coordinates of the lower-right coordinates of the rectangle.

- ✔ If `shape=circ`, use `"x1,y1,r"`, where `"x1,y1"` are the coordinates of the center of the circle and `r` is the circle's radius.

- ✔ If `shape=poly`, use `"x1,y1,x2,y2,x3,y3..."`, where each coordinate pair is one of the vertices of the polygon.

```
<video... />
    <area shape="rect" coords="x1,y1,x2, y2" />
    <area shape="circ" coords="x1,y1,r" />
    <area shape="poly"
        coords="x1,y1, x2, y2, x3, y3, ... xN,yN" />
</video>
```

Take a look at these following examples. They use the `coord` attributes (see bolded lines in the following code) of the `<area>` element to draw out the specific space that the linking area requires. The highlighted areas in Figure 12-2 show you where the links are located. Not every area of your image must be linkable.

```
<img... />
<!-- Draws the rectangle around the one way sign. -->
  <area shape="rect"
        coord="1,30,23,39"
        href="oneway.smi"
        alt="loads one way document"
        target="region1"/>

<!-- Draws the circle around the rail road crossing sign. -->
  <area shape="circ"
        coords="53,8,7"
        href="railway.smi"
        alt="loads rail road document"
        target="region1"/>

<!-- Draws the triangle around the yield sign. -->
  <area shape="poly"
        coords="23,15,39,15,32,28,23,15"
        href="yield.smi"
        alt="loads yield document"
        target="region1"/>

<!-- Draws the octagon around the stop sign. -->
  <area shape="poly"
        coords="8,3,14,3,18,7,18,13,14,17,
                8,17,3,13,3,7,8,3"
        href="stop.smi"
        alt="loads stop document"
        target="region1"/>
</img>
```

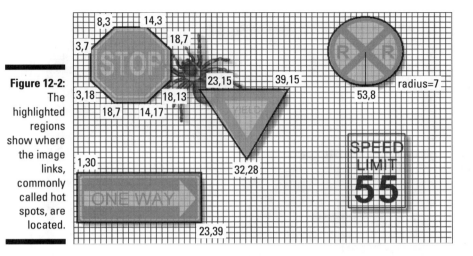

Figure 12-2:
The highlighted regions show where the image links, commonly called hot spots, are located.

You can also designate your hot spot regions based on percentages of the total visible image area. For instance, the following SMIL code (`coords = "0%, 0%, 50%, 50%"`) sets aside an area that encompasses the entire upper-left quarter of an image, no matter what shape and size that image has been fit to. The area is designated from the 0%, 0% corner, or no distance down or over from the top-left corner of the image, to the center of the image, which is 50% down and 50% right of the top-left corner of the image. The second area creates another linking area in the lower-right quadrant of the image, as shown in Figure 12-3.

```
<img src="myimage.gif" ...>
   <area href="audio.ra"
         coords="0%,0%,50%,50%"/>
   <area href="video.rm"
         coords="50%,50%,100%,100%"/>
</img>
```

When no destination is needed

The `nohref` attribute makes sure that the SMIL player knows that the current object has no associated link destination. In other words, this document doesn't open any other document. It's used strictly as a means of creating an action within the document. `nohref` is a *Boolean attribute* — it has only one value when it's present, which value says `nohref=true`. Whenever this value is present, you can use the link to create some action in your presentation but not open another document. One example of using the `nohref` attribute is to create a button to start or stop the playing of a video. The following code, for instance, creates a button that does nothing when pressed. But it does provide an event for other elements to watch for in those other elements' `begin` and `end` attributes.

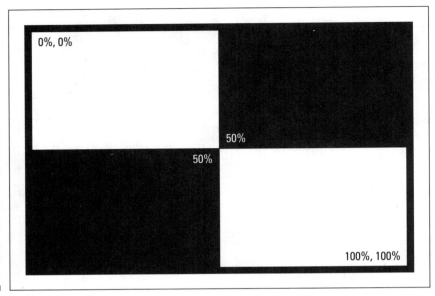

Figure 12-3:
The upper-
left and
lower-right
quadrants of
the image
are covered
by hot spots
or linking
areas,
which are
shown in
white in this
image.

```
<!-- Draws the rectangle around the one way sign. -->
  <area shape="rect"
        coord="1,30,23,39"
        nohref
        alt="starts an activity"
        target="region1"/>
```

Hey . . . shape is important

The shape attribute defines the shape of a clickable area within the media element. The shape attribute is required for the <area> element, and it must have an associated coords attribute to set the dimensions of the specified hot spot. The shape attribute has the following four potential values:

- default: This sets the entire region as the shape.
- rect: This identifies a rectangular region for the hot spot.
- circle: This identifies a circular region for the clickable area.
- poly: This identifies a polygonal region for the hot spot.

The following example code shows the three most used options for the shape attribute with their associated coords designations.

```
<img... />
<!-- Draws the rectangle around the one way sign. -->
  <area shape="rect"
        coord="1,30,23,39"
        href="oneway.smi"
```

```
                  alt="loads one way document"
                  target="region1"/>

<!-- Draws the circle around the rail road crossing sign. -->
  <area shape="circ"
        coords="53,8,7"
        href="railway.smi"
        alt="loads rail road document"
        target="region1"/>

<!-- Draws the triangle around the yield sign. -->
  <area shape="poly"
        coords="23,15,39,15,32,28,23,15"
        href="yield.smi"
        alt="loads yield document"
        target="region1"/>

<!-- Draws the octagon around the stop sign. -->
  <area shape="poly"
        coords="8,3,14,3,18,7,18,13,14,17,
                8,17,3,13,3,7,8,3"
        href="stop.smi"
        alt="loads stop document"
        target="region1"/>
</img>
```

If you have created multiple `<area>` elements that define overlapping areas of an media element with their `coords` attributes, then, as in HTML, the `<area>` that occurs first within the SMIL document takes precedence and directs the destination of your link.

Playing a New Presentation

Playing a new presentation is as simple as linking to it, by using either the `<a>` or `<area>` elements with an `href` attribute. But to really control what's happening on-screen, you need to understand how to control both your new presentation as well as the current one.

Controlling the current presentation's audio level

Sometimes you may want to open another presentation while controlling the current presentation. You can use the `sourceLevel` attribute with either the `<a>` or the `<area>` elements to control the volume of the audio files associated with the current presentation. The value of 25%, in the following example, sets the volume of the current audio files, in the current presentation, to 25% of their current volume.

```
<img src="myimage.gif" ...>
  <area href="audio.ra"
        shape="rect"
        coords="0,0,50,50"
        sourceLevel="25%"/>
  <area href="video.rm"
        shape="rect"
        coords="50,50,100,100"/>
</img>
```

If the current presentation contains no audio file, the sourceLevel attribute is ignored.

Controlling the show

The show attribute determines how a presentation is opened and has the following values:

- ✔ new: The new presentation and the current presentation run simultaneously with the new presentation opening in a new window. The current presentation isn't affected in any way.

- ✔ pause: This value pauses the playing of the current presentation, while opening the new presentation in a new window. It has been deprecated in favor of the pause setting on the sourcePlaystate attribute (which I discuss in the section, "Pausing a Presentation," later in this chapter).

- ✔ replace: This value pauses the current presentation and replaces it in the current window with the new presentation. This is how untargeted links work in HTML and is the default for how links in SMIL work.

```
<a href="someshow.smi"
   show="new"
   sourcePlaystate="pause">
        <video src="display.rm"
        region="region1"/>
</a>
```

Actuating your links

The actuate attribute controls whether a link that's been triggered simply by its time span becoming active is run. What does this mean? Well, if you think of a link being active within a specific text file, that text file can only be active for 3 seconds. Do you want your link in this file to execute itself as soon as the text becomes active, or do you want it to wait until a person has a chance to click it with the mouse pointer? The actuate attribute controls how, and to some degree when, your links are executed. By default, links are only executed onRequest, which is the default value of the actuate attribute, but they can be set to onLoad, which enables the link to be executed as soon as the media element that it's contained within becomes active.

The following sample code activates the link only when the image itself is clicked:

```
<a href="someshow.smi"
    show="new"
    sourcePlaystate="pause"
    actuate="onRequest">
        <img src="display.gif"
            region="region1"/>
</a>
```

The following code executes the link as soon as the image loads:

```
<a href="someshow.smi"
    show="new"
    sourcePlaystate="pause"
    actuate="onLoad">
        <img src="display.gif"
            region="region1"/>
</a>
```

Controlling external influences

As with everything else, SMIL is subject to a variety of external influences. So, you can use the external attribute to decide whether the current application opens the destination file of a link or whether that privilege is given to some other application. If the external attribute is set to true, the link is opened in whatever application the current computer system has designated as an appropriate application for viewing the type of file referenced by the link. If the external attribute is set to false, the current application opens the destination of the link.

If you set the external attribute to true, as I've done in the following sample code, you can't control what application your computer decides to open the destination of the link with through your SMIL document. This function is completely dependent on the computer system that you're using.

```
<a href="someshow.smi"
    show="new"
    sourcePlaystate="pause"
    external="true">
                <img src="display.gif"
        region="region1"/>
</a>
```

If you want more information on controlling the configuration of your computer and its file associations, take a look at one of the following *For Dummies* titles (all published by IDG Books Worldwide, Inc.) that can help you with your particular computer setup:

> *Linux For Dummies,* 3rd Edition, by Dee-Ann LeBlanc, Melanie Hoag and Evan Blomquist
>
> *Mac OS 9 For Dummies* (or *Mac OS 8 For Dummies*) by Bob LeVitus
>
> *Microsoft Windows Me Millennium Edition For Dummies* by Andy Rathbone
>
> *Windows 98 For Dummies* by Andy Rathbone
>
> *Windows CE 2 For Dummies* by Jinjer L. Simon

Setting volume on that new presentation

How many times have you changed channels on your TV only to find some horribly loud commercial playing that makes you immediately hit that mute button? I've done it a hundred times, at least. Companies don't help themselves a bit when their obnoxious commercials chase off viewers. You want to avoid this problem with your own presentations by ensuring that it doesn't blow out your visitors' eardrums. You can use the `destinationLevel` attribute with either the `<a>` or the `<area>` elements to control the volume of the audio files associated with the presentation that's opening. The value of 75% in the following example sets the volume of the new presentation's audio files, in the new presentation, to 75% of the current volume.

```
<img src="myimage.gif" ...>
  <area href="audio.ra"
        shape="rect"
        coords="0,0,50,50"
        destinationLevel="75%"/>
  <area href="video.rm"
        shape="rect"
        coords="50,50,100,100"/>
</img>
```

If the new presentation contains no audio file, the `destinationLevel` attribute is ignored.

Controlling how your new presentation plays

The attribute that you primarily use to control the appearance of a new presentation with both the <a> and the <area> elements is destinationPlaystate. This attribute controls whether the newly opened presentation continues to play or is paused as soon as it opens. Of course, a value of play is the default.

- ✔ play: This setting plays the new presentation as soon as it loads.

- ✔ pause: This setting displays, but then pauses, the new presentation as soon as it loads.

The following code pauses the someshow.smi presentation when it opens. You can pause a presentation when it opens, to give the viewer a chance to select the portion of the presentation that she wants to watch or to make a decision about the order that she wants to view information. You can also do this as a courtesy for the existing presentation screen, enabling it to finish before the new presentation screen takes over.

```
<a href="someshow.smi"
   destinationPlaystate="pause">
         <video src="display.rm"
       region="region1"/>
</a>
```

Pausing a Presentation

One primary attribute that you can use with both the <a> and the <area> elements is a key to pausing a presentation when another is opened. This attribute, sourcePlaystate, controls whether the current presentation continues to play or is paused whenever the new presentation is opened. The actual possible values of sourcePlaystate include the following:

- ✔ play: This setting enables the current presentation to continue playing when a link is traversed.

- ✔ pause: This setting pauses the current presentation when the link is traversed. When the playing of the link's destination is complete, the current presentation continues playing.

- ✔ stop: This setting stops the presentation containing the original link and resets it to its beginning. When the destination presentation completes its own demonstration, the calling presentation doesn't resume automatically.

This attribute is available with both the <a> and the <area> elements and works in conjunction with the show attribute to control the current presentation. In the following example, the current presentation is paused so that the new presentation, someshow.smi, can start playing.

```
<a href="someshow.smi"
    show="new"
    sourcePlaystate="pause">
            <video src="display.rm"
        region="region1"/>
</a>
```

The value of the show attribute controls how the sourcePlaystate attribute works. If the show attribute, which I discuss in more detail in the following section, has a value of new, the current presentation continues to play, as if the sourcePlaystate value is play. If the show attribute has a value of replace, the currently active presentation pauses, as if the sourcePlaystate attribute was set to pause. If the show attribute is used, then the sourcePlaystate is ignored.

Playing Two Presentations

Playing two separate presentations at the same time is quite easy. All you have to do is adjust a few of the default attribute values of some of the <a> and <area> attributes. Just change the value of the show attribute to new and you're all set because a value of show=new enables you to play two presentations in two windows simultaneously. When the following code is executed, both the current presentation and the presentation called mypresentation.smi play simultaneously.

```
<a href="mypresentation.smi"
    show="new">
  <ref src="document.txt"
      region="link_region"/>
</a>
```

In addition to opening multiple copies of the SMIL playing software, you can also force the computer to open different document viewing software. For instance, if you're linking to an HTML file, as I show in the following example code, then you want that file to open in a Web browser. If you were to link to a RealPlayer movie, then you want that movie to open in RealPlayer, just as you want a QuickTime movie to open in Apple QuickTime. By opening documents in the software that's best suited for displaying them, you can get a better quality result for your presentation. In the following code, the combination of the `show=new` and the `external=true` attributes enables you to open the `someweb.html` file in a new Web browser window.

```
<a href="someweb.html"
   show="new"
   external="true">
         <img src="Web_Link.gif"
      region="region1"/>
</a>
```

Starting in the Middle of a Presentation

One of the key bonuses to working with SMIL is the fact that it can link not only to a complete presentation, but also to any portion or any playing time during that presentation. For instance, you can load a presentation to the point that a movie is starting or to a point halfway through it, whether or not that video starts when the presentation starts. In the following example code, you see a link from the current document to the middle of the new presentation. In Chapter 8, you can read about how the `dur`, `begin`, and `end` attributes all work together. You can see how elements are loaded into the document but not active until their `begin` attributes are ready. You can use the `begin` attributes of elements that become active near the middle of a presentation as the destination for a link. This is sort of like warping through time. You are fast-forwarding the presentation to which you're linking to the point at which your destination object itself is active. For instance, in the following code, the link from the current presentation's video element takes you to the playing of `video3` in the second presentation.

Current Presentation

```
<smil>
  <head>
    ...
  </head>
  <body>
    ...
    <a href="nextpresentation.smi#middle">
      <video src="video.rm"/>
    </a>
    ...
  </body>
</smil>
```

New Presentation (nextpresentation.smi):

```
   <smil>
   <head>
    ...
   </head>
   <body>
    ...
    <seq>
      <video src="video.rm"/>
       <par>
         <video src="video2.rm"
                region="region1"/>
         <video id="video3"
                src="video3.rm"
                region="region2"/>
         <text src="text_file.txt"
                region="region_txt"/>
         <text src="text_file2.txt"
                region="title_region"/>
       </par>
    </seq>
    ...
   </body>
</smil>
```

In addition to jumping to the start of a specific element's playing time, you can also jump to a point within the playing time of an element. All you need to do is identify that portion of the element in some fashion, as it has been with the <area> elements in the following example. The <a> element uses the href attribute value of example.smi#act2. This statement says to open the document example.smi and go directly to the element act2. Because you can't go to an element that isn't active, it automatically fast-forwards the example.smi presentation to the point at which the <area> element named act2 becomes active.

Current Presentation

```
<smil>
  <head>
   ...
  </head>
  <body>
    ...
    <a href="example.smi#act2">
      <img id="img1"
           src="map.gif"
           region="img_region"/>
    </a>
    ...
  </body>
</smil>
```

New Presentation (example.smi)

```
<smil>
<head>
...
</head>
<body>
  ...
  <video src="videoplaying.rm">
    <area id="act1"
          nohref
          begin="0s"
          end="5s"/>
    <area id="act2"
          nohref
          begin="5s"
          end="10s"/>
  </video>
  ...
</body>
</smil>
```

As you can see, a lot of options are available for interacting with the information contained within your SMIL presentation and in other SMIL presentations using links. I cover even more examples and options in Chapter 13.

Chapter 13

Using Links, Anchors, and Image Maps

*Y*ou can do so many different things with a link that it behooves you to look at the variety of linking applications that I discuss in this chapter. SMIL provides you with a means of linking to both spatial and temporal (or time) coordinates using anchors within those files. Sounds fancy, huh? It's really quite simple. You can use SMIL links to link to another document, an object within that document, or an object within a specific period of time on that document. The object to which you're linking is called an *anchor*. I've provided examples in this chapter to help clarify the variety of linking options available when you're using anchors to direct the destinations of your links.

I've also included a quick discussion of how to create *multimedia image maps*. If you're familiar with HTML, you already know that an image map is simply an image that has had more than one link applied to it using spatial coordinates and the `<area>` element, which I discuss in Chapter 12. Viewers can roll the mouse pointer over different parts of the image map and click the various links. You can use multimedia image maps for a variety of activities, not just linking, as I show you later in this chapter.

Getting Your Spatial Coordinates Right

Getting the spatial coordinates of your links correct is just as important as getting the timing of your presentation correct. By creating an anchor, you can be sure of getting your spatial coordinates correct for every link that you want to create. Anchors are objects that have an identifiable name that you set by using the id attribute, which can be referenced within a link. By using these anchors, you can easily create a link that opens a presentation to a specific object's location.

Anchors work like suite or apartment numbers for large buildings. The address of the building, for example, 111 Park Street, represents the typical URL of the document that you're loading, as you do in Chapter 12. The apartment number, Apt. 136, points you to a specific location within that building — just as an anchor provides a specific address within your SMIL presentation. So you see, the address 111 Park Street, Apt. 136 simply says, in the language of SMIL, go to the document 111 Park Street, find the object named Apt. 136, and stop there.

Because you can use any area of your SMIL presentation as an anchor, you're in luck — somewhat. Assume for a moment that you have a single area (region) of your presentation screen in which you want to display different information, depending on the selections of the visitor. You can do this by creating a region to serve as the anchor or destination for the information that you want to display. Start with the image shown in Figure 13-1. Assume this image serves as the background for your presentation.

Figure 13-1:
A simple introductory background screen for the presentation of information.

You now need to add regions that hold your links (in this case, an image map serving as a navigational bar) and a region that contains text. Figure 13-2 shows where I've created these regions.

Figure 13-2:
The addition of the image and text regions.

The following SMIL code shows how I've created these regions. For example, the top region, image_region, which is destined to contain the navigational bar, is located 222 pixels down and 122 pixels in from the top-left corner of the presentation area. Its dimensions are 400 x 35 pixels. The lower window, text_region, is destined to contain the rotating text files with the information that's selected from the navigational bar. It sits 285 pixels down and 122 pixels in from the top-left corner of the presentation screen and is 400 x 250 pixels in size.

```
<smil>
<head>
  <layout>
    <root-layout width="800" height="600" />
    <region id="bkg_region"
            width="800" height="600"
            top="0" left="0" />
    <region id="image_region"
            width="400" height="35"
            top="222" left="122"
            fit="hidden" />
    <region id="text_region"
            width="400" height="250"
            top="285" left=122" />
  </layout>
</head>
```

The actual image map, shown in Figure 13-3, is placed in the `image_region`. This image is an image map because it has a variety of `<area>` elements applied to it. Each of these elements is pointing to a specific text file with the `href` attribute of the `<area>` element and is told to target (using the `target` attribute of the `<area>` element, which I discuss in Chapter 12) the new text file to the `text_region` area of the screen. These `<area>` elements are configured so whenever a person clicks in the specifically designated area of the image, the corresponding text files are loaded into the identified `text_region`.

Figure 13-3:
The navigational bar image for loading information.

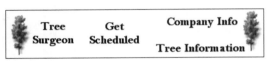

```
<body>
    <img src="nav_bar.jpg"
         region="image_region">
    <area shape="rect"
          coords="40,15,112,65"
          href="surgeon.smi"
          target="text_region"/>
    <area shape="rect"
          coords="125,15,210,65"
          href="schedule.smi"
          target="text_region"/>
    <area shape="rect"
          coords="240,10,360,30"
          href="corporate.smi"i
          target="text_region"/>
    <area shape="rect"
          coords="230,50,375,70"
          href="tree_info.smi"
          target="text_region"/>
    </img>
  </body
</smil>
```

There *is* one catch to this example: The image used for the navigational bar is 400 pixels long and 70 pixels high, but the region itself is only 35 pixels high. This means that a portion of the image, its lower half, is cropped from the screen due to the `fit=hidden` setting in the `image_region` definition, as shown in Figure 13-4. This prohibits any link that's placed in the lower portion of the navigational bar from being used as a link to other documents in this presentation. To avoid having any of your images cropped, stretched out of proportion, or otherwise distorted (as I discuss in Chapter 7), you need to ensure that your images and the regions holding them are at least the same size.

Now whenever someone clicks one of the visible links in your presentation, the contents of that document designated by the links appear in the `text_region`. If you're familiar with HTML and JavaScript, you know how difficult this task can be to re-create using dynamic cross-browser JavaScript with frames and layers . . . yuck. SMIL makes it simple, as long as you have a 2.0-compatible SMIL player.

Figure 13-4:
This is how the presen-tation looks to your visitors.

Getting Your Timing Right

Timing is just as important with links as it is with the remainder of your presentation. The `<actuate>` element, which I discuss in Chapter 12, enables you to determine whether your link must be manually activated (that is, clicked by a visitor), or whether it can be activated just because the element that contains it becomes active. In addition to this type of timing control, you also have control over the time at which the destination document is loaded into the current presentation.

Imagine, for example, that you want to create a series of links to different portions of a documentary on the life cycle of barn cats. You may want one link to the kittenhood years, one to the breeding years, and another to the trials they experience during their old age. In order to link to the different parts of the video, you have to know the timing involved with the video. You have to know when each part of the video starts and how long it lasts. The SMIL document should provide buttons that serve as links to the different portions of the cat video:

✔ You have one button/link that enables viewers to watch the entire program from start to finish.

✔ Other buttons, or links, take viewers to the individual sections of the video so that they can watch each segment individually.

Figure 13-5 shows which portions of the video you're watching when you click on each button. Figure 13-6 shows you what the page actually looks like. If you click the top button shown in Figure 13-6, corresponding to the Cat documentary video line of Figure 13-5, you watch the entire presentation. If you click the second button, you watch the amount of the video that's represented by the Birthing and kittenhood arrow in Figure 13-5 — the childhood. The other buttons enable you to view that part of the video that's discussing the various special topics. The `dur` and `begin` attributes of the image map's `<area>` elements control where the video starts when a viewer presses one of the button links.

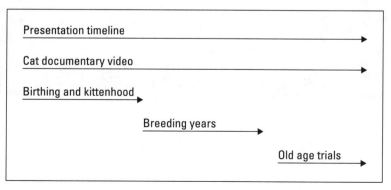

Figure 13-5:
Each of the buttons links to a portion of the video, shown in these timelines.

Presentation timeline

Cat documentary video

Birthing and kittenhood

Breeding years

Old age trials

Figure 13-6:
The layout
of the
presentation
shows each
of the four
buttons/links
that enables
you to
control the
point at
which the
video starts
playing.

```
<smil>
<head>
  <layout>
    <!-- layout of two regions.. one for buttons
         and the other for video. -->
    <root-layout width="800" height="600" />
    <region id="buttons_region"
            width="760" height="50"
            top="730" left="20" />
    <region id="video_region"
            width="760" height="500"
            top="20" left="20" />
  </layout>
</head>
<body>

  <!-- The following code displays both a video
       and a navigation bar. The navigation bar
       has four buttons to control the portion
       of a video that is seen. -->
  <par>
    <video src="cat_video.rm"
           region="video_region" />
    <excl>
      <img src="nav_bar.jpg"
           region="buttons_region">
```

```
        <!-- This area creates a button that when
             clicked plays the entire video. -->
        <area shape="rect"
            coords="0,0,50,35"
            nohref
            begin="0s"
            dur="360s"
            title="watch full video"
            target="video_region" />
        <!-- This area creates a button that when
             clicked plays the first 60s of the video. -->
        <area shape="rect"
            coords="50,0,100,35"
            nohref
            begin="0s"
            dur="60s"
            title="watch birth section"
            target="video_region" />
        <!-- This area creates a button that when
             clicked plays the middle 180s of the video. -->
        <area shape="rect"
            coords="100,0,150,35"
            nohref
            begin="60s"
            dur="180s"
            title="watch midlife section"
            target="video_region" />
        <!-- This area creates a button that when
             clicked plays the last 120s of the video. -->
        <area shape="rect"
            coords="150,0,200,35"
            nohref
            begin="240s"
            dur="120s"
            title="watch end of life section"
            target="video_region" />
        </img>
      </excl>
    </par>
  </body>
</smil>
```

Another Look at Links as Interactions

Image maps can be used to create great interactive links in your SMIL documents. For example, you can create elaborate linking interactions with SMIL and a simple image. It isn't hard. You just have to keep the logic of what you're doing in your head or better yet — if you're like me — on a piece of paper. The following SMIL example isn't too different from this chapter's previous example, but instead of the `<area>` element loading the SMIL documents, the individual media elements are using the SMIL documents to load themselves. By using the clicking of the visitor's mouse to trigger a media element, you have more control over any transitional effects (which I discuss in Chapter 14) that occur within the media, as well as more control over the timing of the media. For example, if you use the `<area>` link to load a document, you can't make it load after a 3-second pause. Tuning the media element to a particular mouse click enables you to incorporate all the timing constraints that are available for your media items.

The presentation, shown in the following example, is composed of three regions in this document that hold a textarea, an image map used for navigation, and a heading image. When the visitor clicks one of the buttons to the left, text appears on-screen replacing images, as shown in Figure 13-7.

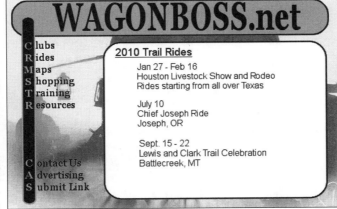

Figure 13-7:
Each option on the menu loads a different text document.

The images and text are all shown in parallel, as you can see from the use of the `<par>` element, but the text itself is set up in an exclusive list (`<excl>`) so that only one text file can be seen at a time. The choice of text file is driven by the visitor's selection of one of the menu option buttons. For example, when a visitor clicks the `<area>` element called *clubs,* the `<text>` document called `clubtxt` is loaded into the `<region>` called `text_region`. Each of the menu buttons, shown to the left side of the screen in Figure 13-7, are mapped with an `<area>` element and are watched by a corresponding `<text>` element. Take a look at the following SMIL code. It may look long, but it's really quite simple, with every menu option set up in the same way as the Clubs button.

```
<smil>
<head>
  <layout>
    <root-layout width="596" height="396" />
    <!-- Identifies the three regions: buttons, text, and
         header. These regions store images and text at
         various points in the playback of this
         presentation. -->
    <region id="buttons_region"
            width="175" height="275"
            top="85" left="0" />
    <region id="text_region"
            width="400" height="275"
            top="100" left="185" />
    <region id="header_region"
            width="596" height="84"
            top="0" left="0" />
  </layout>
</head>
<body>
  <par>
    <!-- Places the header image in the header_region, and
         freezes
         it indefinitely until the presentation is completed
         -->
    <img src=header.gif"
         region="header_region"
         dur="indefinite"
         fill="freeze" />

    <!-- Places the image nav_bar.jpg into the buttons_region
         and freezes it. Then the individual area links are
         mapped with no coordinates. This allows the buttons
         to be used solely as the trigger for the loading of
         the new presentation document, without actually
         loading a new document.
         The visible words in your image (i.e. clubs, etc.)
         are part of the image. The contents of the title
         attributes of the area elements simply provide
         additional information about the document. They have
         no effect on the presentation of the link area or
         the image that link is being applied to.-->
```

```
<img src="nav_bar.jpg"
    region="buttons_region"
    dur="indefinite"
    fill="freeze">
  <area id="clubs"
        shape="rect"
        coords="0,0,150,20"
        nohref

        title="Get list of club activities"
        />
  <area id="rides"
        shape="rect"
        coords="0,20,150,42"
        nohref

        title="Get list of US trail rides."
        />
  <area id="maps"
        shape="rect"
        coords="0,42,150,64"
        nohref

        title="Find maps to rides."
        />
  <area id="shopping"
        shape="rect"
        coords="0,64,150,86"
        nohref

        title="Shop for great gifts"
        />
  <area id="training"
        shape="rect"
        coords="0,86,150,110"
        nohref

        title="Solve your training problems"
        />
  <area id="resources"
        shape="rect"
        coords="0,110,150,132"
        nohref

        title="Find some help"
        />
  <area id="contact"
        shape="rect"
        coords="0,215,150,235"
        nohref
```

```
                       title="Get Contact Information"
  />
      <area id="ads"
            shape="rect"
            coords="0,235,150,260"
            nohref

            title="Place an advertisement"
            />
      <area id="links"
            shape="rect"
            coords="0,260,150,280"
            nohref

            title="Find Related Links"
            />
  </img>

  <!-- Creates a list of files that will play in the
        text_region one at a time, in no particular order.
        Their display is triggered by the click in one of
        the areas defined in the button_region image. -->
  <excl>
    <text id="clubtxt"
          src="club.txt"
          region="text_region"
          dur="indefinite"
          begin="clubs.click" />
    <text id="ridetxt"
          src="ride.txt"
          region="text_region"
          dur="indefinite"
          begin="rides.click" />
    <text id="maptxt"
          src="map.txt"
          region="text_region"
          dur="indefinite"
          begin="maps.click" />
    <text id="shoptxt"
          src="shopping.txt"
          region="text_region"
          dur="indefinite"
          begin="shopping.click" />
    <text id="traintxt"
          src="training.txt"
          region="text_region"
          dur="indefinite"
          begin="training.click" />
```

```
      <text id="restxt"
            src="resources.txt"
            region="text_region"
            dur="indefinite"
            begin="resources.click" />
      <text id="contacttxt"
            src="contact.txt"
            region="text_region"
            dur="indefinite"
            begin="contact.click" />
      <text id="adtxt"
            src="ad.txt"
            region="text_region"
            dur="indefinite"
            begin="ads.click" />
      <text id="linkstxt"
            src="links.txt"
            region="text_region"
            dur="indefinite"
            begin="links.click" />
    </excl>
  </par>
</body>
</smil>
```

SMIL links, such as the ones shown in the previous example, can be performed in a variety of ways. Typically, you'll always be able to find one best way to perform a task, especially when you want to apply different types of animation or transformation effects to your links. In some cases, you can't correctly apply a transformation to the changes that occur in your presentation due to your links.

Chapter 14

Nothing Is Better Than Animations (Except Transformations)

In This Chapter

▶ Animating your presentation properties

▶ Using motion to spice up your presentations

▶ Adding transformations to your presentations

*T*o make your presentation even more interesting and appealing, SMIL offers a series of *animation* and *transformation options*. Animations enable you to move and change the media element based on its available element properties. Transformations enable you to segue between different types of media without that abrupt "here and gone" transition that you've been seeing throughout this book and in the previous versions of SMIL.

SMILe — You're Animated

SMIL provides a mechanism to incorporate animation within your presentations by enabling you to control the settings of the various attributes associated with the media element you're modifying. This doesn't mean that you can actually alter the content of your video or your audio file while it's running. You can, however, change the color of a region or move an image of a bunny around the screen as if it's hopping without creating a lot of animated GIF images. You can even synchronize your animations to a timeline so that you can have every item on your presentation working in sync with each other.

The following four elements work together or individually to create your fully animated presentation:

- ✔ `<animate>`
- ✔ `<animateMotion>`
- ✔ `<animateColor>`
- ✔ `<set>`

Animate your attributes

No, this isn't like trying to put your best attributes (umm . . . foot) forward. You control all your animations by controlling the values of the individual media element's attributes. Some media elements have duration already built into them (for example, video clips, which intrinsically have a set duration). But by animating your media elements, you're creating a new element with a duration built right into the media itself through the use of the dur attribute. You can even repeat an animation multiple times using the repeatCount and repeatDur attributes. A lot of attributes work with SMIL media elements, including the primary attributes, which I discuss in the following sections.

attributeName

The attributeName attribute simply specifies the name of the target attribute whose value will be adjusted.

```
<img src="image.gif"
     width="100" height="100">
  <animate attributeName="width" />
</img>
```

attributeType

The attributeType attribute identifies the type of attribute that you're adjusting. The attribute is set to one of the following case-sensitive values:

- ✔ **CSS:** Identifies the attribute being adjusted as a Cascading Style Sheet attribute. (See Chapter 6 for more about CSS.)
- ✔ **XML:** Identifies the attribute being adjusted as an XML attribute.
- ✔ **auto:** Identifies the attribute being adjusted as one that's associated in either CSS or XML. This is the default.

```
<img src="image.gif"
     width="100" height="100">
  <animate attributeName="width"
           attributeType="CSS" />
</img>
```

targetElement

The targetElement attribute specifies the name of the element whose attributes are being adjusted.

```
<img src="image.gif"
     width="100" height="100">
  <animate attributeName="width"
           attributeType="CSS"
           targetElement="img"/>
</img>
```

accumulate

The accumulate attribute controls whether the movement of the animation is cumulative or whether it's simply a repeat of the original animation movement. This attribute has the following two possible values:

- ✔ sum: Identifies the actions of the animation to be cumulative.

- ✔ none: Identifies the actions of the animation as not cumulative, so the animation appears to be repetitious.

```
<img src="image.gif"
     width="100" height="100">
  <animate attributeName="width"
           attributeType="CSS"
           targetElement="img"
           accumulate="sum"/>
</img>
```

additive

The additive attribute controls whether the values that are affected by the animation increase or decrease as the animation runs. This attribute can have the following values:

- ✔ sum: Specifies that the animation is adding its adjustments to the underlying value of the attribute.

- ✔ replace: Specifies that the animation overrides the attribute values. This is the default.

If you use a value of sum then you're constantly adding to your last base values. When you run an animation that makes an image wider, the image expands to the specified dimension the first time. The second time the animation ran, it expands the same amount and doubles the growth of the original image. If you select replace as the value for your additive attribute then the image never grows past its original destination size.

```
<img src="image.gif"
     width="100" height="100">
  <animate attributeName="width"
           attributeType="CSS"
           targetElement="img"
           accumulate="sum"
           additive="replace"/>
</img>
```

from

When creating an animation, you can specify its starting point, or the original value of the attribute specified with the attributeName attribute, using the from attribute. This attribute can accept any value, but that value must be legal for the attribute identified in the attributeName attribute. The following example uses pixels for its unit of measurement, although you can use any other unit of measurement you like — as long as the SMIL player supports it.

```
<img src="image.gif"
     width="10" height="10">
  <animate attributeName="width"
           attributeType="CSS"
           targetElement="img"
           accumulate="sum"
           additive="replace"
           from="10"/>
</img>
```

to

When creating an animation, you can use the to attribute to specify that the animation is the ultimate destination of the object's attribute specified in the attributeName attribute. This attribute can accept any value, but that value must be legal for the attribute identified in the attributeName attribute. In the following example, the width of the image is being expanded from 10 to 100 pixels.

```
<img src="image.gif"
     width="10" height="10">
  <animate attributeName="width"
           attributeType="CSS"
           targetElement="img"
           accumulate="sum"
           additive="replace"
           from="10"
           to="100"/>
</img>
```

by

The by attribute provides the incremental step value by which the from attribute value reaches the to attribute value. This attribute can accept any value, but that value must be legal for the attribute identified in the attributeName attribute.

```
<img src="image.gif"
     width="10" height="10">
  <animate attributeName="width"
           attributeType="CSS"
           targetElement="img"
           accumulate="sum"
           additive="replace"
           from="10"
           to="100"
           by="5"/>
</img>
```

Get set to go . . .

The <set> element gives you a way to set the values of attributes for a specific duration. You may have always wanted a mute button for your kids, so that you can finish those last 5 minutes of the movie you're watching. Using the <set> element, you can control the values of specified attributes while they're within a specific time frame, but only during that time frame. The <set> element doesn't permanently set the value of your element's attributes.

The <set> element uses all the same attributes as the <animate> element, other than additive and accumulate. Using the repeatDur and repeatCount attributes with <set>, however, is illogical because you can't repeat a static change. If you do use the repeatDur and repeatCount attributes with the <set> element, they simply add to the duration of the <set>.

You can see the <set> element at work in the following example code. It sets the value of the class attribute of the text object to BackLight whenever a visitor moves the mouse over the text. The class BackLight must have already been defined within a Cascading Style Sheet with the appropriate text effects. In order for this example to work, you have to have a SMIL player that supports both SMIL 2.0 and Cascading Style Sheets.

```
<text class="PlainText">
    This will highlight if you mouse over it...
    <set attributeName="class"
        to="BackLight"
        begin="mouseover"
        end="mouseout" />
</text>
```

Add motion with animateMotion

In addition to the <animate> and <set> elements, you can also create motion in your SMIL presentation by using the <animateMotion> element. This element enables you to move a media element along a path. For instance, you can use the <animate> element to move a media element along a single path from point A to point B but only on one axis at a time. The <animateMotion> element enables you to move an object in a straight line from one point on-screen to another, no matter how far away or in what direction that other point may be.

You can specify the direction and destination that the movement takes by using x, y pairs of coordinates for the from, to, and by attributes, rather than for their default horizontal or vertical measurements as the <animate> element uses.

The `<animateMotion>` element uses many of the same attributes as the `<animate>` element. These attributes include the following:

- ✔ dur
- ✔ fill
- ✔ additive
- ✔ accumulate
- ✔ href
- ✔ targetElement
- ✔ from
- ✔ to
- ✔ by

As you may have noticed, the `attributeName` and the `attributeType` attributes are not included in this list. They are unnecessary because the element is moved, which only affects the `top` and `left` attributes. In order for the `<animateMotion>` element to have any effect on your document, you must include at least one of the `from`, `to`, or `by` attributes; otherwise, the animation has no effect. The values of the `from`, `to`, and `by` attribute are expressed as x, y mapping points, so that you can move the object without having to define multiple attributes for each element you're moving.

```
<img src="image1.gif">
    <animateMotion to="100,100"
                   begin="mouseover"
                   end="mouseout" />
</img>
```

Brighten up your world with animateColor

Ever get tired of that old plain background? Do you want to liven it up a little bit when movies are playing or an image is just sitting there? Or maybe you want to change it around as its own effect? Using the `<animateColor>` element, you can specify changes to the color attributes of the various elements in your presentation. The `<animateColor>` element supports all the same attributes as the `<animate>` element, so remembering them is easy:

- ✔ attributeName
- ✔ attributeType
- ✔ dur
- ✔ fill

- ✔ repeatCount
- ✔ repeatDur
- ✔ additive
- ✔ accumulate
- ✔ href
- ✔ targetElement
- ✔ from
- ✔ to
- ✔ by

Just as with the `<animate>` element, the `<animateColor>` element requires the `attributeName` attribute to be present. The value of the `to` attribute can be any of the accepted CSS color names, such as black, white, brown, red, green, blue, and so on.

```
<text class="PlainText">
    This will highlight if you mouse over it...
    <animateColor attributeName="color"
        to="black"
        begin="mouseover"
        end="mouseout" />
</text>
```

Transition Effects — Sneaking In a Change

SMIL has been touted as the medium that will bring TV-like content to the Web. But up to now, with the release of SMIL 2.0, you had no way of bringing common television effects to your SMIL presentations. You're in luck now though: You can now create simple *fades* and *wipes* with your SMIL presentations. What are fades and wipes, you may ask? If you're using a fade, the current image or screen gradually turns into the background color and then forms a new image. It's sort of like blurring your vision as you slowly close your eyes, and then turning your head and "unblurring" it as you slowly open your eyes again, looking at something new. The wipe effect is kind of like passing your hand before your eyes. A wipe effect works just like wiping the dirt off a window. As the bar moves across the screen, the old image is replaced with the new image.

The following code loads a series of images of rodents in a specific order, creating a simple slide show of these images.

```
<body>
...
<seq>
    <img src="rat.jpg" dur="5s" ... />
    <img src="mouse.jpg" dur="5s" ... />
    <img src="hamster.jpg" dur="5s" ... />
    <img src="gerbil.jpg" dur="5s" ... />
</seq>
...
</body>
```

When this presentation plays, you'll see one image disappear and then the other appear in its place. Of course, this can be a bit jarring to the viewer's eyeballs. Using the transition effects from SMIL 2.0, you can add the same fade effect between each of your images or add different effects between each image.

In the following example, I've created a single transition that fades the old image to black before allowing the new image to appear. This transition is used with each image, as you can see by the addition of the transOut attribute associated with each <img> element. I've bolded the lines of transition code to help you spot them quickly.

```
<smil>
  <head>
    ...
    <transition id="fadeblack"
                type="fade"
                subtype="fadeToColor"
                fadeColor="#000000"
                dur="1s"/>
  </head>
  <body>
    ...
    <par>
      <img src="rat.jpg"
           dur="5s"
           transOut="fadeblack"... />
      <img src="mouse.jpg"
           dur="5s"
           transOut="fadeblack" ... />
      <img src="hamster.jpg"
           dur="5s"
           transOut="fadeblack" ... />
      <img src="gerbil.jpg"
           dur="5s"
           transOut="fadeblack"... />
    </par>
    ...
  </body>
</smil>
```

Throughout the rest of this chapter, I show you how to create transitions and add them to your media elements so you can really impress your boss!

Transition effects

The <transition> element creates transitions. This element has a variety of attributes that define the duration of the transition, the type of the transition, and how that transition is used.

Only four types of transitions, shown in Table 14-1, must be supported in a SMIL 2.0-compatible player, although other transitions, such as fade, are also described in the SMIL specification. Because each transition has to have a subtype specified, the four transitions required by the SMIL 2.0 specification also have four default subtypes specified.

Table 14-1	Required Transition Types
Transition Type	*Default Transition Subtype*
barWipe	leftToRight
irisWipe	rectangle
clockWipe	clockwiseTwelve
snakeWipe	topLeftHorizontal

SMIL includes a large variety of other transition types, including all of the transition types and subtypes shown in Table 14-2. Although support for all of these transitions is encouraged, the SMIL specification doesn't require them all to be supported because of the vast number of them. These optional transition effects are broken down into five categories, which I describe in the following list:

- ✔ **Edge wipes:** Wipe effects that occur along the edge of your object. An example of an edge wipe is a left-to-right moving bar that reveals a new image to the left of the bar and the old image to the right of the bar as the bar moves across the image until only the new image is visible.

- ✔ **Iris wipes:** Wipe effects that expand from the center of the media like an eye opening up.

- ✔ **Clock wipes:** A wipe effect that has a rotating arm reaching from the center of the object to its edge, replacing the old image with the new as it sweeps around the center of the object.

- ✔ **Matrix wipes:** Wipe effects that occur by replacing squares in the old image with portions of the new image in a specified pattern.

✔ **Non-SMPTE wipes:** These are the wipe effects that don't really fall into another category and haven't yet been identified by the Society of Motion Picture and Television Engineers (SMPTE). They include such things as fades, which change your screen from an image to a color, an image to another image, or a color to an image, and other wipe effects that haven't been standardized for use in television and movies.

Table 14-2	Optional SMIL Transition Types
Transition Type	*Transition Subtypes*
Edge Wipes	
barWipe	leftToRight [default]
	topToBottom
boxWipe	topLeft [default]
	topRight
	bottomRight
	bottomLeft
	topCenter
	rightCenter
	bottomCenter
	leftCenter
fourBoxWipe	cornersIn [default]
	cornersOut
barnDoorWipe	vertical [default]
	horizontal
	diagonalBottomLeft
	diagonalTopLeft
diagonalWipe	topLeft [default]
	topRight
bowTieWipe	vertical [default]
	horizontal
miscDiagonalWipe	doubleBarnDoor [default]
	doubleDiamond

Transition Type	Transition Subtypes
veeWipe	down [default]
	left
	up
	right
barnVeeWipe	down [default]
	left
	up
	right
zigZagWipe	leftToRight [default]
	topToBottom
barnZigZagWipe	vertical [default]
	horizontal
Iris Wipes	
irisWipe	rectangle [default]
	diamond
triangleWipe	up [default]
	right
	down
	left
arrowHeadWipe	up [default]
	right
	down
	left
pentagonWipe	up [default]
	down
hexagonWipe	horizontal [default]
	vertical

(continued)

Table 14-2 *(continued)*

Transition Type	Transition Subtypes
Edge Wipes	
ellipseWipe	circle [default]
	horizontal
	vertical
eyeWipe	horizontal [default]
	vertical
roundRectWipe	horizontal [default]
	vertical
starWipe	fourPoint [default]
	fivePoint
	sixPoint
miscShapeWipe	heart [default]
	keyhole
Clock Wipes	
clockWipe	clockwiseTwelve [default]
	clockwiseThree
	clockwiseSix
	clockwiseNine
pinWheelWipe	twoBladeVertical [default]
	twoBladeHorizontal
	fourBlade
singleSweepWipe	clockwiseTop [default]
	clockwiseRight
	clockwiseBottom
	clockwiseLeft
	clockwiseTopLeft

Transition Type	Transition Subtypes
	counterClockwiseBottomLeft
	clockwiseBottomRight
	counterClockwiseTopRight
fanWipe	centerTop [default]
	centerRight
	top
	right
	bottom
	left
doubleFanWipe	fanOutVertical [default]
	fanOutHorizontal
	fanInVertical
	fanInHorizontal
doubleSweepWipe	parallelVertical [default]
	parallelDiagonal
	oppositeVertical
	oppositeHorizontal
	parallelDiagonalTopLeft
	parallelDiagonalBottomLeft
saloonDoorWipe	top [default]
	left
	bottom
	right
windshieldWipe	right [default]
	up
	vertical
	horizontal

(continued)

Table 14-2 *(continued)*

Transition Type	Transition Subtypes
Matrix Wipes	
snakeWipe	topLeftHorizontal [default]
	topLeftVertical
	topLeftDiagonal
	topRightDiagonal
	bottomRightDiagonal
	bottomLeftDiagonal
spiralWipe	topLeftClockwise [default]
	topRightClockwise
	bottomRightClockwise
	bottomLeftClockwise
	topLeftCounterClockwise
	topRightCounterClockwise
	bottomRightCounterClockwise
	bottomLeftCounterClockwise
parallelSnakesWipe	verticalTopSame [default]
	verticalBottomSame
	verticalTopLeftOpposite
	verticalBottomLeftOpposite
	horizontalLeftSame
	horizontalRightSame
	horizontalTopLeftOpposite
	horizontalTopRightOpposite
	diagonalBottomLeftOpposite
	diagonalTopLeftOpposite
boxSnakesWipe	twoBoxTop [default]
	twoBoxBottom
	twoBoxLeft

Transition Type	Transition Subtypes
	twoBoxRight
	fourBoxVertical
	fourBoxHorizontal
waterfallWipe	verticalLeft [default]
	verticalRight
	horizontalLeft
	horizontalRight
Non-SMPTE Wipes	
pushWipe	fromLeft [default]
	fromTop
	fromRight
	fromBottom
slideWipe	fromLeft [default]
	fromTop
	fromRight
	fromBottom
fade	crossfade [default]
	fadeToColor
	fadeFromColor

Each of these transition filters requires a number of different settings in order to configure themselves correctly. I show only the main transition effects in this book, but you can get more information on each of these other transitions from the World Wide Web Consortium Web site located at www.w3.org.

The transition element

The <transition> element, typically located in the <head> of your SMIL document, sets all the parameters that control how the transition appears. Because the <transition> is created once and located in the SMIL document <head>, it can be referenced from any number of locations within the SMIL presentation. In order to completely describe how a transition appears and functions, you need to use the following attributes. I describe these attributes in more detail in the following sections of this chapter.

- ✔ `type`: Identifies the type of transition to take place.
- ✔ `subtype`: Identifies the specific transition within the selected type category.
- ✔ `dur`: The length of the transition.
- ✔ `startProgress`: Indicates the point at which the transition should start.
- ✔ `endProgress`: Indicates the point at which the transition should end.
- ✔ `direction`: Indicates the direction the transition will move.
- ✔ `faceColor`: Controls the change of a fade transition to a specific color.
- ✔ `borderWidth`: Sets the width of the border of the transition area.
- ✔ `borderColor`: Sets the color of the border of the transition area.

In addition to these attributes, the `<transition>` element can have the `<param>` element as a child. The purpose of the `<param>` element is to provide a generic means of supplying parameters to extended transition effects. The `<param>` element's values are dependent on the software that's viewing the document. To find out more about the `<param>` element and how it works with different SMIL players, check out the W3C Web site at `www.w3.org`.

In the following sections, I provide examples and detailed information about the attributes of the transition element. They build upon each other showing how each attribute works with the others to define exactly how an individual transition behaves.

Deciding on a type

The `type` attribute is required to set the type of transition effect that takes place. It must be one of the types that I've listed in Table 14-2 or a specific transition provided by the software that's viewing the SMIL presentation.

```
<transition id="fadeblack"
            type="fade" />
```

Setting up a subtype

The `subtype` attribute provides you with an optional way of further describing the type of effect that you're using. It has to be one of the types that I've listed in Table 14-2 or a specific transition provided by the software that's viewing the SMIL presentation.

```
<transition id="fadeblack"
            type="fade"
            subtype="fadetocolor"/>
```

Controlling the duration

In transitions, the `dur` attribute works the same as when you use it in the timing modules that I discuss in Chapter 8. All the transitions that I've listed in Table 14-2 have a duration of 1 second by default. You can increase this time, which is the amount of time it takes for the transition to complete once it's started.

```
<transition id="fadeblack"
            type="fade"
            subtype="fadetocolor"
            dur="2s"/>
```

Starting your transition

You can use the `startProgress` attribute to control the amount of progress, through the specified transition, that appears to take place before the transition effect becomes visible. For instance, if the `startProgress` attribute is set to .25, the transition appears to be 25% complete when it becomes visible to the visitor. The default value of this attribute is 0, or the beginning of the transition.

```
<transition id="fadeblack"
            type="fade"
            subtype="fadetocolor"
            dur="2s"
            startProgress=".25"/>
```

Ending your transition

You can use the `endProgress` attribute to control the amount of progress, through the specified transition, that appears to be left to execute when the transition effect closes. For instance, if the `endProgress` attribute is set to .75, the transition appears to be 75% complete when it ends. The default value of this attribute is 1, or the end of the transition. If both the `startProgress` and the `endProgress` values are the same, then the transition appears fixed for the duration of the transition.

```
<transition id="fadeblack"
            type="fade"
            subtype="fadetocolor"
            dur="2s"
            startProgress=".25"
            endProgress=".75"/>
```

Controlling the direction

The `direction` attribute has one task: to control the direction that the transition runs. This attribute has two values: `forward` and `reverse`. The direction specified by forward and reverse is controlled by the effect that was selected in the `type` and `subtype` fields. For instance, a `barWipe` transition `type`, with a `subtype` of `leftToRight`, would wipe left-to-right with `direction=forward` and right-to-left with `direction=reverse`. As you may imagine, the default value of this attribute is forward. In order for this attribute to have an effect, you must use a *geometric transition* — essentially one of the wipe effects that moves the screen in a specific direction, or overwrites the screen with a particular shape. Fade transitions cannot be geometric transitions because they don't have a direction or shape applied to them while the change is being made.

```
<transition id="fadeblack"
            type="fade"
            subtype="fadetocolor"
            dur="2s"
            startProgress=".25"
            endProgress=".75"
            direction="forward" />
```

Fading colors

The fadeColor attribute doesn't work for all situations. It's only available if type="fade" and subtype="fadeToColor" or subtype="fadeFromColor". If this situation exists, the fadeColor attribute specifies either the starting or ending color of the fade transition. The default value of this attribute is black, but the attribute supports any of the standard Cascading Style Sheets (CSS2) system colors, which I've listed in Table 14-3.

Table 14-3	Valid CSS Color Names and Codes
Name	*Hex Value*
Aqua	00FFFF
Black	000000
Blue	0000FF
Fuchsia	FF00FF
Gray	808080
Green	008000
Lime	00FF00
Maroon	800000
Navy	000080
Olive	808000
Purple	800080
Red	FF0000
Silver	C0C0C0

Name	Hex Value
Teal	008080
White	FFFFFF
Yellow	FFFF00

You can find out more about CSS2 coloring at `www.w3.org/Style/CSS`.

```
<transition id="fadeblack"
            type="fade"
            subtype="fadetocolor"
            dur="2s"
            startProgress=".25"
            endProgress=".75"
            fadeColor="yellow"/>
```

Setting the wipe edge border

You can control the appearance of your transition edge during a wipe effect by using the `borderWidth` and the `borderColor` attributes. The `borderwidth` attribute sets the width of the border created along the edge of the wipe. The default value of `borderWidth` is 0, which draws no border. The `borderColor` attribute controls the color of the border that's drawn (if one is drawn) along the edge of the wipe effect. Although the default color value for this attribute is black, you can use any of the colors provided for in the CSS2 specification (refer to Table 14-3).

```
<transition id="fadeblack"
            type="fade"
            subtype="fadetocolor"
            dur="2s"
            startprogress=".25"
            endprogress=".75"
            fadecolor="yellow"
            borderwidth="1"
            bordercolor="orange"/>
```

Adding transitions to media elements

After you know how to create your transitions, you have to add them to the individual media elements to which they're applied. You can do this by specifying the `transIn` and `transOut` attributes as a part of the media element.

```
<img transIn="fadein" transOut="fadeout" ... />
```

A transition specified by the `transIn` attribute begins at the beginning of the element's active duration, whereas transitions specified by the `transOut` attribute end at the end of the media's active duration or fill state. If neither of these attributes is specified, no transition is used on the media. When these attributes *are* used, however, they can specify as many transition IDs as you want (in a semicolon-separated list, of course).

```
<img transIn="fadein; wipeRed; fadeOut" ... />
```

This list provides the software a way of falling back if the first transition listed can't be supported. This enables you, as the presentation creator, to provide a variety of possible transitions that can be used by different software, with different support levels. Take the previous code, for example. If the transition named "fadein" can't be displayed, the transition "wipeRed" will be used. If the "wipeRed" transition doesn't work, the "fadeOut" transition will be used.

You must follow a few rules when applying a transition to a media element:

- ✔ The transition must begin with or end with the beginning or ending of the media element's duration.

- ✔ Transitions happen during the active duration of the media element to which they are applied, plus any fill period that has been applied to them.

- ✔ The active duration of the media element that's being transitioned to should overlap the duration of the media element that you're transitioning from. If this can't be the case, the background of the area behind the media should be used in the transition.

- ✔ If both the transIn and transOut transitions are specified for a media element and they overlap, the effect of the transIn transition takes precedence. The transOut transition is ignored and not performed.

- ✔ Because transitions imply the passage from the display of one media element to another, they don't repeat.

Filling in a transition

In addition to the transIn and transOut attributes, you can specify a new value for your fill media element attribute that enables you to place the transition in the fill area after a media element finishes playing rather than have the transition overwrite the media itself.

```
<smil>
  <head>
  ...
    <transition id="starTrans"
    type="starWipe"
    subtype="fivePoint"
            dur="5s" />
  ...
```

```
</head>
<body>
...
<video src="video_25.rm"  dur="30s" fill="transition"
        transOut="starTrans" ... />
...
</body>
</smil>
```

This statement uses the `starTrans` transition value of the `transOut`
attribute to fill in the amount of space left over by the transition fill time.

Setting up a slide show

After adding the `fill` and `transIn` attributes, the example slide show (from
the beginning of the section, "Transition Effects — Sneaking In a Change,"
earlier in this chapter) now looks like the following:

```
<smil>
  <head>
    ...
    <transition id="starTrans"
                type="starWipe"
                subtype="fivePoint"
                dur="2s" />
    ...
  </head>
  <body>
    <seq>
    <img src="rat.jpg"
         dur="10s"
         fill="transition"... />
    <img src="mouse.jpg"
         dur="10s"
         fill="transition"
         transIn="starTrans" ... />
    <img src="hamster.jpg"
         dur="10s"
         fill="transition"
         transIn="starTrans" ... />
    <img src="gerbil.jpg"
         dur="10s"
         transIn="starTrans" ... />
    </seq>
  </body>
</smil>
```

Now the presentation plays in the following fashion:

1. **At 0 seconds, the** `rat.jpg` **image loads.**

2. **At 10 seconds, a 1-second keyhole transition from** `rat.jpg` **to** `mouse.jpg` **begins.**

3. **At 12 seconds,** `mouse.jpg` **is fully displayed and remains displayed for 8 more seconds until 20 seconds.**

4. **At 20 seconds, a 2-second keyhole transition from** `mouse.jpg` **to** `hamster.jpg` **begins.**

5. **At 22 seconds,** `hamster.jpg` **is fully displayed for 8 more seconds until 30 seconds.**

6. **At 30 seconds, a 2-second left-to-right wipe begins from** `hamster.jpg` **to** `gerbil.jpg`**.**

7. **At 32 seconds,** `gerbil.jpg` **is fully displayed for 8 more seconds until 40 seconds.**

8. **At 40 seconds, the presentation ends.**

All these transitions take place while each of the images is visible without subtracting from the image's display time. In this example, the transitions occur at the beginning of each image's active duration.

Notice the importance of `fill="transition"`. If I hadn't specified `fill="transition"` on `rat.jpg`, `mouse.jpg`, and `hamster.jpg`, the transitions at 10, 20, and 30 seconds would have taken place between the background of the playback area (or the default background color, depending on how the layout language is specified) instead of the previous image in the sequence.

Part V
Multimedia from the Ground Up

The 5th Wave   By Rich Tennant

"Give him air! Give him air! He'll be okay. He's just been exposed to some raw SMIL code. It must have accidently flashed across his screen from the server."

In this part . . .

*I*f you feel like you just can't envision the whole picture, then this part's for you. Within these chapters, you can see how to turn a blank SMIL document (and a modicum of understanding about SMIL commands) into a full-blown radio station playing sounds from yesteryear. Perhaps you prefer watching a silent movie. If you aren't into the regal entertainment of the 1920s, then maybe producing your own cartoon would suit you best. Whatever your tastes, you can do all this and more using the examples and commands that I step you through within the following chapters.

Chapter 15

Building Your Own Radio Station

In This Chapter
▶ Building the foundation
▶ Setting locations
▶ Timing your music
▶ Hearing the results

*S*etting out to create your own online radio station is a long, arduous process. In this chapter, I show you a sample of an online radio station that, although it gets you started, highlights only the very basics. When you create a series of music files that you want to play in conjunction with text on-screen, you must

✔ Define the structure and navigation system of your SMIL document, as I discuss in Chapter 3, so that you have the proper structure from which to work, including all the files that go into the document.

✔ Define all areas that you use in the presentation by using the `<region>` element. Within the regions, include everything that holds text, images, video, or audio tracks. For a refresher on using the `<region>` element to set up regions, see Chapter 7.

✔ Get your timing right. (This is the tough part.) Listen to all the music that you plan to have your station play and write down its duration. Doing so enables you to appropriately time interactions, commercials, breaks, and other parts of your radio station's playing schedule.

After you've accomplished all that, you come to the easy part: You get to sit down and watch/listen to your presentation to make sure it works just the way that you want it to.

Laying Out the Foundation

Before you can start developing your SMIL-based radio station, you have to create all the files, whether music, text, or images, that you need to use within the presentation. Trust me on this. If you're creating your content as you're creating the SMIL document, you're only giving yourself more headaches.

In the case of this radio station, you have six files to create, in addition to the actual SMIL document:

- ✔ The radio station logo (an image)
- ✔ The radio station motto
- ✔ The Play Now heading
- ✔ The Play Next heading
- ✔ The scrolling marquee containing the name of the currently playing song
- ✔ The scrolling marquee containing the name of the song that's playing next

Placing the radio station logo

Create your own logo for the radio station. The logo that I've made, shown in Figure 15-1, is a simple, small 100 x 100 pixel image. Place your logo in the RadioImage region specified in the `<layout>` section of the SMIL document. For more information on the `<layout>` element, see the section, "Controlling Your Locations," later in this chapter.

Figure 15-1:
A simple
logo.

You can find this image on the CD as `logo.gif` in the `Examples\Chapter15` directory.

Placing the radio motto

A motto is typically a very simple statement used in advertising, and this case is no different. In this RealText document, shown in the following code, you use a few of the most basic RealText commands to create a simple heading that you place across the top of the SMIL presentation. See Appendix F on the CD for more detailed information about the individual RealText commands that I use in this file, as well as in the other examples throughout this chapter. RealText is a RealNetworks language that's used to provide formatted text input into RealPlayer presentations. The formatting of this language is almost a subset of HTML and SMIL with a few additional formatting elements.

Specifically, the following RealText document creates a `window`, or a region to use SMIL terminology, in your SMIL document that has a black background, a width of 280 pixels and a height of 35 pixels. It contains the text "The Best Country, in the Country" in white, slightly larger than normal, characters.

You can find this document on the CD as `stationtext.rt` in the `Examples\ Chapter15` directory.

```
<window
    type="generic"
    bgcolor="black"
    duration="1"
    width="280"
    height="35"
    extraspaces="ignore"
>

    <pos y="0"/>
    <font color="white" size="+1">
        <center>
            <i>The Best Country, in the Country</i>
        </center>
    </font>
</window>
```

Setting up the Play Now heading

Setting up the static headings for the presentation is relatively easy when you're using RealText and SMIL. The RealText document that makes up the Play Now heading uses many commands that are very close in nature and appearance to their HTML counterparts. If you're familiar with HTML, using SMIL and RealText is a cinch for you.

The following RealText document creates a window with a black background with the dimensions of 150 x 30 pixels. In this window, the file places the text "NOW PLAYING" in italicized white letters.

You can find this file on the CD as `nowplay.rt` in the `Examples\Chapter15` directory.

```
<window
    type="generic"
    bgcolor="black"
    duration="1"
```

```
    width="150"
    height="30"
    extraspaces="ignore"
>

    <pos y="0"/>
    <font color="white" size="-1">
        <center>
            <i>NOW PLAYING</i>
        </center>
    </font>
</window>
```

Setting up the Play Next heading

This RealText document takes care of the formatting required to create nicely formatted text on your SMIL document. This text creates a single heading: PLAY NEXT. You use the `<region>` element to specify the placement of this heading. I discuss the `<region>` element more in Chapter 7.

The following RealText document creates a window with a black background with the dimensions of 150 x 30 pixels. In this window, the file places the text "PLAY NEXT" written in italicized white letters.

You can find this file on the CD as `playnext.rt` in the `Examples\Chapter15` directory.

```
<window
    type="generic"
    bgcolor="black"
    duration="1"
    width="150"
    height="30"
    extraspaces="ignore"
>

    <pos y="0"/>
    <font color="white" size="-1">
        <center>
            <i>PLAYING NEXT</i>
        </center>
    </font>
</window>
```

Setting up the Play Now marquee

The radio station document that you're building uses the controls available with RealText to format, color, time, and scroll the information that will appear in the marquee under the Play Now heading. You can find more details on each of the RealText elements and attributes that I use in this file in Appendix F, which is on the CD.

The following RealText document creates a ticker tape-styled text window with a black background. It moves the phrase "The SMIL Boogie" slowly across the 120 x 30 pixel window. This time, the text is orange.

You can find this file located on the CD as `marqplay.rt` in the `Examples\ Chapter15` directory.

```
<window
    type="tickertape"
    bgcolor="black"
    crawlrate="20"
    duration="1"
    width="120"
    height="30"
    extraspaces="ignore"
>

<pos y="0"/>
    <font color="orange">
        <center>
            <b>The SMIL Boogie</b>
        </center>
    </font>
</window>
```

Setting up the Play Next marquee

This is another basic RealText file that uses the controls available with RealText to format, color, time, and scroll the information that you want to appear in the marquee (perhaps the name of the next song that you're playing). You can find more details on each of the RealText elements and attributes that I use in this file in Appendix F, which is on the CD.

The following RealText document creates a ticker tape-styled text window with a black background. It moves the phrase "The HTML Foxtrot" slowly across the 120x30 pixel window. This time, the text is orange.

You can find this file located on the CD as `marqnext.rt` in the `Examples\ Chapter15` directory.

```
<window
    type="tickertape"
    bgcolor="black"
    crawlrate="20"
    duration="1"
```

```
    width="120"
    height="30"
    extraspaces="ignore"
>

<pos y="0"/>
<font color="orange">
<center>
<bi>The HTML FoxTrot </b>
</center>
</font>
</window>
```

Setting up the SMIL file

After you create all the pieces, you're ready to start working on the SMIL file itself. To ensure that you don't forget any important information, start with the basics. As you can see in the following code, you set aside the `<smil>` element (along with the `<head>`, `<meta>`, `<layout>`, and `<body>` elements) so that you can add them as you develop your presentation.

```
<smil>
  <head>
    <meta name="author"
       content="Heather Williamson"/>
    <meta name="title"
       content="Your Radio Station"/>
    <meta name="copyright"
       content="(c) 2000"/>
    <meta name="description"
       content="Web based country radio with a real
                      Internet twist.">
    <meta name="keywords"
       content="internet, smil, radio, music, country
                      radio, exotic music">
    <layout>
    </layout>
  </head>
  <body>
  </body>
</smil>
```

Including `<meta>` elements within your presentation is always a good idea. These elements enable search engines to register your SMIL page and provide links to the information it contains.

Controlling Your Locations

After you start your SMIL document, you need to sort out the various regions that you're using in the presentation to display text, images, and videos. This sample doesn't have any video content, but it does use five text fields, an image field, and another simple empty field that provides background color for the entire presentation. Although you're using a lot of audio files, you don't have to specify a region for them because audio doesn't actually appear on-screen. Audio files can play outside of a region, or you can simply place them inside one of your other regions, if you have problems with some SMIL players not recognizing your audio.

Use the <layout> element to provide boundaries on the specific section of the SMIL document that you're using to create the document structure. You can find out more about the <layout> and the <root-layout> elements in Chapter 6.

Within the entire <layout> area of the document are a series of regions. Each of these regions contains one piece of information within the presentation. In this example, a single region exists for each file that I describe in the section, "Laying Out the Foundation," earlier in this chapter. I discuss the <region> element in detail in Chapter 7 if you have any questions about it or its attributes.

```
<layout>
     <root-layout height="200" width="300"/>
     <region id="background"
          left="0" top="0"
          height="200" width="300"
          z-index="0"
          fit="fill"
          background-color="#000000"/>
     <region id="radioFigure"
          left="10" top="90"
          height="100" width="100"
          z-index="3"
          fit="fill"/>
     <region id="RadioStations"
          left="9" top="10"
          height="35" width="280"
          z-index="4"
          fit="fill"/>
     <region id="NowPlay"
          left="125" top="50"
          height="30" width="150"
          z-index="6"/>
     <region id="NextPlay"
          left="128" top="125"
          height="30" width="150"
          z-index="5"/>
```

```
     <region id="PlayingMarq"
          left="135" top="85"
          height="30" width="140"
          z-index="2"/>
     <region id="NextMarq"
          left="135" top="158"
          height="30" width="140"
          z-index="1"/>
</layout>
```

As I discuss in Chapter 7, you have to provide each of the regions with an identity and a location. Without the id attribute, you can't use the region to contain any information. Without the location and dimension attributes, the region becomes relatively useless unless you simply want to play an audio file within it.

Setting the Timing for Your Music

The hardest part of setting up any SMIL file is getting the timing right; that's why I devote so many pages to timing in this book (see Chapters 8, 9, 10, and 11). Within the timing system, you can set information to appear in a sequence (seq) or in parallel (par).

As you can see from the following SMIL code, this document uses a series of <seq> and <par> elements to create a stacked structure enabling the static content of the SMIL page to appear when it first opens and stay visible the entire time the presentation is open. It then uses an embedded <seq> element to play a series of songs in order and show the text associated with them. For more information on the individual <seq> and <par> elements, see Chapters 9 and 10 respectively. For more information on the individual media commands such as <textarea>, <img>, and <audio>, check out Chapter 2.

In this SMIL document, the <seq> element plays all its child elements, the <par>, and any other banners or text files that you want to display. Within the first child <par> of the <seq> element, place the various text files that you want displayed simultaneously, such as the logo, the stationtext.rt and the Now Playing and Playing Next headings. The music files are then added in time to the changing contents of the information about each song.

```
<body>
  <seq>
    <par system-language="en"
        endsync="first">
      <textstream id="nowplay"
            src="nowplay.rt"
            region="NowPlay"
            fill="freeze"
```

```
                    system-language="en"
                    system-bitrate="9"/>
        <textstream id="stationtext"
                src="stationtext.rt"
                region="RadioStations"
                fill="freeze"
                system-language="en"
                system-bitrate="226"/>
        <img id="radioface"
            src="radioface.gif"
            region="radioFigure"
            fill="freeze"
            system-language="en"
            system-bitrate="12000"/>
        <textstream id="playnext"
                src="playnext.rt"
                region="NextPlay"
                fill="freeze"
                system-language="en"
                system-bitrate="9"/>
        <seq>
            <par system-language="en" endsync="first">
                <textstream id="marqplay"
                        src="marqplay.rt"
                        region="PlayingMarq"
                        system-language="en"
                        system-bitrate="9"
                        repeat="10"/>
                <textstream id="marqnext"
                        src="marqnext.rt"
                        region="NextMarq"
                        system-language="en"
                        system-bitrate="9" repeat="10"/>
                <audio id="zok"
                        src="z-ok.wav"
                        system-bitrate="352800"/>
            </par>
            <par>
                <!-- Add another song here -->
            </par>
            <par>
                <!-- Add another song here -->
            </par>
            <par>
                <!-- Add another song here -->
            </par>
        </seq>
    </par>
    <!-- Add any banners, text, or advertisements that play
        during the music here -->
    </seq>
</body>
```

Listening to the Results

After you've created RealText documents that appear within your regions and images and audio files, you're all done. You have created your SMIL presentation document with the sole focus of playing a series of audio files while providing information for the listeners about the songs. Now, you need to see the results of your handy work. Figure 15-2 shows a sample of what your document will look like after you've created it and sent it out to draw millions of listeners to your favorite kind of music.

Figure 15-2: The completed radio station, as shown in RealPlayer.

The following sample of code shows the radio station code in its entirety:

```
<smil>
  <head>
    <meta name="author"
      content="Heather Williamson"/>
    <meta name="title"
      content="Your Radio Station"/>
    <meta name="copyright"
      content="(c) 2000"/>
    <meta name="description"
      content="Web based country radio with a real
              Internet twist.">
    <meta name="keywords"
      content="internet, smil, radio, music, country
              radio, exotic music">
    <layout>
      <root-layout height="200" width="300"/>
      <region id="background"
          left="0" top="0"
          height="200" width="300"
          z-index="0"
          fit="fill"
```

```
                    background-color="#000000"/>
        <region id="radioFigure"
            left="10" top="90"
            height="100" width="100"
            z-index="3"
            fit="fill"/>
        <region id="RadioStations"
            left="9" top="10"
            height="35" width="280"
            z-index="4"
            fit="fill"/>
        <region id="NowPlay"
            left="125" top="50"
            height="30" width="150"
            z-index="6"/>
        <region id="NextPlay"
            left="128" top="125"
            height="30" width="150"
            z-index="5"/>
        <region id="PlayingMarq"
            left="135" top="85"
            height="30" width="140"
            z-index="2"/>
        <region id="NextMarq"
            left="135" top="158"
            height="30" width="140"
            z-index="1"/>
    </layout>
</head>
<body>
    <seq>
        <par system-language="en"
            endsync="first">
        <textstream id="nowplay"
                src="nowplay.rt"
                region="NowPlay"
                fill="freeze"
                system-language="en"
                system-bitrate="9"/>
        <textstream id="stationtext"
                src="stationtext.rt"
                region="RadioStations"
                fill="freeze"
                system-language="en"
                system-bitrate="226"/>
        <img id="radioface"
            src="radioface.gif"
            region="radioFigure"
            fill="freeze"
            system-language="en"
            system-bitrate="12000"/>
```

```
        <textstream id="playnext"
            src="playnext.rt"
            region="NextPlay"
            fill="freeze"
            system-language="en"
            system-bitrate="9"/>
    <seq>
      <par system-language="en" endsync="first">
        <textstream id="marqplay"
            src="marqplay.rt"
            region="PlayingMarq"
            system-language="en"
            system-bitrate="9"
            repeat="10"/>
        <textstream id="marqnext"
            src="marqnext.rt"
            region="NextMarq"
            system-language="en"
            system-bitrate="9" repeat="10"/>
        <audio id="zok"
            src="z-ok.wav"
            system-bitrate="352800"/>
      </par>
      <par>
        <!-- Add another song here -->
      </par>
      <par>
        <!-- Add another song here -->
      </par>
      <par>
        <!-- Add another song here -->
      </par>
    </seq>
  </par>
  <!-- Add any banners, text, or advertisements that play
       during the music here -->

    </seq>
  </body>
</smil>
```

If you have any questions about the commands that I use in this example, I describe each of these commands in detail in other areas of the book (check out the index or the cross-references throughout this chapter).

You can find the contents of this file on your CD in the file `radio.smi` in the `Examples\Chapter15` directory.

Chapter 16

Revisiting the Silent Movie Era

- -

In This Chapter

▶ Building the foundation for your silent movie

▶ Setting the locations for your regions

▶ Controlling the timing of your background music

▶ Viewing the results

- -

Creating your own silent movie is actually quite simple, depending on how long you want your movie to be. I show you only the very basics in this chapter's sample, but it should be enough to get you started. You have to do the following things when you're creating a silent movie with background music and animations:

1. Design the foundation of your SMIL document so that you have the proper structure from which to work and create all the files that go into the document.

2. Define the regions to be used in the presentation. These regions need to include everything that holds text, images, and audio tracks. (Although audio tracks don't appear on-screen, they still need to be in a region: Some SMIL players won't play anything that's not in a region.)

3. Schedule your timing.

4. Finally, watch your presentation to make sure it works just the way you want.

You may be thinking that a silent movie shouldn't have any sound at all. Traditionally, silent movies had orchestras playing in the pit at the theatre and the actors/actresses didn't speak. Subtitles enabled the viewers to see what the actors/actresses were saying. Although this movie has background music, you really are creating a traditional silent movie.

Laying Out the Foundation

Before you can get started with developing your SMIL-based silent flick, you have to set up all the files, whether they're music, text, or images that you're going to use in the presentation. You don't want to be creating content as you're creating the SMIL code; it only compounds your stress.

In the case of this silent movie, you have six files to create, in addition to the actual SMIL document:

✔ The movie background (an image)

✔ The movie's animated characters

✔ The music soundtrack

✔ The three text files that serve as the movie's subtitles

The movie background

This background, shown in Figure 16-1, is a simple image that is 600 x 400 pixels. It's placed in the background region as specified by the `<layout>` element in the SMIL document's `<head>`:

```
<img id="background"
     src="background.jpg"
     region="Background"
     systemBitrate="12000"/>
```

You can see this background image on the CD as `background.jpg` in the `Examples\Chapter16` folder. This image is in full color, contains no animations, and is strictly a flat background image.

Figure 16-1:
The simple background for your silent movie.

The movie animation characters

All movies need characters. This movie has two simple characters, a little butterfly that flits across the screen and lands on an Easter egg in the grass and a small bug that bounces across the bottom of the screen. This butterfly, shown in Figure 16-2, is a simple animated GIF image with a transparent background enabling you to move it all over the screen. The second character in the movie is a transparent GIF image of a little bug, also shown in Figure 16-2, that uses SMIL animation commands to move it in small arcs partway across the screen.

```
<img id="butterflyanim"
     src="butterflyanim.gif"
     region="Animation"
     systemLanguage="en"
     systemBitrate="12000"/>

<img id="bug"
     src="bug.gif"
     region="Bugg"
     systemLanguage="en"
     systemBitrate="12000"
     begin="10s"
     dur="27s"
     fill="freeze"/>
```

Figure 16-2:
A butterfly
and bug
to use for
animation.

You can see these images — in full color — on the CD as butterflyanim. gif and bug.gif in the Examples\Chapter16 folder. The butterflyanim. gif file contains the animated image of the butterfly, while the bug.gif contains no animations. It is strictly a flat image that's moved by animation elements contained within the SMIL document. Unless you're using Internet Explorer 5.5, you'll see white backgrounds around your images when you open these images in most SMIL players. Internet Explorer is the only SMIL player that currently supports transparent GIF images.

The soundtrack

Because one audio file is playing in the background of your silent movie, you need to include that audio file in your document's media definitions. You do this by using the `<audio>` media element, which you can see in the following code. For more about the `<audio>` media element, see Chapter 2.

```
<audio id="soundeffect"
       src="soundeffect.wav"
       region="Audio"
       systemLanguage="en"
       systemBitrate="178488"
       repeatCount="2"/>
```

You can find this audio file on the CD as `soundeffect.wav` in the `Examples\Chapter16` folder.

This element requires a reference to the address of the `<audio>` element; add this reference by using the `src` attribute. The `id` attribute provides a name for the sound, so scripts and other elements can reference it as part of their `begin` and `end` attribute values. You can find out more about the various rules for the `begin` and `end` attribute values in Chapter 8. One of the many benefits of using SMIL is that you can control the start or ending of media elements by tying these events to the start or end of other elements within the SMIL presentation. The `region` attribute provides the name of the region that's created to hold this particular audio file. The `repeatCount` attribute ensures that the `soundeffect.wav` file is played twice so that it has enough length to play during an intro, the movie, and its credits (if any exist).

The soundtrack that I've used in this SMIL presentation sample is a wav file, although you can use whatever type of audio file that's supported by the SMIL player that's seeing your presentation. This means that while you could use a RealAudio file in a presentation that's viewed by RealPlayer, you couldn't use that type of file with a presentation that's viewed in QuickTime. You can find out more about file types in Chapter 2.

You can have multiple objects in each region, including multiple audio files within each region. Some SMIL players won't display objects, or play audio files, that aren't included in a region.

The two test attributes, `systemLanguage` and `systemBitrate`, test the `<audio>` element and allow it to play only if the presentation viewer's computer is using English and has an accessible bit rate over 178,488 bits (about 178.5 kilobits). Both of these tests have to be met before the audio file will play. Even if they aren't met, the remainder of the silent movie works, except for those items that use the start, or the playing time, of this audio file as their marker for beginning themselves.

The subtitles

Subtitles are an integral part of your silent movie experience. You can create your subtitle files quite simply by typing the actual text that you want to appear as a subtitle into its own text file. For example, if you wanted your subtitle to read, "Oh George, do you have to go?!??", then you place that text into your subtitle file.

You have two choices when creating files to use as subtitles. You can create a series of plain text files that can be displayed in succession, with the timing controls being placed in the hands of a sequence (<seq>) element. Or, you can create the subtitle files in the form of RealText documents and include the timing controls for the text within the RealText file. The files that I've used in the following example use plain text files for subtitles.

```
<text id="subtitletext"
        src="text1.txt"
        region="subtitles"
        dur="3s" />
    <text id="subtitletext"
        src="text2.txt"
        region="subtitles"
        dur="5s" />
    <text id="subtitletext"
        src="text3.txt"
        region="subtitles"
        dur="2s" />
```

You can find these text files on the CD as `text1.txt`, `text2.txt`, and `text3.txt` in the `Examples\Chapter16` folder.

The SMIL file

After you've created all the pieces for your SMIL presentation and you've built their individual media elements, you're ready to start putting together all the pieces that go into the SMIL presentation. The basic structure of this silent movie file is the same as for Chapter 15's radio station. In the following code, I've created the <smil> element (as well as the <head>, <meta>, <layout>, and <body> elements) so that a variety of search engines can index this silent movie. The elements that are specifically looked at by the search engines are `meta name="keywords"` and `meta name="description"`.

```
<smil>
  <head>
    <meta name="author"
      content="Heather Williamson"/>
    <meta name="title"
      content="Your First Silent Movie"/>
```

```
   <meta name="copyright"
      content="(c) 2000"/>
   <meta name="description"
      content="SMIL based silent, full color movie,
               with a lovely soundtrack."/>
   <meta name="keywords"
      content="internet, smil, butterfly, movie,
               exotic music"/>
   <layout>
     <!-- Region definitions are placed here -->
   </layout>
  </head>
  <body>
    <!-- Media elements are placed here. -->
  </body>
</smil>
```

<meta> elements are one of the primary ways that search engines can sort and index your presentation. You should always include them in your presentation if you want search engines to find it.

Controlling Your Locations

After creating the structure for your SMIL document, create the individual regions that hold your information. Regions, which I discuss in Chapter 7, are part of the layout of the document. Regions define the interior areas that's used to create the visible formatting of your presentation. The <layout> and the <root-layout> elements, both of which I discuss in Chapter 6, control the outer limits of your presentation area.

In the following code, a <region> is created to hold the video, background, subtitles, and audio files.

```
<layout>
  <root-layout height="400"
               width="600"/>
  <region id="Background"
          left="0" top="0"
          height="400" width="600"
          z-index="0"/>
  <region id="Animation"
          left="0" top="0"
          height="400" width="600"
          z-index="1"/>
  <region id="Audio"
          left="0" top="0"
          height="1" width="1"
          z-index="1"/>
```

```
  <region id="Bugg"
          left="0" top="340"
          height="100" width="600"
          z-index="3" />
  <region id="subtitles"
          left="0" top="360"
          height="40" width="600"
          z-index="4" />
</layout>
```

✔ The `<root-layout>` element identifies the outside dimensions (400 x 600) of the presentation.

✔ The `Background` region has been created to contain the background image.

✔ The `Animation` region contains the animated GIF image of a butterfly.

✔ The `Bugg` region contains the image of the bug that's animated using the `<animation>` elements and attributes included with SMIL.

✔ The `Subtitles` region contains the subtitle text to go along with any dialog the bug or the butterfly may speak.

As I discuss in Chapter 7, you have to provide each of the regions with an `id` attribute and a location. Without the `id` attribute, the region can't be used to contain any information. Without the `location` and `dimension` attributes, the region can't contain anything that has dimension: All you can do is play an audio file within it.

Setting the Timing for Your Movie

The timing of your presentation is integral to ensuring that it plays correctly and makes a good impression on the presentation's visitor. Within the timing system, you can set information to appear in a sequence (`<seq>`), exclusively (`<excl>`), or in parallel (`<par>`).

In the following SMIL code, this document uses a single `<par>` element with an embedded `<seq>` element to create a stacked structure that displays the contents of the presentation when the document first opens, and which keeps that content visible while the presentation remains open. The `<seq>` displays the text files associated with the movie in order so that they appear in time to everything else that's happening on-screen.

For more information on the `<par>` element, see Chapter 10. For more information on the individual media commands, such as `<text>`, `<img>`, and `<audio>`, check out Chapter 2. I discuss the `<animation>` elements in Chapter 14.

In the following code, the `<par>` element contains the background image, the animated butterfly GIF, the sound effects audio file, and the picture of the bug so that they all appear simultaneously. The `<par>` element also contains the `<seq>` that controls the display of the subtitle text required to understand the dialog in a silent movie.

The lines of code that I've bolded in the following example are those that directly deal with the timing of the various parts of the presentation. In this example, the animated butterfly image starts 5 seconds after the background loads and the audio file starts immediately, lasting for its intrinsic duration but repeating for at least 45 seconds. The image of the bug loads 10 seconds after the background loads and lasts for 27 seconds, during which time it's animated by the `<animateMotion>` element, which bounces the bug in a rough arc through a series of 4 hops — lasting roughly 5 seconds — partially across your screen.

```
<par system-language="en">
    <img id="background"
        src="background.jpg"
        region="Background"
        systemBitrate="12000"
        fill="freeze" />
    <img id="butterflyanim"
        src="butterflyanim.gif"
        region="Animation"
        systemLanguage="en"
        systemBitrate="12000"
        begin="+5s" />
    <audio id="soundeffect"
        src="soundeffect.wav"
        region="Audio"
        systemLanguage="en"
        dur="media"
        repeatDur="45s"/>
    <img id="bug"
        src="bug.gif"
        region="Bugg"
        systemLanguage="en"
        systemBitrate="12000"
        begin="10s"
        dur="27s">
        <animateMotion path="c( 3 5 7 5 10 0)"
                        dur="5s"
                        accumulate="sum"
                        repeatCount="4" />
    </img>
    <seq>
        <text id="subtitletext"
            src="text1.txt"
            region="subtitles"
            dur="3s" />
```

```
        <text id="subtitletext"
              src="text2.txt"
              region="subtitles"
              dur="5s" />
        <text id="subtitletext"
              src="text3.txt"
              region="subtitles"
              dur="2s" />
    </seq>
  </par>
```

The GRiNS SMIL 2.0 player is the only SMIL player that currently supports the `<animateMotion>` element applied to the Bugg image. None of the other SMIL players will play this presentation's animation correctly. Even GRiNS doesn't display the presentation correctly because it can't display the transparent portion of the images as they move about on-screen.

Hearing and Watching the Results

You've created your images, subtitles, and audio files; you're standing by ready to add to your presentation; "What's next?" you ask. Well, you're all done. You've created your SMIL presentation document, which you've designed so that a single audio file plays while a butterfly and a bug move around in front of a background image on-screen, their conversation appearing as subtitled bits. Now you need to see the results of your handiwork. Figure 16-3 is a sample of what your document looks like when you send it out to draw in millions of watchers.

Figure 16-3:
The completed SMIL silent movie, as shown in RealPlayer 8.

Now that you've seen your creation, do you remember how it all went together? In the previous sections of this chapter, I show you all the pieces but never the code in one large piece. If you have any questions about the commands that I've used in this sample, browse through this book. You can find each of these commands, which I describe in Parts II and III, along with other examples of how to use them.

You can find the contents of this file on your CD as `silent_movie.smi` in the `Examples\Chapter16` folder.

```
<smil>
  <head>
    <meta name="author"
       content="Heather Williamson"/>
    <meta name="title"
       content="Your First Silent Movie"/>
    <meta name="copyright"
       content="(c) 2000"/>
    <meta name="description"
       content="SMIL based silent, full color movie,
                with a lovely soundtrack."/>
    <meta name="keywords"
       content="internet, smil, butterfly, movie,
                exotic music"/>
    <layout>
      <root-layout height="400"
                   width="600"/>
      <region id="Background"
              left="0" top="0"
              height="400" width="600"
              z-index="0"/>
      <region id="Animation"
              left="0" top="0"
              height="400" width="600"
              z-index="1"/>
      <region id="Audio"
              left="0" top="0"
              height="1" width="1"
              z-index="2"/>
      <region id="Bugg"
              left="0" top="340"
              height="60" width="62"
              z-index="3" />
      <region id="subtitles"
              left="0" top="360"
              height="40" width="600"
              z-index="4" />
    </layout>
  </head>
  <body>
    <par system-language="en">
      <img id="background"
```

```
                    src="background.jpg"
                    region="Background"
                    systemBitrate="12000"
                    fill="freeze" />
        <img id="butterflyanim"
                    src="butterflyanim.gif"
                    region="Animation"
                    systemLanguage="en"
                    systemBitrate="12000"
                    begin="+5s"  />
        <audio id="soundeffect"
                    src="soundeffect.wav"
                    region="Audio"
                    systemLanguage="en"
                    dur="media"
                    repeatDur="45S"/>
        <img id="bug"
                    src="bug.gif"
                    region="Bugg"
                    systemLanguage="en"
                    systemBitrate="12000"
                    begin="10s"
                    dur="27s">
            <animateMotion path="c( 3 5 7 5 10 0)"
                            dur="5s"
                            accumulate="sum"
                            repeatCount="4" />
        </img>
        <seq>
            <text id="subtitletext"
                    src="text1.txt"
                    region="subtitles"
                    dur="3s" />
            <text id="subtitletext"
                    src="text2.txt"
                    region="subtitles"
                    dur="5s" />
            <text id="subtitletext"
                    src="text3.txt"
                    region="subtitles"
                    dur="2s" />
        </seq>
    </par>
  </body>
</smil>
```

You can create many different effects by using SMIL; this sample silent movie
just contains a few. SMIL enables you to combine whichever types of media
files you want to create a presentation — your only concern is what the SMIL
players support. As SMIL grows as a language and receives more support
from the various software vendors, you'll find that you can include a more
varied selection of media in your presentations. And you won't have to worry
about whether or not everyone can view your presentation.

Chapter 17

Producing Your Own Cartoon

● ●

In This Chapter

▶ Creating your cartoon's foundation

▶ Setting the locations for your regions

▶ Controlling the timing of background music and voices

▶ Viewing the results

● ●

*C*reating your own cartoon is actually quite simple, depending on how long you want your cartoon to be, that is. In this chapter, you create a simple cartoon of two fish having a little chat. Although this is a very simple cartoon, it requires the same care that a larger production would; the only difference is that in this cartoon, you're working with a smaller number of objects. When you're creating a cartoon with background music and still images, you must do the following three things:

✔ **Create the image files and record the audio files that comprise the visual and audio content of the presentation.** These are the files that are referenced, placed, timed, and animated by the media and animation/ transformation elements in your SMIL document.

✔ **Write the SMIL code for your document.** This code includes the regions, media definitions, meta elements, and any animation or transformation controls that you want to use.

✔ **Time the audio files so that they correspond to the animations that you're using with your images.** You need to be sure to record your audio files (both voice tracks and background music) prior to attempting to program your presentation's timing; otherwise, you'll most likely have to redo all your timing work because you won't know how long your sound files last.

Laying Out the Foundation

The easiest way to start working on your cartoon is to create the visual and audio media that go into it. Creating a storyboard (which I talk about in

Chapter 3) and then creating the files that go along with the storyboard is the best way to do this.

In the case of this cartoon, you have three image files to create and a variety of audio tracks, in addition to the actual SMIL document:

- ✔ The cartoon background (an image)
- ✔ The cartoon still characters (there are two)
- ✔ The music soundtrack
- ✔ The voice tracks for each character

You can create your image files using a simple graphics editor, such as Paint Shop Pro, which is on the CD accompanying this book. You can record your voice tracks using a microphone and your computer's built-in sound manipulation software. Windows 95 and 98 both enable you to record .wav files with your sound card and the Sound Recorder software that ships with the Windows operating systems. I'm not aware of any sound recording software that ships on a Macintosh automatically, but you can download software from www.tucows.com.

The cartoon background

The background that I'm using for this cartoon, shown in Figure 17-1, is a very simple image of 400 x 400 pixels. It's placed in the background region as specified by the `<layout>` element contained within the SMIL document's `<head>`.

```
<img id="background"
     src="background.jpg"
     region="Background"
     systemBitrate="12000"/>
```

You can find this image on the accompanying CD as background.jpg in the Examples\Chapter17 folder.

The cartoon's animated characters

All movies need characters. This movie has two simple characters, both fish. Fred is a small, green and yellow fish that flits about the screen trying to get Maggie to notice him. Maggie floats about gently, wondering why this small pesky Fred fish keeps bugging her.

Figure 17-1:
The back-
ground for
the creation
of your
cartoon.

Fred is created with a simple transparent GIF image, shown in Figure 17-2, which has been animated using the SMIL animation commands. His location and position are controlled using the `<animate>` element, with both the `top` and `left` attributes being moved by a specific amount until Fred has reached his new location over the course of a 5-second period.

Most SMIL players do not currently support transparent GIF images. Actually, only Internet Explorer 5.5 supports them. As SMIL becomes more popular, you should see more and more SMIL players supporting transparent GIF images.

You can find the image of Fred on the accompanying CD as `fredfish.gif` in the `Examples\Chapter17` folder.

Maggie, shown in Figure 17-3, swims in a lazy way across the screen. I use the `<animateMotion>` element to create a few shallow arcs that move up and then down as she moves across the screen.

Figure 17-2:
Fred is a
small, yet
colorful fish.

```
<img id="Fred"
     src="fredfish.gif"
     region="FredBox"
     systemLanguage="en"
     systemBitrate="12000">
  <seq repeatCount="3">
    <animate attributeName="top"
             by="20"
             dur="5s" />
```

```
<animate attributeName="left"
        by="10"
        dur="5s" />
    <animate attributeName="top"
        by="-25"
        dur="5s" />
    <animate attributeName="left"
        by="5"
        dur="5s" />
    </seq>
</img>
```

Figure 17-3:
Maggie is bigger and more colorful than Fred!

```
<img id="Maggie"
    src="maggiefish.gif"
    region="MaggieBox"
    systemLanguage="en"
    systemBitrate="12000">
    <seq repeatCount="2">
    <animateMotion path="c( 3 10 13 10 20 0)"
                    dur="5s"
                    accumulate="sum"
                    repeatCount="1" />
    <animateMotion path="c( -3 10 -13 10 -20 0)"
                    dur="5s"
                    accumulate="sum"
                    repeatCount="1" />
    </seq>
```

You can find this image on your CD as `maggiefish.gif` in the `Examples\Chapter17` folder.

Setting up background music

Now that you have the three images ready to go for your cartoon, you're ready to start working on the soundtrack. This soundtrack needs to be something soft and cute. I've recorded some seashore sounds off my keyboard for this. (Please forgive the obvious lack of professional music. I am not, after all, a professional musician.)

```
<audio id="soundeffect"
       src="seasounds.wav"
       region="Audio"
       systemLanguage="en"
       systemBitrate="178488"
       repeatDur="2"/>
```

You can find this audio file on your CD as `seasounds.wav` in the `Examples\` `Chapter17` folder.

Setting up voice tracks

In addition to the background sound track, you also need to record voice tracks for each of your fish. Fred should sound like a frantic boy trying to find some way of impressing Maggie. Maggie, on the other hand, is just trying to find some way to get Fred to leave her alone.

```
<audio id="FredVoice1"
       src="fred1.wav"
       region="Audio"
       systemLanguage="en"
       systemBitrate="178488"
       begin="2s"
       repeatDur="1"/>
<audio id="FredVoice2"
       src="fred2.wav"
       region="Audio"
       systemLanguage="en"
       systemBitrate="178488"
       begin="8s"
       repeatDur="1"/>
<audio id="MaggieVoice1"
       src="maggie1.wav"
       region="Audio"
       systemLanguage="en"
       systemBitrate="178488"
       begin="5s"
       repeatDur="1"/>
<audio id="MaggieVoice2"
       src="maggie2.wav"
       region="Audio"
       systemLanguage="en"
       systemBitrate="178488"
       begin="10s"
       repeatDur="1"/>
```

You can find these audio files on your CD in the `Examples\Chapter17` folder, as `fred1.wav`, `fred2.wav`, `maggie1.wav`, and `maggie2.wav`.

Setting up the SMIL file

You've now created all the pieces required to create your SMIL presentation — other than the SMIL document itself. In Chapters 15 and 16, I show you how to create the basic structure of your SMIL document, as shown in the following code. I've modified the contents of the `<meta>` elements to fit this example:

```
<smil>
  <head>
    <meta name="author"
       content="Heather Williamson"/>
    <meta name="title"
       content="Your First Cartoon"/>
    <meta name="copyright"
       content="(c) 2000"/>
    <meta name="description"
       content="SMIL based full color cartoon,
              with a lovely soundtrack, and
              voice tracks."/>
    <meta name="keywords"
       content="internet, smil, fish, cartoon,
              seashore, music, voice tracks"/>
    <layout>
       <!-- Regions definitions are placed here -->
    </layout>
  </head>
  <body>
     <!-- Media elements are placed here. -->
  </body>
</smil>
```

Your next task is to create the individual regions for each object in your cartoon.

Setting Up Regions

As I discuss in Chapter 6, you use the `<layout>` element to demarcate the specific section of the SMIL document that's used to create the document structure. Within the entire `<layout>` area of the document is a series of regions. Each of these regions contains one of the visual objects used within the presentation. In the case of this cartoon, you have to create a separate region for each object because those objects and regions are being moved around the screen using animation elements that are a part of the SMIL 2.0 recommendation. If you have any questions about the `<region>` element or its attributes, see Chapter 7.

```
<layout>
  <root-layout height="400"
               width="400"/>
  <region id="Background"
          left="0" top="0"
          height="400" width="400"
          z-index="0"/>
  <region id="FredBox"
          left="0" top="0"
          height="114" width="158"
          z-index="1"/>
  <region id="Audio"
          left="0" top="0"
          height="1" width="1"
          z-index="1"/>
  <region id="MaggieBox"
          left="0" top="340"
          height="186" width="123"
          z-index="3" />
</layout>
```

As I discuss in Chapter 7, you have to provide each of the regions with an identity and a location. Without the id attribute, the region can't be used to contain any information because a media element has no way to reference it. Without the location and dimension attributes, the region becomes relatively useless unless you simply want to play an audio file within it.

Setting Your Cartoon's Timing

In this example, I'm using timed animations and timed audio files. This makes the timing on this cartoon much more difficult than it was for the silent movie example in Chapter 16 or the radio station example in Chapter 15. As you can see from the following SMIL code, this cartoon uses a single <par> element, which displays the contents of the presentation when the document first opens and continues to display these contents while the presentation remains open. For more information on the <par> element, see Chapter 10.

For each animated image, a <seq> element controls the movement of the animations. Because the animations repeat themselves, the sequence uses a repeatCount attribute to control the number of times the animations run. Because the <seq> element is contained within the <par> element, the sequences of animations each run simultaneously, whereas their individual animation steps, contained within the <seq> event, run sequentially.

If this process sounds confusing, take a look at Chapter 9 for more information on using <seq> and its effects. For more information on the individual media commands, such as <img> and <audio>, check out Chapter 2. I discuss the animation elements in Chapter 14.

```
<par system-language="en">
  <!-- Fred's image loads immediately upon the Par element
       loading. Then a set of 4 animate elements will
       repeat three times while Fred is bounced around
       the screen.-->
  <img id="Fred"
       src="fredfish.gif"
       region="FredBox"
       systemLanguage="en"
       systemBitrate="12000">
    <seq repeatCount="3">
      <animate attributeName="top"
               by="20"
               dur="5s" />
      <animate attributeName="left"
               by="10"
               dur="5s" />
      <animate attributeName="top"
               by="-25"
               dur="5s" />
      <animate attributeName="left"
               by="5"
               dur="5s" />
    </seq>
  </img>
  <!-- Maggie's image loads immediately upon the par element
       loading. Then a set of 2 animateMotion elements will
       repeat 2 times while Maggie is gliding around
       the screen.-->
  <img id="Maggie"
       src="maggiefish.gif"
       region="MaggieBox"
       systemLanguage="en"
       systemBitrate="12000">
    <seq repeatCount="2">
      <animateMotion path="c( 3 10 13 10 20 0)"
                      dur="5s"
                      accumulate="sum"
                      repeatCount="1" />
<animateMotion        path="c( -3 10 -13 10 -20 0)"
                      dur="5s"
                      accumulate="sum"
                      repeatCount="1" />
    </seq>
  </img>
  <!-- The sound effects file loads immediately upon the par
       element loading. It will repeat itself twice. -->
  <audio id="soundeffect"
         src="seasounds.wav"
         region="Audio"
         systemLanguage="en"
         systemBitrate="178488"
         repeatDur="2"/>
```

```
<!-- The fred1.wav files loads 2 seconds after the start of
     the presentation. -->
<audio id="FredVoice1"
       src="fred1.wav"
       region="Audio"
       systemLanguage="en"
       systemBitrate="178488"
       begin="2s"
       repeatDur="1"/>
<!-- The fred2.wav files loads 8 seconds after the start of
     the presentation. -->
<audio id="FredVoice2"
       src="fred2.wav"
       region="Audio"
       systemLanguage="en"
       systemBitrate="178488"
       begin="8s"
       repeatDur="1"/>
<!-- The maggie1.wav files loads 5 seconds after the start
     of the presentation. -->
<audio id="MaggieVoice1"
       src="maggie1.wav"
       region="Audio"
       systemLanguage="en"
       systemBitrate="178488"
       begin="5s"
       repeatDur="1"/>
<!-- The maggie2.wav files loads 10 seconds after the start
     of the presentation. -->
<audio id="MaggieVoice2"
       src="maggie2.wav"
       region="Audio"
       systemLanguage="en"
       systemBitrate="178488"
       begin="10s"
       repeatDur="1" />
</par>
```

Hearing and Watching the Results

You've created your images and audio files and are standing by ready to
watch your cartoon, correct? Well, you're done. This cartoon uses the two
fish as characters in front of a watery background. You have controlled what
they say with the audio soundtracks and what they do with the SMIL animation elements. Now, you need to see the results of your efforts. Figure 17-4 is
a sample of what your cartoon looks like.

Figure 17-4:
The completed SMIL cartoon, as shown in RealPlayer 8.

Now that you've seen your creation, do you remember how it all went together? In the previous sections of this chapter, I show you all the pieces, but I never present the code in one large piece. Well, here it is:

```
<smil>
  <head>
    <meta name="author"
        content="Heather Williamson"/>
    <meta name="title"
        content="Your First Cartoon"/>
    <meta name="copyright"
        content="(c) 2000"/>
    <meta name="description"
        content="SMIL based full color cartoon,
                 with a lovely soundtrack, and
                 voice tracks."/>
    <meta name="keywords"
        content="internet, smil, fish, cartoon,
                 seashore, music, voice tracks"/>
<layout>
    <root-layout height="400"
                 width="400"/>
    <region id="Background"
            left="0" top="0"
            height="400" width="400"
            z-index="0"/>
    <region id="FredBox"
            left="0" top="0"
            height="114" width="158"
            z-index="1"/>
    <region id="Audio"
```

```
                    left="0" top="0"
                    height="1" width="1"
                    z-index="1"/>
        <region id="MaggieBox"
                left="0" top="340"
                height="186" width="123"
                z-index="3" />
    </layout>
  </head>
  <body>
    <par system-language="en">
<!-- Fred's image loads immediately upon the Par element
     loading. Then a set of 4 animate elements will
     repeat three times while Fred is bounced around
     the screen.-->

    <img id="Fred"
         src="fredfish.gif"
         region="FredBox"
         systemLanguage="en"
         systemBitrate="12000">
       <seq repeatCount="3">
          <animate attributeName="top"
                   by="20"
                   dur="5s" />
          <animate attributeName="left"
                   by="10"
                   dur="5s" />
          <animate attributeName="top"
                   by="-25"
                   dur="5s" />
          <animate attributeName="left"
                   by="5"
                   dur="5s" />
       </seq>
     </img>
<!-- Maggie's image loads immediately upon the par element
     loading. Then a set of 2 animateMotion elements will
     repeat 2 times while Maggie is gliding around
     the screen.-->
<img id="Maggie"
         src="maggiefish.gif"
         region="MaggieBox"
         systemLanguage="en"
         systemBitrate="12000">
       <seq repeatCount="2">
          <animateMotion path="c( 3 10 13 10 20 0)"
                         dur="5s"
                         accumulate="sum"
                         repeatCount="1" />
```

```
                <animateMotion path="c( -3 10 -13 10 -20 0)"
                               dur="5s"
                               accumulate="sum"
                               repeatCount="1" />
        </seq>
    </img>
  <!-- The sound effects file loads immediately upon the par
       element loading. It will repeat itself twice. -->
<audio id="soundeffect"
         src="seasounds.wav"
         region="Audio"
         systemLanguage="en"
         systemBitrate="178488"
         repeatDur="2"/>
  <!-- The fred1.wav files loads 2 seconds after the start of
       the presentation. -->
<audio id="FredVoice1"
         src="fred1.wav"
         region="Audio"
         systemLanguage="en"
         systemBitrate="178488"
         begin="2s"
         repeatDur="1"/>
  <!-- The fred2.wav files loads 8 seconds after the start of
       the presentation. -->

<audio id="FredVoice2"
         src="fred2.wav"
         region="Audio"
         systemLanguage="en"
         systemBitrate="178488"
         begin="8s"
         repeatDur="1"/>
  <!-- The maggie1.wav files loads 5 seconds after the start
       of the presentation. -->

<audio id="MaggieVoice1"
         src="maggie1.wav"
         region="Audio"
         systemLanguage="en"
         systemBitrate="178488"
         begin="5s"
         repeatDur="1"/>
  <!-- The maggie2.wav files loads 10 seconds after the start
       of the presentation. -->

<audio id="MaggieVoice2"
         src="maggie2.wav"
         region="Audio"
```

```
                    systemLanguage="en"
                    systemBitrate="178488"
                    begin="10s"
                    repeatDur="1" />
        </par>
      </body>
    </smil>
```

If you have any questions about the commands used in this sample, look back through this book. I describe each of these commands in detail in other areas of the book, along with other examples of how to use them.

You can find the contents of the preceding file on your CD as `cartoon.smi` in the `Examples\Chapter17` folder.

Part VI
The Part of Tens

The 5th Wave   By Rich Tennant

"I did this report with the help of a satellite view atmospheric map from the National Weather Service, research text from the Jet Propulsion Laboratory, and a sound file from 'The Barfing Lungworms' new CD."

In this part . . .

In this great Part of Tens, I introduce you to ten rules for designing a multimedia site in Chapter 18. I include a collection of information, hints, and tips handed down from Gutenberg and his first printing press. If that isn't enough for you, take a look at Chapter 19 and some useful research sites. In this chapter, you find a listing for some of the most informative SMIL-related Web sites on the Internet. As you start using SMIL, you may find that the aggravations I list in Chapter 20 are ones that you also experience. If you haven't yet, you will! Either way, this information is sure to bring a SMILe to your face.

Chapter 18

Top Ten Rules for Designing a Multimedia Site

In This Chapter
▶ Navigating smoothly
▶ Designing layout
▶ Using color
▶ Cleaning up the look
▶ Working with photographs and artwork
▶ Jazzing up your site

*Y*ou can design a SMIL presentation in almost as many ways as there are presentations. In this chapter, I discuss various design tips that you may want to keep in mind. I highlight the most important ones and give you great suggestions for smart multimedia design.

Design Sensible Navigation Methods

No matter how much time you take designing your presentation, you must be aware of how your viewers maneuver through your information. Without an interface they can easily understand, your visitors fail to find their way to your storefront and may simply leave. Think about your Macintosh or Windows computer. No matter what type of software you're running, the menus are similar with a similar screen structure. You automatically know the basics of using your particular software because you've used software like it before. Likewise, your visitors need to feel the same comfort within your SMIL presentation.

When designing your navigation system, keep in mind that your visitors ask themselves two questions on every page of your Web site: "Where am I?" and "Where am I going?" If you keep these two questions in mind, you find that you can easily include a navigational system in your presentation design. Often referred to as a *navigation bar* or *navigation panel*, this system, shown in Figure 18-1, enables the visitors to easily discern their current location and enables them to go to any other location in your SMIL presentation. Thus, they get to answer both of their questions with every change to your presentation.

In the document shown in Figure 18-1, every time that you select one of the options, such as portfolio, beneath the logo and company name, the half-circle graphic to the right of the company name changes to reflect the title of the new page you're viewing.

Figure 18-1:
This page heading provides links to other primary locations on this Web site and lets you know where you are by the change in the half-circle graphic on the right edge of the company name.

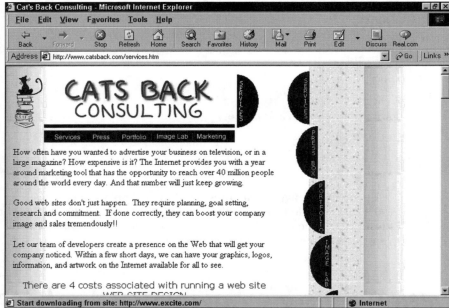

Make sure that your visitors can easily discern the navigational buttons or text. To do this, give graphical buttons a raised appearance or separate your text with pipes (|) or some other type of characters that visually separate information on your page, such as hyphens, lots of white space, or even a series of periods.

You can also use a *rollover* trick with your buttons (as you would on an HTML page) that enables the visitor to access more information while you maintain a very tight design of your pages. Rollover images provide you with a variety of images that you can use depending on the location of a visitor's mouse. For example, when your presentation loads, you can have a button that says home in blue text on a white background, but when a visitor places the mouse pointer over the top of it, the button changes to white text on a blue background. This effect of swapping one image for another is called a rollover. These types of effects make the navigation of your page more enjoyable and give the entire presentation an added feeling of interactivity.

Create a Clean Layout

Two schools of thought prevail regarding Web page design: *KISS* and *chaos*. The KISS (Keep It Simple, Stupid) school of thought directs you to design simple pages with solid, often light-colored backgrounds, standard black text, and easily identifiable, almost common-looking navigational bars in a format that anyone familiar with computers, and especially the Internet, understands. This type of design makes the decision-making and formatting process quite easy for the developer. You, the developer, know exactly where all the information needs to appear. This type of construction, shown in Figure 18-2, is often highly structured and tends to create a series of deliberate rules for laying out information and graphics, which may include the following:

- ✔ Navigation bar appears on the left side
- ✔ Copyright always appears on the bottom of the page
- ✔ Image always appears just below article title and above article text

By making the entire presentation appear rigid, these rules sometimes eliminate the appearance of the simplicity of the design. The site may be very easy for you to maintain, but your visitors tend to see the rigid format rather than the simplistic structure. But most importantly, your visitors are able to easily get from one part of the site to another.

The chaos method, shown in Figure 18-3, incorporates the use of a variety of freeform elements, giving the impression of a relaxed presentation composition. The relaxation of this type of design brings a feeling of simplicity to the presentation, no matter how many elements appear within each page or how hard they are for you to maintain and update. The pages look simple because they have a loose appearance, without the rigid structure of many presentations.

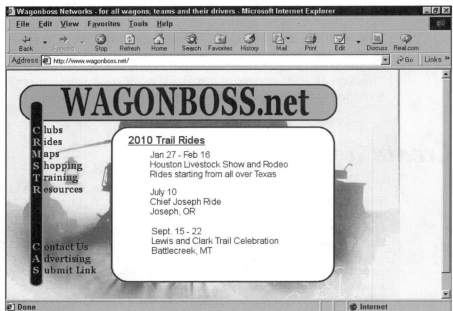

Figure 18-2:
This presentation uses a fixed structure, which has a tendency to remove the simple appearance of the three objects that appear over the background.

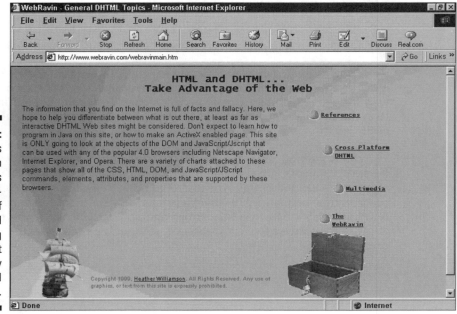

Figure 18-3:
This presentation includes timed movements of objects and rotating pictures, yet has a very simple and open layout.

You must decide how you want your pages to appear and what method you're most comfortable using to reach your goal.

Coordinate Colors

All colors are good colors: Don't ever let anyone tell you differently. All colors can be used together to create an effect, as long as those colors create the effect that you want. The key to using colors within your presentation effectively is to remember that not everyone sees colors the same way or likes the same colors. Some colors and shades, however, tend to evoke specific feelings, or meanings, for all people.

Take a sienna-shaded photograph. The typical viewer thinks, "old, antique" rather than "boy, that photo is dirty." We just naturally link those rusty shades of brown to things that are old. Other colors evoke a sense of independence or strength. When designing your presentation, you have to think about how people are going to interpret your colors. Pale pinks and pale blues tend toward a softer appearance while browns and reds have a stronger, more rustic appearance.

When designing your pages, avoid the obvious color choices, such as pure red (#FF0000), green (#00FF00), and blue (#0000FF), to attain a more professional appearance. These colors are cliché and so common in everyday life that they don't provide any new information to our senses and, therefore, are hard to work into professional designs.

Because you can use any of the millions of different colors that our eyes can see, you can easily alter the shades of color — which can all be described using *hexadecimal notation,* such as #FF0000 for red — on your presentations to evoke the type of emotional response on your visual presentation that you may want. Within the hexadecimal number, the first pair of digits represents the amount of red (RR) in the color, the second the amount of green (GG), and the third the amount of blue (BB): #RRGGBB. In Table 18-1, I provide an interpretation of the various feelings evoked by different shades of color on the color wheel.

Table 18-1	Color Zones
Colors	*Color Interpretations*
Black	Dark; becomes heavy without proper balance.
White	Unless toned down with other colors, usually too bright for most uses.
Blue	Psychologically tranquilizing; sets a reserved mood and makes things appear distant.
Aqua	Peaceful, non-intrusive, and almost relaxing.
Green	Dark colors express keen interest in a subject.

(continued)

Table 18-1 *(continued)*

Colors	Color Interpretations
Dark green with slight yellow	Strikes feelings of deep, intense earnestness without the least sign of pallor or dimness.
Yellow-green	Often too natural and leaves a slight sense of swampy, damp heat.
Yellow	Fiery emotion; heat
Light brown	Reminiscent of age, ancient relics, old books, and a historical strength.
Brown	Suggestions of cultivated objects, such as paper, wood, or brick.
Red	Alerts intensity and provokes feelings of emergency.
Magenta	The cooler side of red imparts a sense of the artificial, of modern commercial sales and marketing gimmicks. This range of colors tends to bring up thoughts of today and today's fast pace, rather than any historical or solid background.

Heighten Contrast between Text and Backgrounds

Legible text is your primary goal when setting up your backgrounds and your text objects. No one wants to read dark blue text on a black background! You ensure the legibility of your text when you have a high level of contrast between the text and the background. Obviously, black text on a white background is the most legible combination. But, if you're worried about how boring white and black are, you can try other color combinations that maintain a high color differentiation without sacrificing legibility.

You can create highly legible text on a background in the following ways:

✔ **Decrease background saturation.** This lightens the background from its otherwise bright color so it's a few shades darker than white. You remove the stark unnatural look that white can have without losing the easy legibility of dark text.

✔ **Make the background and text color varying shades of the same color hue.** When you're working on a light background, darker text of the same hue brings out the slight color left in the background. When you reverse this effect, using a dark background with text in an almost white color of the same hue, you yield a similar effect, although not as cohesive appearing. This system enables you to alter the colors of your links and image borders to work with the same, or compatible, hue and add further depth to your presentation's color scheme.

✔ **Use light text over a dark background.** This scheme works quite well; although, because the computer screen's backlight increases the text luminance, you can create the impression of glowing text. Because your monitor has its own light source, which appears to come from behind the text on your screen, the letters can achieve an almost "glow in the dark" effect to them. You encounter only one major problem with light text on dark backgrounds: printing. Many color printers print your light-colored text on white pages, without converting the text to a gray-scale value. This makes the text almost impossible for any of your visitors to read after they print a copy of your presentation.

Use Fonts Effectively

Fonts can truly make or break your Web site. You must maintain a delicate balance: Too many fonts can give your visitors a headache whereas too few fonts can leave your site with a boring monotone appearance. Follow these rules and, generally, your use of fonts will be effective:

✔ **Two's company, three's a crowd.** Limit the number of fonts you use. Okay, although this is a great rule, it isn't always true. Typically, one typeface for headings and one for body text is all you really need. It's fine to introduce a third typeface to highlight a special portion of a document — just be sure that it doesn't clash with your other typeface selections.

✔ **Use serif fonts in your headings.** *Serifs* are the little "feet" on the ends of each leg of a letter that help lead your eye from one character to another. Using fonts with serifs in headings helps make them flow across your screen.

✔ **Use *sans-serif* fonts in your body text.** Sans-serif fonts, or fonts without serifs, are easier to read on a computer screen. (This is the exact opposite of conventional wisdom about printed media.)

✔ **Reserve specialty fonts for special purposes.** Specialty fonts, such as cursive or any that are dripping decorative goo, are great to use for special headings. They aren't generally legible enough to use in the body of your document.

Even with these rules, you need to remember that only a few fonts are available to everyone (a term I use loosely). If you specify a special font, such as Cooper Black, viewers who don't have that specific font on their computers just see the text in one of the old standbys, such as Arial or Times. Although they get boring, it's sometimes best to keep with one of these fonts. Luckily, a few alternative fonts such as Garamond (a replacement for the serif font Times) or Verdana (a good sans-serif replacement) are widely available.

Gauge Sizes Appropriately

If you're used to designing graphics for use on printed mediums, you're in for a shock. Graphics that are seen on a computer screen must be much smaller than those seen in print. Just assume that graphics used on the Internet are roughly half the size of the same graphic used on printed mediums. When planning your presentation, you need to think about the visible screen limitations of your viewers' systems. If they're using a WebTV system, for instance, horizontal scrolling is impossible, so your presentations have to be viewable within a small 544-pixel width. Computer screens have a variety of resolutions that can show as few as 600 pixels across the screen, or more than 1200. Your biggest challenge in designing any SMIL presentation is designing it so it looks good in *all* screen resolutions.

To fit within all computer screen resolutions, you have to limit yourself to a 580 pixels wide by 350 pixels high presentation layout. If you want to cater to the WebTV crowd, you should limit yourself to a 544 pixel wide by a 376 pixel high design. Your visitors can scroll vertically to read more of the information in your documents. Realistically, rarely can you limit yourself entirely to space limitations. But, if you can create your design so vertical scrolling is allowed but horizontal scrolling isn't needed, you're that much closer to pleasing your visitors.

Use Photographs to Draw Attention to Content

To add a sense of real life to your presentation, you must use photography. Photos give you a complex series of life-like figures that add a human element to the variety of your document's illustrative graphics. Photos provide your presentation with a

- Face to make them feel at home. Give your visitors someone to look at. If this is your presentation about you, put a picture of yourself on the presentation. If it's a presentation about your company, then put a picture of all company employees as a group on your presentation. By adding a face to the company name, you can make your visitors feel better about working with you. On the Internet, this is the only way to recreate that feeling of walking into your favorite restaurant and having your favorite waitress bring your coffee and cream without needing to be asked, just because she recognized you when you walked in the door.

- Picture of products for viewing before a visitor purchases the product. Human beings like to touch things. Well, touch-technology hasn't been figured out yet for the Internet, just like we're still waiting for *scratch-n-sniff* to hit the Internet, but you can at least enable your visitors to see what they're buying.

✔ Glimpse into the creative and artistic image of the company. If you're trying to sell your company or services, then your visitors need to see where you're coming from. They need to be able to understand that, "Yes, she works in a warehouse! But . . . she has great light for painting! And her view of the ocean can't be beat."

✔ Navigational method for traversing through various portions of the presentation. Photographs make great navigational aids. You can show a picture of your building and visitors will know that if they click it, they will soon be greeted with company information. And if visitors see a picture of a laptop computer on a computer sales site, then they're able to get information on laptops, not desktops, from that location.

When using photographs, be aware of the edges of the photos. By fading out the edges to match the background color or pattern, you can reduce the harsh rectangular appearance of photo edges. The use of a human face within your photo provides a solid eye-catching point within your presentation that draws the attention of the visitor. In addition to monitoring the shape and content of photos, you need to be aware of the colors within the photographs. At times, the real color of a photo is too green or too blue for the colors existing on your SMIL document. By building your design around a photograph, you avoid this problem. If you add a photo to your presentation near the end of the development process, you may have to recolor the photo or remove large portions of the photo background to merge your design and the photo in a pleasing fashion.

Make Art Work for You

When you're working with pieces of art, just as when working with photographs, you have to think of the shape, color, and size of the artwork when you initially design your presentation. Artwork can add or detract from your presentation just as a photograph can. Just like photographs, you can order artwork to meet your specific needs, or you can find clipart that's "close enough for government work." Artwork can be more easily modified to fit within the scheme of your design. You can also hire an artist to modify artwork that you've previously created or purchased. Unlike photographs, art often becomes the centerpiece of your entire presentation. If you're going to plan the appearance of your entire presentation around a single illustration, you need to have that illustration before you start planning the rest of your presentation. This is definitely a situation where you need the egg before the chicken.

Add Animations Wisely

Whether the animation on your SMIL presentation is done using SMIL commands, JavaScript, Flash movies, or just simple animated GIFs, they all have to work within your design without overwhelming your visitor. Too much of the wrong style of animation — whether it's video or a blinking text banner — may make your visitors leave your presentation to find some other way of getting the information they need.

When designing your animations, it's important that you create your animations so that they follow certain rules. It wouldn't look right to you, or your visitors, if an animated GIF-snake bent at right angles or if a jumping fish simply rose and fell out of the water like a yo-yo. Animations that don't follow the accepted rules of physics, gravity, and organic flow do nothing more than create an unsettling sense of *wrongness* for your presentation visitors.

Make Your Site Look Dynamic

Making your site look dynamic is actually quite simple. You don't have to add moving lights or rollover images to your pages. All you have to do is add a *naturally dynamic* image or graphic to your page. A naturally dynamic image expresses a motion within its theme. A car driving by, a person running across a parking lot, a mother swinging her child in her arms, or a seal diving into the ocean all add a sense of motion and energy to your presentation. The best part is that you can achieve this motion and energy without programming a lot of flashy movement and swapping images.

When you're adding images with a strong sense of motion to your presentation, leave empty space around the image so it has a chance to extend its internal movement about the screen. Framing a dynamic picture restricts its motion. When you're providing this picture with space, also be aware of where that space is and what that space does to the image's motion.

For example, if you have more empty space behind an object than in front of it, you create the optical illusion of slowing down. Having more space in front of, rather than behind, the image makes the image accelerate into the activity shown within the document. I don't mean to say that you want a perfectly symmetrical frame of empty space around the dynamic image. Symmetry also tends to slow down the motion of the image and make it less invigorating. By adding a sense of asymmetrical acceleration to the image, you can increase the interest and energy created with your SMIL document rather than provide tranquility to the site. Of course, tranquility may be your goal.

Chapter 19

Top Ten SMIL Research Sites

● ●

In This Chapter

▶ Accessing online SMIL resources

▶ Finding multimedia information online

● ●

A wide variety of SMIL resources are available through the Internet. These resources range from specifications of the SMIL language, to tutorials on implementing SMIL, to software that reads it or creates it. The following resources should help you with your further explorations of the SMIL language.

World Wide Web Consortium

```
www.w3.org
```

Whether you're looking for technical information or just something to play with, the World Wide Web Consortium site, shown in Figure 19-1, contains information about the actual development and implementation of the SMIL standard and its upcoming changes. Although it doesn't contain many examples or even a tutorial, the site is the primary source to visit for the hard, cold facts.

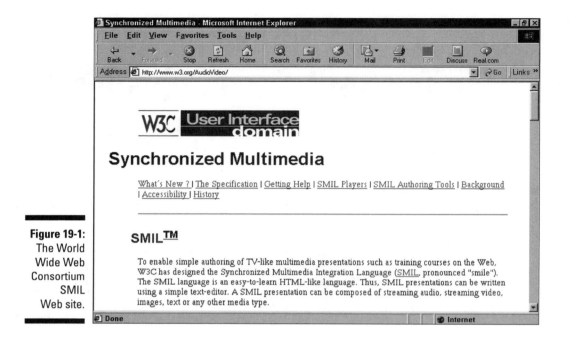

Figure 19-1:
The World
Wide Web
Consortium
SMIL
Web site.

Streaming Media World

www.streamingmediaworld.com

This is a great site where you can immerse yourself in SMIL and its multimedia cohorts. You can find everything from Flash direction to the best in SMIL information at the Streaming Media World site, shown in Figure 19-2. The site, devoted to the world of electronic streaming multimedia, is actually a conglomeration of Web sites combined to make one complete interactive multimedia resource on the Internet. From here, you can get design advice, tips on creating eye-catching yet fast-loading videos, and the latest news about what software companies and standards organizations are doing with the multimedia creation tools used today. You'll also find a series of tutorials that are appropriate for everyone from the beginner to the professional.

Figure 19-2:
The
Streaming
Media
World Web
site offers
practically
every type
of help
when it
comes
to SMIL
and other
media types.

RealNetworks

`http://realnetworks.com/devzone/index.html`

RealNetworks provides a full library and tool kit for working with SMIL (although it uses its own RealText and RealPics languages in addition to SMIL). At the RealNetworks DevZone, shown in Figure 19-3, you can access discussion groups, create contacts within the industry, and create your own mentor program to help guide you, whether you're a beginning or professional developer. If you're designing SMIL presentations primarily for playing within RealNetworks software, you *must* see this site.

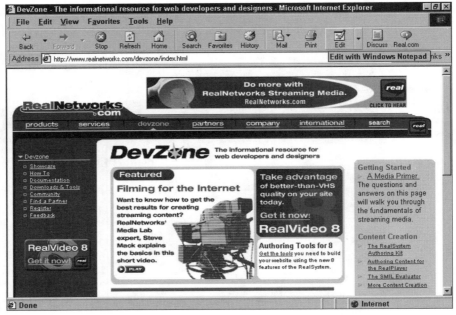

Figure 19-3:
The Real-
Networks
DevZone
provides
information
and exam-
ples of all
types of
SMIL- and
RealPlayer-
compatible
media.

developer.com

```
http://developer.earthweb.com/dlink.index-jhtml.72.950.-.
          0.jhtml
```

Check out the developer.com site (Figure 19-4) and delve into a vast number
of tutorials on SMIL, XML, and all other Internet development technologies.
In addition to these tutorials, you can access software, read the news, talk to
industry professionals, discover upcoming trade shows, and hold online
discussions with everyday SMIL developers, SMIL beginners, or SMIL gurus.

Figure 19-4:
An XML
tutorial
Web site.

Builder.com

http://builder.com

Whether you're looking for types of software to use in creating your SMIL
pages or just some simple information, you can find it at Builder.com
(Figure 19-5). This site contains everything from text editors to SMIL development software, from hundreds of image and sound editing programs to
creation programs. A variety of tutorials, covering all types of streaming
multimedia with some specific discussions on SMIL thrown in, await you.
Check out the Web Development Graphics and Multimedia section for information on designing SMIL sites. And, last but not least, don't forget to search
for all things SMIL.

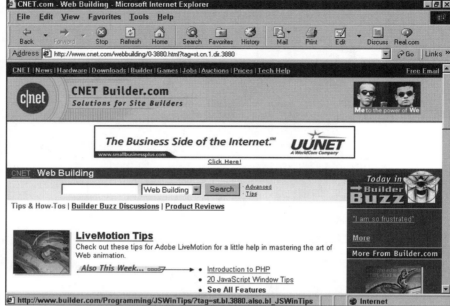

Figure 19-5:
Use Builder.
com to find
a multitude
of infor-
mation on
electronic
media
design and
development.

QuickTime Site

```
www.apple.com/quicktime/
```

If you go for the up-and-coming players in the software world, check out Apple QuickTime. From this Web site, shown in Figure 19-6, you can collect all the information you need on Apple QuickTime: development software, server software, and a variety of tutorials on creating streaming media documents and presentations. Although this site is focused primarily on developing for the QuickTime player, the techniques you find here work for all players that work with your final SMIL document.

Figure 19-6:
The Apple QuickTime Web site provides links to free and commercial software, as well as development tutorials and VR authoring guides.

helio

http://helio.org

If you want to find out more about SMIL and use Helio's SOJA SMIL player, the helio Web site (Figure 19-7) is a must-see. It has tutorials, software, and design tips for all levels of SMIL developers. The site continually updates its tutorials, so expect it to change and grow as SMIL standards change and grow.

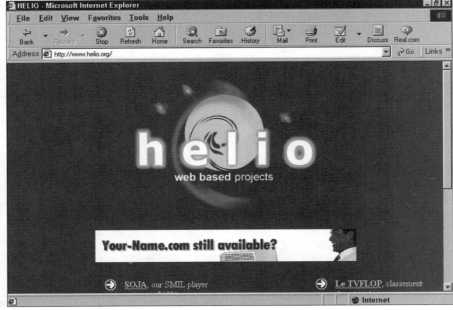

Figure 19-7:
Visit the
helio Web
site to
access both
the helio
player and
a SMIL
tutorial.

WebDeveloper.com

```
http://webdeveloper.com/multimedia
```

The WebDeveloper's Web site, shown in Figure 19-8, contains information relating to all types of SMIL and RealNetworks technologies. You can find reviews of SMIL-compatible software, tutorials, and links to software downloads. This site has a wealth of information and many links to other Internet resources.

Figure 19-8:
The
WebDevel-
oper.com
site provides
information
on all Web-
related tech-
nologies —
including
great
kernels of
information
on SMIL
and its
streaming
media
brethren.

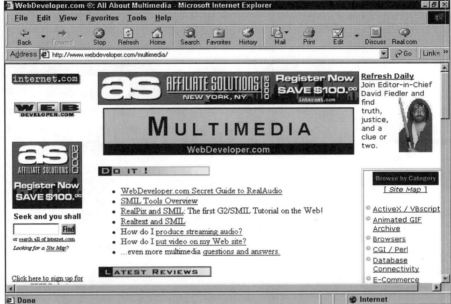

Figure 19-8:
The WebDeveloper.com site provides information on all Web-related technologies — including great kernels of information on SMIL and its streaming media brethren.

webtechniques.com

http://webtechniques.com

This site (Figure 19-9) is primarily a resource for articles, a few small SMIL tutorials, and other tutorials and articles on Web-related technology. To easily access SMIL content, search for *SMIL* or *streaming media*. This links you to quite a few articles on SMIL, its technology, how to use it, how to implement it, and a few thoughts about where it can take the streaming media world.

Figure 19-9:
The web-
techniques.
com Web
site provides
a good
resource
for articles
about SMIL.

XML.com

http://xml.com

XML.com, shown in Figure 19-10, provides you with information on all things
XML-related. To get information directly related to your projects, you can
search for specific articles on SMIL. If you want to know more about SMIL and
its origins, you can check out the variety of XML documents on this site that
provide a close look at SMIL's parent language. You may gain some insight
into your own development of SMIL.

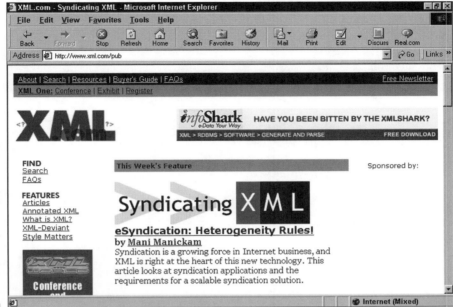

Figure 19-10:
XML.com provides plenty of information about XML and its child languages, including SMIL.

Chapter 20

Top Ten SMIL Aggravations

Do you have days when nothing goes your way? If you're working with computers, you may have those days more frequently than your friend, the tiger trainer, has. As you find out while working with SMIL, most of the problems with SMIL aren't with the language or what you can do with it; they're with the companies and software that support it. With that said, jump with me now into the world of headaches and frustration.

SMIL Is the Only Link between Players

Think about it for a second. What's the link between Netscape Navigator and Internet Explorer? HTML. What's the link between RealPlayer and QuickTime? SMIL. Do any other links exist? Not really. Other than SMIL, both of these prime-time players have their own languages, their own supported movie formats, their own everything. SMIL is their primary link. You probably shouldn't expect a presentation that you designed for one of these players to play perfectly within the other, unless you're using very strict SMIL code. Most of the SMIL editors available today are leaning toward support for RealPlayer's implementation of SMIL because it has been the primary player for much longer than Apple QuickTime.

Specifications Change Frequently

How many times have you driven to your preferred coffee joint and found that your favorite cup of java has just gone up in price? The SMIL specification, like coffee prices, is always changing, morphing, growing, shrinking, becoming easier to understand, and then twice as difficult to understand. You can't stop the SMIL specification . . . at least not in the near future.

As frustrating as this is for a developer like you, who always likes to use the latest and the greatest, this pattern of constant changes ensures you that the eye of the Web Big Brother (the World Wide Web Consortium at www.w3.org) is looking at SMIL and sees it as something worth considering. This constant change gives SMIL developers a good reason to continue their work: They can be assured that their favorite multimedia format isn't destined to go the way of the dinosaurs (at least not this year).

Not All SMIL Players Can Use All Media

Now just a second. SMIL can use anything, right? Well, any media. *SMIL* can incorporate any type of media into a presentation. *SMIL players,* however, have their limitations. If RealPlayer can't display WMF files, you can't use WMF files in a SMIL presentation that you're going to play on RealPlayer. If QuickTime can't play audio CD tracks, you have to find a new format to save your audio files in — if you want QuickTime to play them. You can't go to Germany and order a beer if you only know English. Likewise, SMIL players can't understand file types that they haven't been created to use. To find out what kind of media your particular SMIL player uses, go to its creator's Web site. If you're using RealPlayer, visit www.realnetworks.com. If you're using Apple QuickTime, go to www.quicktime.com.

SMIL Can't Do Everything Director Does

To put it simply, SMIL can't do what Director does because the SMIL files aren't as large and SMIL doesn't cost as much. *Director* is a very expensive program (okay, expensive according to this author's budget) that enables you to create totally interactive multimedia CDs. It has its own built-in language, called Lingo, and can do practically anything you want it to do as far as a multimedia presentation is concerned. Director, which supports multiple time lines, is a full development package that provides you with the ability to actually create complex animations that move, speak, and literally leap off the screen. SMIL doesn't cost you anything; the knowledge you need to use it is free; and because SMIL is free and a team of vastly knowledgeable volunteers is developing it, it's limited by some very focused goals:

- ✔ The files must be small enough to share over the Internet.
- ✔ The files must be easily legible to computers and humans alike.
- ✔ SMIL must provide multimedia in a format that can be easily incorporated into existing tools.

As great as Director is, it doesn't create small enough files to be readily accessible over the Internet. It doesn't create documents that you can read without using Directory. And it doesn't support a format that can be easily incorporated into existing Multimedia players, at least not without installing a plug-in. Director is a great tool, if you know Lingo and don't want to share files over the Internet (they're just too big). Rome wasn't built in a day. Give SMIL a few years, and it just may give Director a run for its money.

SMIL Is So Dang Picky about Tags!

If you're writing your SMIL code yourself and you aren't using an editor, I commend you. SMIL is a picky language — which it inherited from its father, XML. XML has a whole list of rules that SMIL also has to follow. These rules include the following:

- ✔ Element and tag names are case-sensitive, so your opening and closing tags have to match.
- ✔ Opening tags must have closing tags.
- ✔ Empty tags can't have closing tags, but they must have their closing slash (/). In SMIL, you can't get by with using HTML's accepted <P> elements without a closing slash; in SMIL, you have to use </P>.
- ✔ You must properly pair tags. For instance, you can't have the following:

```
<SWITCH> <PAR> </SWITCH> </PAR>
```

The tag pairs aren't properly matched. SMIL and XML (which I discuss further in Appendix C) require that you match your tag pairs properly, as shown in the following:

```
<SWITCH> <PAR> </PAR> </SWITCH>
```

- ✔ Comments can't occur within a tag, nor can they be stacked within themselves.
- ✔ Your tags are case-sensitive. For instance, <par> </par> and <PAR> </PAR> are two separate sets of tags.

SMIL Isn't Supported in All Web Browsers

Microsoft forgot about SMIL for awhile. Microsoft became interested in its HTML+TIME plan and pulled out its SMIL specification support at the last minute. In the latest releases of Internet Explorer 5.5, however, SMIL is coming back. The release of Internet Explorer 6.0 is surely going to provide even more support for SMIL (I'm rubbing my magic glass ball here). Netscape Navigator 6, on the other hand, doesn't currently provide any support for SMIL files, although it hasn't yet been released in its final form. (At the time of this writing, no word on the Netscape or Mozilla Web sites confirms plans for supporting SMIL.)

SMIL Doesn't Support Two Timelines

SMIL doesn't enable you to use two timelines, but luckily for you, you don't really need two timelines. If you use a bit of math, or check out the hints in Chapter 8, you can easily figure out the relationship between two activities that have separate stimuli and find the one time in which they both occur. Or, you can just use a relational time in your SMIL code. The old phrase "Time stops for no man" holds true in SMIL with one addition: "Time starts for no developer."

Not Many SMIL Editors Exist Yet

SMIL editors are out there, and more are coming all the time. The Real Slides how software and Sausage Software's SMIL Composer are just the beginning. With the RealNetworks Streaming Media Starter Kit, a SMIL development powerhouse, you can see the truly advanced features of SMIL at work in a graphical interface. Of course, this kind of power has a price. Where you can get basic copies of the Real Slideshow and Sausage's SMIL Composer for free, you're going to have to pay in excess of $500 for the full Starter Kit — and that's without the RealNetworks RealServer software.

And what about Mac users? Well, they're pretty much left out in the cold. Right now few, if any, Macintosh-based SMIL development packages are available, and the majority of the big design houses are havens for Macintosh users. SMIL can't survive without software that's designed to work with the way a designer, not an engineer, thinks. You can find out about some of the editors that are available for SMIL in Chapter 1.

SMIL Is Small, but Its Contents Are So Big

Ever wonder why SMIL is so small, but its contents are so big? That's easy! SMIL was designed to be small, but many of the movie formats and image and audio file structures were not designed to be streamed. They weren't designed with the Internet and slow connections in mind. Besides, think about how much information one frame of a video has to store. Because every frame of a video is essentially one flat image, you can easily expect a video file to be as many times larger than an image file as the video has frames. Audio files are the same way: Sound takes up a lot of space. Unfortunately, an easy way to convert the full range of nuances of the human voice into a small compact package hasn't been discovered yet.

Text, on the other hand, is amazingly compact. Because we can represent every character of the alphabet with a single number, the SMIL files have it made. SMIL documents are created from straight text, avoiding the bulk associated with trying to compress binary files.

SMIL Software Has Its Share of Bugs

I hope you weren't expecting SMIL software to be bug-free. Bugs, those little, creepy crawlies that work their way into any piece of software — including your SMIL documents — are a permanent part of computer life. Software without bugs is like a picnic without ants; the picnic may be a lot quieter, but the challenge is gone.

Actually, most SMIL software is pretty good. Developers have had so much experience with HTML and XML languages that they're getting things done right the first time around with SMIL. Since its incorporation in RealPlayer G2, SMIL has become increasingly important to the Real family of software to the point that even their own RealPics and RealText language are simply extensions of the SMIL format, or is the SMIL format an extension of them? Hmm. Well, whatever, the biggest hindrance to the smooth playing of SMIL files is the bandwidth of the Internet, not the software that's doing the playing.

Part VII
Appendixes

The 5th Wave   By Rich Tennant

"I don't mean to hinder your quest for knowledge; however, it's not generally a good idea to try and download the entire Internet."

In this part . . .

*N*eed a reference? A tip? A quick question answered? Or do you just want some help in understanding the *whys, wherefores,* and *whats* of SMIL? The appendixes in this part can help you get a deeper understanding of SMIL.

Appendix A tells you about the different SMIL players and editors available at the time this book went to press at the end of 2000. As you'll see, not too many are available. Keep checking the World Wide Web Consortium's Web site (www.w3.org/AudioVideo) for announcements regarding new software. Appendix B contains copies of the two Document Type Definitions (DTD) used with SMIL 1.0 and SMIL 2.0. Appendix C introduces you to the foundation language of SMIL: XML. If you want to delve deeper into SMIL, other than the commands explained throughout this book, be sure to read Appendix C.

As you continue perusing the Appendixes, you'll see that Appendix D is all about the CD-ROM that accompanies this book. In this appendix, you find a listing of all the software included on the CD, instructions on using the software, and the minimum system requirements necessary to use the CD and its contents. The CD also contains a couple of additional appendixes that you might find helpful. Appendix E is a sorted list of all the elements and attributes used in SMIL 2.0. Appendix F provides you with references for RealText and RealPics — the proprietary HTML-like languages that work with the RealNetworks RealPlayer software. So don't forget to check out these two appendixes.

Appendix A

SMIL Composers and Players

A variety of software programs allow you to both view and create your SMIL presentations. None of them are flush and full of features, but they do what they do quite well. I'd say that most of the editors that allow you to create SMIL documents without having to know the code yourself are "teen-age" software and are still trying to work out what they are and how they're going to do what they want to do. Many of the SMIL players that allow you to view but not create SMIL presentations are quite mature.

At the time of this writing, most of the software, whether it's a SMIL editor or a SMIL player, available on the Internet for SMIL doesn't yet support the SMIL 2.0 commands and standards. If you're just looking for some tools, you can check out some of these SMIL 1.0 editors that get you started and even work with the SMIL 2.0 players:

✔ SMIL Composer from Sausage Software (freeware: www.sausage.com)

✔ GRiNS SMIL 1.0 Composer from Oratrix (shareware: www.oratrix.com)

✔ RealSlideshow 2.0 from RealNetworks (free basic version: www.realnetworks.com)

✔ Homesite 4.0 with the SMIL extensions from Allaire (demo version: www.allaire.com)

✔ Fluition by Confluent (Macintosh) (demo version: www.confluenttechnologies.com)

✔ VEON Studio (commercial, no demo: www.veon.com)

✔ lp Studio by Labyrinten (demo version: www.prodworks.com)

- ✔ T.A.G. Composer by Digital Renaissance (demo version: www.digital-ren.com)
- ✔ MAGpie by NCAM (demo version: www.wgbh.com/webaccess/magpie)

GRiNS . . . Playing Better SMIL

Oratrix, a company known for its work with multimedia software and formats, currently has two editors on the market. Both of these editors are used for working with multimedia presentations. The first one of these editors, simply called the GRiNS Editor, is primarily focused on developing for RealPlayer software, using the RealNetworks proprietary languages RealPix and RealText, which I discuss in Appendix F on the CD. These languages are similar to SMIL but are not identical; therefore, documents written in these languages aren't fully supported in other SMIL players.

The second editor available through Oratrix is the GRiNS SMIL Editor. This program creates SMIL 1.0-compatible presentations that any SMIL player can view, whether the player is from Apple, RealNetworks, or Microsoft. Because this editor is meant to work with SMIL 1.0, you won't find any way to create SMIL animations or transformations, but you will be able to use all the timing and layout elements that were supported in SMIL 1.0.

Oratrix has also released its SMIL Player 2, which supports the SMIL 2.0 specification. With the release of a SMIL player supporting SMIL 2.0, I hope it won't be too long before Oratrix has a SMIL 2.0 editor available, as well. GRiNS supports the SMIL animation and transformation controls but doesn't support transparent GIFs. The version of the GRiNS Player for SMIL 2.0 available at the time of this writing (see Figure A-1) seems to support all the new features included in the SMIL 2.0 specification.

Netscape Navigator 6 and SMIL

Netscape Navigator 6 recognizes SMIL files as a part of the XML document language and therefore requires that the SMIL document have a style sheet in order to be visible. With the additions of the RealPlayer and Apple QuickTime plug-ins, Netscape should be able to play SMIL files in a fashion similar to the Microsoft HTML+TIME implementation of SMIL. Of course, until both Netscape Navigator 6 and the SMIL 2.0 specification are actually released, it's anyone's best guess how much SMIL playing support will be built into Netscape Navigator 6 and how much we will continue to depend on the primary SMIL players like RealPlayer and QuickTime for viewing our Web-based SMIL presentations. Take a look at the Netscape Navigator 6 interface in Figure A-2.

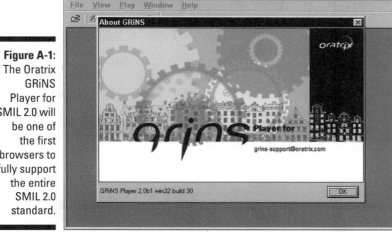

Figure A-1:
The Oratrix
GRiNS
Player for
SMIL 2.0 will
be one of
the first
browsers to
fully support
the entire
SMIL 2.0
standard.

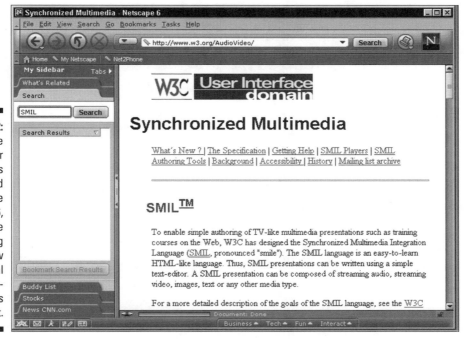

Figure A-2:
With the
vast number
of changes
in SMIL and
Netscape
Navigator 6,
it will be
interesting
to see how
the final
implementa-
tion works
out.

Internet Explorer 5.5 and SMIL

The release of Internet Explorer 5.5, shown in Figure A-3, includes support for many of the SMIL 2.0 modules. Internet Explorer now supports the Timing and Synchronization, BasicAnimation, SplineAnimation, BasicMedia, MediaClipping, and BasicContentControl modules. Microsoft claims that it doesn't support SMIL, but its own brand of SMIL, called HTML+TIME, is practically identical to the existing SMIL specification. The system that Microsoft has implemented enables you to easily embed your SMIL timing code directly within your HTML file by using XML Namespaces. You can find more information on the HTML+TIME concept at `http://msdn.microsoft.com/workshop/Author/behaviors/htmltime.asp`.

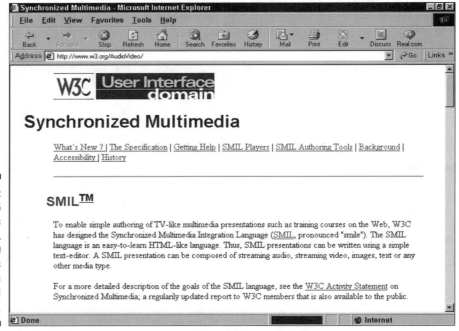

Figure A-3:
IE 5.5 integrates the HTML and SMIL 2.0 specifications into its own brand called HTML+TIME.

XMLInstance Edits SMIL

XMLInstance, shown in Figure A-4, isn't a SMIL editor, but it is an XML editor. (XML is SMIL's daddy.) XMLInstance, by TIBCO Extensibility, enables you to edit and create XML files and includes a SMIL Document Type Definition (DTD), which enables you to create and automatically format SMIL documents, while ensuring that they're valid. How? Because XMLInstance does all the checking and validating for you. XMLInstance uses the SMIL DTD to force you to use the proper elements and attributes together so that you can't make an invalid document. Of course, it doesn't do anything for your design or to control your timing: You're still responsible for making sure that the timing is correct. This product just ensures that you're using the proper document structure so that your SMIL documents are viewable in any SMIL 2.0 software.

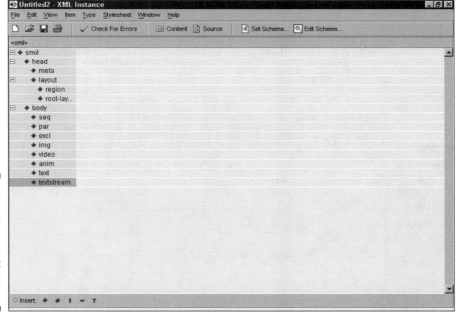

Figure A-4: XMLInstance provides you with a structured environment for creating documents.

The Validator

You can validate your SMIL documents online by using the CWI SMIL Validator located at `www.cwi.nl/~media/symm/validator/` and shown in Figure A-5. This is a simple online validator that allows you to enter your own SMIL code for validation. You can also have the validator look directly at a document that you've previously placed online. The validator allows you to use one of a variety of definitions of the SMIL language so that you know exactly how your document stacks up to the current specifications for both SMIL and XHTML.

The process of validating a SMIL document is actually quite complex. The validating software must read the SMIL document and compare that to the appropriate SMIL DTD and decide whether or not the document meets all the rules that have been specified within the DTD. If the SMIL document meets the rules, then the document is considered valid. If the SMIL document does not meet the rules, errors will occur, and the Validator will point them out to you. Any error that occurs within a SMIL presentation can cause problems when a SMIL player is viewing that presentation. By validating your presentations before letting the public view it, you may be able to forego the standard complaints that your presentation isn't working for a noticeable percentage of your visitors.

Figure A-5:
The CWI SMIL Validator enables you to check your SMIL 2.0 documents without worrying about quirks in RealPlayer, QuickTime, or the browser.

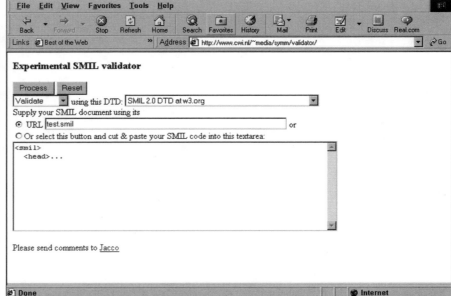

Appendix B

The SMIL Document Type Definitions

*D*ocument Type Definitions (DTDs) are used as a dictionary-like reference for all the commands, elements, and their descriptive attributes that are available for use with SMIL documents.

All XML Namespaces point to DTDs. A Document Type Definition is a series of instructions that identify all the allowable elements and attributes that can be used in a document. Imagine a large dictionary just for that particular type of document. Just as the English dictionary lists all of the words and phrases that can be used in the proper version of the English language, the SMIL DTD identifies what commands (elements) can be used with a SMIL document. In addition, DTDs also specify what attributes can be used with each element and the values that can be used with that attribute. This is like your desktop dictionary telling you which prefix or suffix is usable with a particular word. Attributes simply provide more information about the element that is being looked at. Read this appendix for more information on the SMIL Document Type Definitions.

The hard task now is to find the document viewer that can read your SMIL, your Scalable Vector Graphics (SVG), as well as all your graphics and all your content — video, audio, and text.

With the release of the SMIL 2.0 standard, you can expect improvements in both the current SMIL readers and players, as well as more interest in SMIL from other software vendors, especially those software developers that want to add an element of timing to their document presentations.

DTDs are the control documents for SMIL support. They let the SMIL players know what is a good element or attribute and which ones are bad. You can read more about DTDs on the World Wide Web Consortium Web site located at `www.w3.org`. Here are some quick rules for reading DTDs that may help you understand what these documents contain, without having to read a full book on XML and DTDs:

- ✔ Each element that's available for use with SMIL presentations is identified with the `<!ELEMENT ...>` tag.

- ✔ Each attribute is identified with an `<!ATTLIST ...>` tag.

- ✔ `<!ENTITY ...>` tags identify groups of attributes so you don't have to identify the same attribute multiple times.

- ✔ Comments about the contents of the DTD are included in the `<!-- -->` tags. Comments may cover a single line, or multiple lines, but all the text between these two tags is considered a *comment*.

SMIL 1.0 DTD

The *SMIL 1.0 DTD* was designed to work with SMIL software for the original SMIL 1.0 specification. This DTD was created so that all software wanting to support SMIL 1.0 would have a reference for the elements and attributes that can be used. SMIL players that support SMIL 2.0 don't have to support SMIL 1.0, but you can encourage many of them to do so by applying a DTD to your SMIL documents. You can do this by adding the `<!DOCTYPE>` command to your SMIL presentation following your opening `<smil>` element. This command ensures that the SMIL player knows where to look to find the instruction book for the presentation that you create.

```
<smil>
   <!DOCTYPE smil PUBLIC "-//W3C//DTD SMIL 1.0//EN"
            "http://www.w3.org/TR/REC-smil/SMIL10.dtd">
   <head>
   ...
   </head>
   <body>
   ...
   </body>
</smil>
```

The `<!DOCTYPE>` command shown here points to the SMIL1.0 DTD. You should not use this command with documents written based on the SMIL 2.0 DTD. If you want to use the appropriate command for referencing the SMIL 2.0 DTD, it is:

```
<!DOCTYPE smil PUBLIC "-//W3C//DTD SMIL 2.0 Basic//EN"
         "http://www.w3.org/TR/REC-smil/smilbasic2020.dtd">
```

The following code is the SMIL 1.0 DTD. This document provides all the instructions for implementing SMIL 1.0 within a SMIL player. You can help enforce support for SMIL 1.0 by attaching this document, as previously described, to your SMIL presentation.

```
<!--
    This is the XML document type definition (DTD) for SMIL
    1.0.
    Date: 1998/06/15 08:56:30
    Authors: Jacco van Ossenbruggen <jrvosse@cwi.nl>
             Sjoerd Mullender       <sjoerd@cwi.nl>

    Further information about SMIL is available at:
    http://www.w3.org/AudioVideo/
-->

<!-- Generally useful entities -->
<!ENTITY % id-attr "id ID #IMPLIED">
<!ENTITY % title-attr "title CDATA #IMPLIED">
<!ENTITY % skip-attr "skip-content (true|false) 'true'">
<!ENTITY % desc-attr "
        %title-attr;
            abstract    CDATA #IMPLIED
            author             CDATA  #IMPLIED
            copyright   CDATA #IMPLIED
">


<!--========== SMIL Document ====================-->
<!--
    The root element SMIL contains all other elements.
-->
<!ELEMENT smil (head?,body?)>
<!ATTLIST smil
        %id-attr;
>


<!--============== The Document Head ==================-->
<!ENTITY % layout-section "layout|switch">
<!ENTITY % head-element "(meta*,((%layout-section;),
          meta*))?">
<!ELEMENT head %head-element;>
<!ATTLIST head %id-attr;>


<!--========== Layout Element ====================-->
<!--
    Layout contains the region and root-layout elements
    defined by smil-basic-layout or other elements
    define an external layout mechanism.
```

```
-->
<!ELEMENT layout ANY>
<!ATTLIST layout
        %id-attr;
        type CDATA        "text/smil-basic-layout"
>


<!--=========== Region Element ===================-->
<!ENTITY % viewport-attrs "
        height            CDATA       #IMPLIED
        width             CDATA       #IMPLIED
        background-color  CDATA       #IMPLIED
">

<!ELEMENT region EMPTY>
<!ATTLIST region
        %id-attr;
        %title-attr;
        %viewport-attrs;
        left              CDATA       "0"
        top               CDATA       "0"
        z-index           CDATA       "0"
        fit          (hidden|fill|meet|scroll|slice) "hidden"
        %skip-attr;
>

<!--=========== Root-layout Element ===================-->
<!ELEMENT root-layout EMPTY>
<!ATTLIST root-layout
        %id-attr;
        %title-attr;
        %viewport-attrs;
        %skip-attr;
>


<!--=========== Meta Element ===================-->
<!ELEMENT meta EMPTY>
<!ATTLIST meta
        name    NMTOKEN #REQUIRED
        content CDATA    #REQUIRED
        %skip-attr;
>


<!--=========== The Document Body ===============-->
<!ENTITY % media-object
          "audio|video|text|img|animation|textstream|ref">
<!ENTITY % schedule "par|seq|(%media-object;)">
<!ENTITY % inline-link "a">
<!ENTITY % assoc-link "anchor">
<!ENTITY % link "%inline-link;">
<!ENTITY % container-content "(%schedule;)|switch|(%link;)">
```

```
<!ENTITY % body-content "(%container-content;)">

<!ELEMENT body (%body-content;)*>
<!ATTLIST body %id-attr;>


<!--========= Synchronization Attributes ===========-->
<!ENTITY % sync-attributes "
       begin   CDATA   #IMPLIED
       end     CDATA   #IMPLIED
">


<!--======= Switch Parameter Attributes =============-->
<!ENTITY % system-attribute "
    system-bitrate            CDATA        #IMPLIED
    system-language           CDATA        #IMPLIED
    system-required           NMTOKEN      #IMPLIED
    system-screen-size        CDATA        #IMPLIED
    system-screen-depth       CDATA        #IMPLIED
    system-captions           (on|off)     #IMPLIED
    system-overdub-or-caption (caption|overdub)   #IMPLIED
">


<!--========= Fill Attribute =====================-->
<!ENTITY % fill-attribute "
       fill    (remove|freeze)     'remove'
">


<!--========== The Parallel Element =================-->
<!ENTITY % par-content "%container-content;">
<!ELEMENT par     (%par-content;)*>
<!ATTLIST par
       %id-attr;
       %desc-attr;
       endsync CDATA             "last"
       dur     CDATA             #IMPLIED
       repeat  CDATA             "1"
       region  IDREF             #IMPLIED
       %sync-attributes;
       %system-attribute;
>


<!--========== The Sequential Element ================-->
<!ENTITY % seq-content "%container-content;">
<!ELEMENT seq     (%seq-content;)*>
<!ATTLIST seq
       %id-attr;
       %desc-attr;
       dur     CDATA             #IMPLIED
       repeat  CDATA             "1"
       region  IDREF             #IMPLIED
       %sync-attributes;
       %system-attribute;
>
```

```
<!--========== The Switch Element ==================-->
<!-- In the head, a switch may contain only layout elements,
     in the body, only container elements. However, this
     constraint cannot be expressed in the DTD (?), so
     we allow both:
-->
<!ENTITY % switch-content "layout|(%container-content;)">
<!ELEMENT switch (%switch-content;)*>
<!ATTLIST switch
        %id-attr;
        %title-attr;
>


<!--========== Media Object Elements ==================-->
<!-- SMIL only defines the structure. The real media data is
     referenced by the src attribute of the media objects.
-->

<!-- Furthermore, they have the following attributes as
     defined in the SMIL specification:
-->
<!ENTITY % mo-attributes "
        %id-attr;
        %desc-attr;
        region      IDREF           #IMPLIED
        alt         CDATA           #IMPLIED
        longdesc    CDATA           #IMPLIED
        src         CDATA           #IMPLIED
        type        CDATA           #IMPLIED
        dur         CDATA           #IMPLIED
        repeat      CDATA           '1'
        %fill-attribute;
        %sync-attributes;
        %system-attribute;
">


<!--
    Most info is in the attributes, media objects are empty
    or contain associated link elements:
-->
<!ENTITY % mo-content "(%assoc-link;)*">
<!ENTITY % clip-attrs "
        clip-begin      CDATA   #IMPLIED
        clip-end        CDATA   #IMPLIED
">

<!ELEMENT ref           %mo-content;>
<!ELEMENT audio         %mo-content;>
<!ELEMENT img           %mo-content;>
<!ELEMENT video         %mo-content;>
<!ELEMENT text          %mo-content;>
<!ELEMENT textstream    %mo-content;>
<!ELEMENT animation     %mo-content;>
```

```
<!ATTLIST ref               %mo-attributes; %clip-attrs;>
<!ATTLIST audio             %mo-attributes; %clip-attrs;>
<!ATTLIST video             %mo-attributes; %clip-attrs;>
<!ATTLIST animation         %mo-attributes; %clip-attrs;>
<!ATTLIST textstream        %mo-attributes; %clip-attrs;>
<!ATTLIST text              %mo-attributes;>
<!ATTLIST img               %mo-attributes;>


<!--========== Link Elements ====================-->

<!ENTITY % smil-link-attributes "
        %id-attr;
        %title-attr;
        href            CDATA                   #REQUIRED
        show            (replace|new|pause)     'replace'
">


<!--========== Inline Link Element ==================-->
<!ELEMENT a (%schedule;|switch)*>
<!ATTLIST a
        %smil-link-attributes;
>


<!--========== Associated Link Element ============-->
<!ELEMENT anchor EMPTY>
<!ATTLIST anchor
        %skip-attr;
        %smil-link-attributes;
        %sync-attributes;
        coords          CDATA       #IMPLIED
>
```

SMIL 2.0 DTD

The *SMIL 2.0 DTD* was created to work with SMIL software that surpasses
the element support provided in the original SMIL 1.0 specification. SMIL 2.0
software doesn't have to provide support for the SMIL 1.0 DTD, but it also
doesn't prohibit support for that DTD. In other words, you can have software
that supports only SMIL 1.0, both SMIL 1.0 and 2.0, or just SMIL 2.0. You'll find
no restrictions on what type of DTD support that must be provided by SMIL
software. With the new release of SMIL 2.0, however, you can probably bet
that most of the new SMIL players will be supporting SMIL 2.0.

Unlike SMIL 1.0 — with only 1 DTD that covers the entire language — SMIL 2.0
is broken out into 11 different DTDs and 2 driver DTDs that provide the glue
to hold the other 11 together. The following DTD is the SMIL Basic Language
Module DTD. This is the primary document that provides the instructions for
linking and working with all the effects available with SMIL presentations.

```
<!-- ============================================= -->
<!-- SMIL 2.0 Basic DTD ===================== -->
<!-- file: SMIL20Basic.dtd

    This is SMIL 2.0 Basic, a proper subset of SMIL 2.0.

    Copyright 1998-2000 World Wide Web Consortium
    (Massachusetts Institute of Technology, Institut
    National de Recherche en Informatique et en Automatique,
    Keio University).
    All Rights Reserved.

    Permission to use, copy, modify and distribute the SMIL
    Basic DTD and its accompanying documentation for any
    purpose and without fee is hereby granted in perpetuity,
    provided that the above copyright notice and this
    paragraph appear in all copies.  The copyright holders
    make no representation about the suitability of the DTD
    for any purpose.

    It is provided "as is" without expressed or implied
    warranty.

        Author:    Jacco van Ossenbruggen, Kenichi Kubota
        Revision:  $Id: smil-DTD.html,v 1.13 2000/09/21
        01:39:23 tmichel Exp $

-->
<!-- This is the driver file for the SMIL Basic DTD.

    Please use this formal public identifier to identify it:

    "-//W3C//DTD SMIL 2.0 Basic//EN"
-->

<!ENTITY % NS.prefixed "IGNORE" >
<!ENTITY % SMIL.prefix "" >

<!-- Define the Content Model -->
<!ENTITY % smil-model.mod
    PUBLIC "-//W3C//ENTITIES SMIL 2.0 Basic Document Model
    1.0//EN"
    "smilbasic-model-1.mod" >

<!-- Modular Framework Module  ................... -->
<!ENTITY % smil-framework.module "INCLUDE" >
<![%smil-framework.module;[
<!ENTITY % smil-framework.mod
    PUBLIC "-//W3C//ENTITIES SMIL 2.0 Modular Framework
    1.0//EN"
    "smil-framework-1.mod" >
%smil-framework.mod;]]>
```

```
<!--     The SMIL 2.0 Basic Profile supports the lightweight
         multimedia features defined in SMIL language. This
         profile includes the following SMIL modules:

                 SMIL 2.0 BasicLayout Module
                 SMIL 2.0 BasicLinking Module
                 SMIL 2.0 BasicMedia and MediaClipping Modules
                 SMIL 2.0 Structure Module
                 SMIL 2.0 BasicInlinTiming, SyncbaseTiming,
         EventTiming and BasicTimeContainers Modules
                 (with restrictions of single time container)
                 SMIL 2.0 BasicContentControl and
                 SkipContentControl Modules
-->
<!ENTITY % layout-mod
  PUBLIC "-//W3C//ELEMENTS SMIL 2.0 Layout//EN"
  "SMIL-layout.mod">
    %layout-mod;

<!ENTITY % link-mod
  PUBLIC "-//W3C//ELEMENTS SMIL 2.0 Linking//EN"
  "SMIL-link.mod">
    %link-mod;
<!ENTITY % BasicLinkingModule "INCLUDE">

<!ENTITY % media-mod
  PUBLIC "-//W3C//ELEMENTS SMIL 2.0 Media Objects//EN"
  "SMIL-media.mod">
    %media-mod;

<!ENTITY % struct-mod
  PUBLIC "-//W3C//ELEMENTS SMIL 2.0 Document Structure//EN"
  "SMIL-struct.mod">
%struct-mod;

<!ENTITY % timing-mod
  PUBLIC "-//W3C//ELEMENTS SMIL 2.0 Timing//EN"
  "SMIL-timing.mod">
%timing-mod;

<!ENTITY % control-mod
  PUBLIC "-//W3C//ELEMENTS SMIL 2.0 Content//EN"
  "SMIL-control.mod">
%control-mod;
```

To read all the DTDs that work with SMIL 2.0, go to the World Wide Web Consortium's SMIL DTD pages at: `www.w3.org/TR/2000/WD-smil20-20000921/smil-DTD.html`.

Appendix C

The XML Background

SMIL is just one instance of an *XML application*. Now don't let that scare you. XML (*Ex*tensible *M*arkup *L*anguage) is simply a language that enables you to create a system of defining your own information, however you want to do that. You have no reason to be scared. Actually, if you've created one of the SMIL presentations examples that I discuss in this book, you've already created an XML document — and you didn't even know it!

Documents Working Together

One of the uniquely useful things about XML-based documents is that you can use multiple languages together within them. Because of its XML foundations, SMIL works the same way. Because you can embed SMIL documents within other XML-based documents or HTML files and you can embed those other languages within SMIL presentations, you can use SMIL with other languages, such as the following:

- ✔ Vector Markup Language (VML)
- ✔ MathML
- ✔ Broadcast HTML (bHTML)
- ✔ Scalable Vector Graphics (SVG)

As a developer, you can use SMIL with any document technology, as long as a player is available that can correctly read all the document languages that you use. Right now the biggest drawback for working with existing XML formats is finding readers that are capable of reading all these languages. At the time of this writing, some document readers can display XML but haven't been programmed to properly act on each SMIL command. Likewise, some SMIL players can't tell one XML command from another; they can read only SMIL documents.

Software that can do it all — view your XML documents, HTML pages, and SMIL presentations — isn't quite here yet, but I discuss a number of SMIL players and editors in Appendix A. What I mean to say is, if you're going to work with SMIL, stick to SMIL. If you try to merge SMIL with some complex home-grown XML document structure, you may end up with a maze of information you can't extract yourself from.

You can find information on VML, MathML, bHTML, and SVG at the World Wide Web Consortium page at `www.w3.org`.

Although it may be best to not use SMIL with other XML document languages that you create yourself, there's nothing wrong with using SMIL inside a HTML document or with other tried-and-true XML languages that you *know* are supported by your SMIL player. In the following example, I've incorporated both SMIL and a single SVG object into the same file (players are available that can read this particular combination). As you can see, the programming can look complicated, but you can easily refer to the chapters of this book in which I discuss these elements to understand what each does. The SVG commands are identified by the `svg:` preface for both the software reading the presentation and you — so you can tell the difference between the SVG and the SMIL code easier.

```
<smil xmlns:svg="http://www.w3.org/Graphics/SVG/SVG-
        19991203.dtd">
    <head>
        <layout>
            <root-layout height="196" width="136"/>
            <region id="slug_Region" left="0" top="0"
                    height="100" width="106" z-index="1"/>
            <region id="slime_Region" left="0" top="0"
                    height="196" width="136" z-index="0"/>
        </layout>
    </head>
    <body>
        <seq>
            <video id="composer" src="media/slug.rm"
                    region="slug_Region"
                    system-bitrate="13178"/>
            <par>
            <img id="sausage" src="media/slime.rp"
                    region="slime_Region"
                    system-bitrate="12000"/>
                <svg:svg width="2cm" height="5cm">
                    <svg:ellipse rx="30" ry="50" />
                </svg:svg>
            </par>
        </seq>
    </body>
</smil>
```

As you can see from this sample code, the embedded SVG code, shown here bolded, is simply treated as an additional object within the body of the SMIL presentation. It is treated no differently than an image or a video object. In order for both the SMIL code and the SVG code to be properly displayed, your SMIL player must have the ability to properly display the SVG code. It also must understand each element and identify which markup tag goes with SMIL and which with SVG. This is where XML Namespaces come into the picture.

The XML Namespace Requirement

You use *XML Namespaces* to identify which portion of the document belongs to which language. An XML Namespace is an identifier that enables you to load information that controls one language into a document that's primarily using another language. You can think of an XML Namespace as a link to a French-English dictionary when all you read and speak is English.

Look at the lines that use the SVG code, which I've bolded in the SMIL code example in the preceding section. Each of these lines starts with the identifier `svg:`. This identifier refers the document reader, such as the SMIL player, to the following statement that's been added to the opening SMIL document declaration (the opening `<smil>` element statement):

```
xmlns:svg="http://www.w3.org/Graphics/SVG/SVG-19991203.dtd"
```

The `svg:` is an XML Namespace identifier. This statement is used to direct the document reader, such as the SMIL player, to the SVG Document Type Definition (DTD), which you can read about in the following section. This DTD provides information on how to display the SVG elements included within the SMIL statements. The remaining elements — without the `svg:` preface — are interpreted as belonging to the SMIL document and are treated as such.

By using XML Namespaces, you can include a SMIL presentation within an XML document or add a SMIL presentation into an HTML document. The ability of the software being used to display that document correctly depends on its ability to read and use the DTD that's associated with each document language, whether SMIL or XML, that was used within the presentation.

SMIL 2.0

The current primary concern of SMIL developers is the new SMIL recommendation called SMIL 2.0. This new specification builds on the existing SMIL recommendation — expanding it, modularizing it, and making sure it works well with the Document Object Model (DOM) — so that SMIL, like HTML, can be easily modified using scripting languages.

The Document Object Model is simply a mapping of how documents should be created. If you think about a *For Dummies* book, for example, it traditionally has a cover, an introduction, a table of contents, chapters, and an index. In order for you to understand how to use the book, you must know what each part of the book is and what it does. Just as your grade school teacher helped you understand the various elements or parts that make up a book, the Document Object Model teaches SMIL programmers and developers about the parts of SMIL presentations.

The goal of the SMIL 2.0 specification is to make SMIL available throughout all XML-based languages. For example, in XHTML documents, SMIL would provide all the timing commands used in that language. In this draft, a few of the commands that were provided for in SMIL 1.0 have been deprecated in favor of other commands that are more DOM-friendly. In addition, the previously used (in SMIL 1.0) hyphenated commands have been changed to mixed-case commands. For example, the `repeat-count` attribute has been replaced with `repeatCount`.

The tradition has changed. Unlike most other W3C standards that continue to require support for a previous version of a standard, SMIL 2.0 doesn't require that new players support the deprecated elements and attributes. Players that support the SMIL media type, however, will be required to support both the SMIL 1.0 and the SMIL 2.0 commands. This change enables new players to use the new style of DOM-compatible SMIL rather than the previous, relatively non-DOM-friendly version.

The Working Draft is broken into a variety of modules that help segment the uses of SMIL, making it easily included in any other XML-based document language. These modules include the following:

- ✔ **Animation Module:** Provides a means of adding a timing and a composing mechanism to a timeline to control multiple animations.

- ✔ **Content Control Module:** Enables you to select content on your site based upon the values of a series of attributes.

- ✔ **Layout Module:** Enables you to control the special layout of your visual content.

- ✔ **Linking Module:** Enables you to relate documents to specific pieces of content, content to content, and documents to document fragments.

- ✔ **Media Object Module:** Enables you to declare the types of media that are used in your SMIL multimedia display.

- ✔ **Metainformation Module:** Describes the document for either a computer or a human reader.

- ✔ **Structure Module:** Defines the actual structure of the document parts.

✔ **Timing and Synchronization Module:** Provides a means of controlling timing structure, timing controls, and temporal relationships between the individual document objects.

✔ **Transition Effects Module:** Identifies the controls and commands used to create transitions between document objects.

The SMIL media type

Because SMIL documents, like HTML documents, automatically download files of a multitude of types from a multitude of sources and those files are automatically accessed by a variety of software, security has to be a concern. By creating media types, you can increase the security of all the portions of your SMIL document from the document itself to the individual media types it uses. By having recognizable media types, such as the MIME type for HTML (text/html) or for GIF images (image/gif), you can force the computer to only open files that it has registered software for. In other words, if a computer doesn't have software that recognizes a particular type of file, the user of that computer will be asked for instructions on how the computer should handle that type of file.

The SMIL media type is still considered a work in progress, but it is used to define SMIL documents so that they are easily read and recognized by SMIL-compliant players and editors. The identification of a specific SMIL media type enables players and editors to recognize the character set that's being used by the document quickly so that it's able to display the document contents without delay.

In addition to the concerns of character set and document recognition by the media type development group are the concerns of security. Because multimedia documents require the ability to use an *infinite loop* structure, or, in other words, constantly repeating code that seemingly has no end, many concerns arise regarding players that don't provide a break out, or stop button, for use with these files. Infinite loops become a security risk by overloading the memory of your computer and causing it to crash, or by having the SMIL player take up so many resources on your computer that other software ends up with corrupted files through crashes and cluttered memory.

Interoperability, security, and document readability and recognition are other concerns that are addressed in the SMIL media type draft. To find out more information about it and where it may lead SMIL, check out the following Web site: `www.ietf.org/internet-drafts/draft-hoschka-smil-media-type-04.txt`.

SMIL accessibility features

With the growth of the Internet, the World Wide Web Consortium is deeply concerned with the inherent Accessibility Features of all the standards and recommendations that they release. SMIL is no different. SMIL provides an easy means of bringing multimedia content to millions of Internet denizens. Many of these people may be vision- or hearing-impaired. SMIL needs to be accessible for everyone.

A variety of challenges faces developers of SMIL documents who strive to meet the accessibility needs of all users. The primary challenges of these developers center on providing alternative content and timing that alternative content with the primary content so that it isn't confusing to the visitor.

Providing content that all visitors can access is really only polite. If you walk into a room of friends and acquaintances who are speaking a language that you don't understand, you probably feel left out of the group and don't want to come back. If your friends take the time to speak the language that you understand, even if they lapse every so often, you're able to follow the conversation, feel like a part of the group, and will return the next time. Your SMIL documents need to take the same care with your readers. For readers who can't see your multimedia content, provide descriptive audio. For readers who can't hear your audio, provide visible written text.

The next key to making your multimedia site accessible is to have all your accessibility options timed together. You're familiar with the bouncing ball singalong that kids' shows use. Learn a little bit from them. Using these types of devices, blind users can hear the song, and deaf users can follow along with the beat and the words without losing their place or feeling left out of the group. It's a win-win situation for all.

SYMM and SMIL

The work that the World Wide Web Consortium has been doing on *Synchronized Multimedia Modules (SYMM)* is based on SMIL 1.0. This simply propels the use of SMIL further into the main stream of Internet development.

The SYMM modularization project allows for the break-up of SMIL into a variety of modules, or component parts, that can be separated and used in a variety of other applications. For instance, you can use a layout module in a variety of applications to control the basic design of your application or document. You can use a timing module to control the synchronization of events contained within the document or application.

By modularizing SMIL, without changing its content, you give it a much wider realm of possible uses than just the control of Internet multimedia content. The constant development of the SYMM module structure allows a collective look at all the activity taking place in the development of the Hypertext Markup Language (HTML), eXtensible Markup Language (XML), eXtensible Stylesheet Language (XSL), and Cascading Style Sheets (CSS). By combining this overall look at SMIL and its brethren, the group of developers working on SYMM can modify, or suggest modifications, to SMIL that uses the pre-existing standards and commands to provide the same type of functionality that it's already providing but in a more familiar manner for the developer. And we all know that the more comfortable developers are with the tools that they're using, such as SMIL, the more they'll use it.

Appendix D

About the CD

● ●

*H*ere is some of the cool stuff that you'll find on the *SMIL For Dummies* CD-ROM:

- ✔ Apple QuickTime: a close second for SMIL player popularity

- ✔ RealSlideshow: a picture presentation and slide show creation software from RealNetworks

- ✔ SMIL Composer: a simple, yet thorough, SMIL editor

- ✔ Hot Dog Pro: an HTML editor that can pretty much do it all

- ✔ Dreamweaver: another HTML editor that can do it all

- ✔ Allaire Homesite: for the code-lover in all of us, an HTML editor with expansion capabilities that can be made to support SMIL

- ✔ BBEdit: the most popular HTML editor for Macintosh users

- ✔ WinZip: the famous Windows compression program

- ✔ Stuffit: the best-loved Macintosh compression program

- ✔ Shockwave and Flash Plug-in: just one more way to view multimedia on the Internet

- ✔ Paint Shop Pro: a simple-to-use, yet advanced graphics editor for all styles of graphics

System Requirements

Make sure that your computer meets the minimum system requirements in the following list. If your computer doesn't match up to most of these requirements, you may have problems using the contents of the CD. You need

- ✔ A PC with a Pentium 120 or faster processor, or a Mac 604 PowerPC or faster processor

- ✔ Microsoft Windows 95 or later, or Mac OS system software 7.55 or later.

- ✔ At least 32MB of total RAM installed on your computer. For best performance, we recommend at least 64MB of RAM installed.

✔ At least 300MB of hard drive space available to install all the software from this CD. (You need less space if you don't install every program.)

✔ A CD-ROM drive — double-speed (2x) or faster.

✔ A sound card for PCs. (Mac OS computers have built-in sound support.)

✔ A monitor capable of displaying at least 65K colors.

✔ A modem with a speed of at least 28,800 bps.

If you need more information on the basics, check out *PCs For Dummies,* 7th Edition, by Dan Gookin; *Macs For Dummies,* 6th Edition, by David Pogue; *iMac For Dummies,* by David Pogue; *Windows 98 For Dummies,* or *Windows 95 For Dummies,* 2nd Edition, both by Andy Rathbone (all published by IDG Books Worldwide, Inc.).

Using the CD with Microsoft Windows

To install items from the CD to your hard drive, follow these steps:

1. **Insert the CD into your computer's CD-ROM drive.**

2. **Click the Start button and choose Run from the menu.**

3. **In the dialog box that appears, type** d:\start.htm.

   Replace *d* with the proper drive letter for your CD-ROM if it uses a different letter. (If you don't know the letter, double-click the My Computer icon on your desktop and see what letter is listed for your CD-ROM drive.)

   Your browser opens, and the license agreement is displayed. If you don't have a browser, Microsoft Internet Explorer and Netscape Communicator are included on the CD.

4. **Read through the license agreement, nod your head, and click the Accept button if you want to use the CD.**

   After you click Accept, you're taken to the Main menu. This is where you can browse through the contents of the CD.

5. **To navigate within the interface, click any topic of interest to take you to an explanation of the files on the CD and how to use or install them.**

6. **To install software from the CD, simply click the software name.**

   You'll see two options: to run or open the file from the current location or to save the file to your hard drive. Choose to run or open the file from its current location, and the installation procedure continues. When you finish using the interface, close your browser as usual.

Using the CD with a Mac

To install items from the CD to your hard drive, follow these steps:

1. **Insert the CD into your computer's CD-ROM drive.**

   In a moment, an icon representing the CD you just inserted appears on your Mac desktop. Chances are, the icon looks like a CD-ROM.

2. **Double-click the CD icon to show the CD's contents.**

3. **Double-click** start.html **to open your browser and display the license agreement.**

   If your browser doesn't open automatically, open it as you normally would by choosing File⇨Open File (in Internet Explorer) or File⇨Open⇨Location in Netscape (in Netscape Navigator) and select *SMIL For Dummies*. The license agreement appears.

4. **Read through the license agreement, nod your head, and click the Accept button if you want to use the CD.**

   After you click Accept, you're taken to the Main menu. This is where you can browse through the contents of the CD.

5. **To navigate within the interface, click any topic of interest to take you to an explanation of the files on the CD and how to use or install them.**

6. **To install software from the CD, simply click the software name.**

   You'll see two options: to run or open the file from the current location or to save the file to your hard drive. Choose to run or open the file from its current location, and the installation procedure continues. When you finish using the interface, close your browser as usual.

What You'll Find on the CD

The following sections are arranged by category and provide a summary of the software and other goodies you'll find on the CD. If you need help with installing the items provided on the CD, refer back to the installation instructions in the preceding section.

Shareware programs are fully functional, free trial versions of copyrighted programs. If you like particular programs, register with their authors for a nominal fee and receive licenses, enhanced versions, and technical support. *Freeware programs* are free, copyrighted games, applications, and utilities. You can copy them to as many computers as you like — free — but they have no technical support. *GNU software* is governed by its own license, which is included inside the folder of the GNU software. No restrictions limit the distribution of this software. See the GNU license for more details. Trial, demo, or evaluation versions are usually limited either by time or functionality (such as being unable to save projects).

Converters and editors

BBEdit and BBEdit Lite, from Bare Bones Software

For Macintosh. *Commercial. Demo is available.* BBEdit is a high-performance HTML and text editor for the Macintosh. It's designed and crafted for the editing, searching, transformation, and manipulation of text. BBEdit provides an array of general-purpose features that are useful for a wide variety of tasks and includes many features that have been specifically developed in response to the needs of Web authors and software developers. If you want to find out more, check out www.bbedit.com.

Dreamweaver, from Macromedia

For Macintosh, Windows 95/98 and NT 4.0 or later. *Commercial. Demo is available.* Dreamweaver enables you to create cross-browser dynamic HTML sites using a very clear and easy WYSIWYG interface. The Dreamweaver advanced interface and site management tools provide you with access to the nitty-gritty details of working with your Web sites. All of the Dreamweaver menus are based on XML and can be modified right in Dreamweaver. It also enables you to modify your SMIL files, although it isn't set up with predefined commands for SMIL. Go to www.macromedia.com.

Homesite, from Allaire

For Windows 95/98 and NT 4.0 or later. *Commercial. Demo is available.* Homesite has an intuitive *WYSIWYN* (what you see is what you need) interface, which gives you access to all the primary site-building tools. Homesite helps you increase your productivity, enhance your ability to manage projects efficiently, and deploy your site easier and faster, all while supporting the latest Web technologies. Visit www.allaire.com for more information.

Hot Dog Pro, from Sausage Software

For Windows 95/98 and NT 4.0 or later. *Commercial. Demo.* This demo version of Hot Dog Pro is good for 30 days from the date of first installation, and it does just about everything you need. It is fully functional and provides you with access to modifying just about any type of XML for HTML document you could want. You can look at its Web site at www.sausage.com.

RealSlideshow, from RealNetworks

For Windows 95/98 and NT 4.0 or later. *Commercial. Free basic version is available.* You can't talk about SMIL, or any multimedia for that matter, without talking about RealNetworks software. The RealSlideshow software comes in a free Basic version and a commercial Professional version. The free version only lets you create slide shows of images, but the professional version enables you to add text captions, audio files, and just about any other multimedia effect you want. Check out `www.realnetworks.com`.

SMIL Composer, from Sausage Software

For Windows 95/98 and NT 4.0 or later. *Freeware.* This small editor creates SMIL documents for playing with RealNetworks RealPlayer, but they can also be viewed in just about any other SMIL player available. With its succinct WYSIWG layout screen and code developer, SMIL Composer is great for working with audio, video, still images, and text. Visit `www.sausage.com`.

Handy tools

Acrobat Reader 4.0, from Adobe Systems

For Macintosh and Windows. *Evaluation version.* With this handy graphics program, you can view and print Portable Document Format (PDF) files, such as the two appendix files in PDF format that are included on the CD. To get more information about Acrobat Reader, visit the Adobe Systems Web site at `www.adobe.com`.

Shockwave and Flash Plug-in, from Macromedia

For Macintosh, Windows 95/98/Me, Windows NT. *Freeware.* The Flash plug-in is one of the staple plug-ins used with Web sites. This plug-in provides you with the ability to read Flash movies. Flash movies are small, multimedia presentations that can incorporate sound, video, still images, and text into a very easy-to-read and quick-to-download presentation. Flash presentations are used on a lot of sites to provide a splash screen or to create the entire Web site. Check out `www.macromedia.com` for more info. (***Note:*** If you don't have Netscape installed and are using Internet Explorer, you must download the ActiveX version of this plug-in from `www.macromedia.com`.)

Paint Shop Pro 7, from Jasc Software, Inc.

For Windows 95/98/Me, Windows NT. *Shareware.* Paint Shop Pro is a favorite for creating graphics. It definitely gives graphic designers the most bang for their buck with the shortest turn around time for learning the program. And it also is the only fully functional graphics design program that lets you try it out *before* you buy it. Take a look at `www.jasc.com`.

Stuffit, from Aladdin Systems, Inc.

For Macintosh. *Shareware.* This is the most popular expansion and compression software for the Macintosh. The wide variety of encoding algorithms that Stuffit can work with include BinHex, ZIP, gzip, TAR, EXE files, UNIX compress, UUencode, and MIME. Stuffit can expand files that have been created on all three primary operating systems: Macintosh, Unix, and Windows. To find out more, go to www.aladdinsys.com.

WinZip, from Nico Mak Computing

For Windows 95/98/Me, Windows NT. *Shareware.* Face it: WinZip is probably the most popular expansion and compression program currently used on any PC that's connected to the Internet or is owned by someone that buys a lot of computer books. This little program appears on almost every computer book CD that I buy, so I couldn't let you get away without seeing it. It provides built-in support for all the popular Internet file formats, such as ZIP, self-extracting EXE files, TAR, gzip, UNIX compress, UUencode, BinHex, and MIME. You can add ARJ, LZH, and ARC file support through the use of links to external programs. WinZip can even work directly with your virus scanning software to check each file as it's expanded. What more could you ask for in a compression program? Visit www.winzip.com.

SMIL player

Apple QuickTime Player 4.0, from Apple

For Macintosh, Windows 95/98 and NT 4.0 or later. *Freeware.* Apple QuickTime Player is a great multimedia player that supports SMIL, as well as its own proprietary QuickTime format. QuickTime supports AppleScript, synchronized audio and video, and links to remote URLs. Go to www.apple.com to check out the Apple Web site.

Web browsers

Internet Explorer 5.5, from Microsoft.

For Mac and Windows. *Commercial product.* This is the popular, powerful Web browser that's packed with all the latest features for today's cybertravels. It's also free, which makes it a true bargain. This program is updated frequently, so check out the Microsoft Web site at www.microsoft.com.

Netscape Communicator 4.7, from Netscape

For Windows and Mac. *Commercial version.* This free suite of programs includes a full-featured browser (Navigator), e-mail program (Messenger), and an HTML editor (Composer). This program is updated frequently, so be sure to check out `www.home.netscape.com`.

Sample files from the author

All the examples provided in this book are located in the Examples directory on the CD and work with Macintosh, Linux, Unix, and Windows 95/98/NT and later computers. These files contain much of the sample code from the book. Many examples in this book aren't included on the CD because no players fully support the SMIL 2.0 standard, which is what the examples are written in. You can browse these files directly from the CD, or you can copy them to your hard drive and use them as the basis for your own projects in multimedia presentations. The structure of the examples directory is

```
Examples/Chapter1
```

Not every chapter has an accompanying example folder. Chapters 15, 16, and 17 each contain one of the three most complete examples. You can find these examples in the `Examples/Chapter15`, `Examples/Chapter16`, and `Examples/Chapter17` directories, respectively.

To run the individual examples within these folders, open the `.smi` files. If you double-click a `.smi` file in Windows, it's automatically loaded into the SMIL player installed on your computer.

Appendixes on the CD

A couple of additional appendixes are available in a PDF file on the CD. If you don't have Adobe Acrobat Reader on your computer, it's also included on this CD. Be sure to install it first so that you'll be able to open these appendixes.

If you want to find out more about SMIL 2.0 elements and attributes, or if you want to enhance your SMIL presentations by using the RealNetworks proprietary languages RealPix and RealText, these appendixes are just the ticket.

Links to resources

The CD contains links to every Web site discussed in this book, and many of these links will take you to places that can provide you with tutorials and lots more technical information. By clicking <u>Links from the Book</u> on the CD interface, you have access to many resources that can help you learn and use SMIL.

If You've Got Problems of the CD Kind

I tried my best to compile programs that work on most computers with the minimum system requirements. Alas, your computer may differ, and some programs may not work properly for some reason.

The two likeliest problems are that you don't have enough memory (RAM) for the programs that you want to use or that you have other programs running that are affecting the installation or running of a program. If you get error messages, such as `Not enough memory` or `Setup cannot continue`, try one or more of the following methods and then try using the software again:

- **Turn off any antivirus software that you have on your computer.** Installers sometimes mimic virus activity and may make your computer incorrectly believe that it's infected with a virus.

- **Close all running programs.** The more programs you're running, the less memory is available to other programs. Installers also typically update files and programs; if you keep other programs running, installation may not work properly.

- **In Windows, close the CD interface and run demos or installations directly from Windows Explorer.** The interface itself can tie-up system memory or even conflict with certain kinds of interactive demos. Use Windows Explorer to browse the files on the CD and launch installers or demos.

- **Have your local computer store add more RAM to your computer.** This is, admittedly, a drastic and somewhat expensive step. If you have a Windows 95 PC or a MacOS computer with a PowerPC chip, however, adding more memory can really increase the speed of your computer and enable more programs to run at the same time.

If you still have trouble installing the items from the CD, please call the IDG Books Worldwide Customer Service phone number: 800-762-2974 (outside the U.S.: 317-572-3993).

Index

●●

• *U* •

• *V* •

• *W* •

IDG Books Worldwide, Inc.,
End-User License Agreement

READ THIS. You should carefully read these terms and conditions before opening the software packet(s) included with this book ("Book"). This is a license agreement ("Agreement") between you and IDG Books Worldwide, Inc. ("IDGB"). By opening the accompanying software packet(s), you acknowledge that you have read and accept the following terms and conditions. If you do not agree and do not want to be bound by such terms and conditions, promptly return the Book and the unopened software packet(s) to the place you obtained them for a full refund.

1. **License Grant.** IDGB grants to you (either an individual or entity) a nonexclusive license to use one copy of the enclosed software program(s) (collectively, the "Software") solely for your own personal or business purposes on a single computer (whether a standard computer or a workstation component of a multiuser network). The Software is in use on a computer when it is loaded into temporary memory (RAM) or installed into permanent memory (hard disk, CD-ROM, or other storage device). IDGB reserves all rights not expressly granted herein.

2. **Ownership.** IDGB is the owner of all right, title, and interest, including copyright, in and to the compilation of the Software recorded on the disk(s) or CD-ROM ("Software Media"). Copyright to the individual programs recorded on the Software Media is owned by the author or other authorized copyright owner of each program. Ownership of the Software and all proprietary rights relating thereto remain with IDGB and its licensers.

3. **Restrictions on Use and Transfer.**

    (a) You may only (i) make one copy of the Software for backup or archival purposes, or (ii) transfer the Software to a single hard disk, provided that you keep the original for backup or archival purposes. You may not (i) rent or lease the Software, (ii) copy or reproduce the Software through a LAN or other network system or through any computer subscriber system or bulletin-board system, or (iii) modify, adapt, or create derivative works based on the Software.

    (b) You may not reverse engineer, decompile, or disassemble the Software. You may transfer the Software and user documentation on a permanent basis, provided that the transferee agrees to accept the terms and conditions of this Agreement and you retain no copies. If the Software is an update or has been updated, any transfer must include the most recent update and all prior versions.

4. **Restrictions on Use of Individual Programs.** You must follow the individual requirements and restrictions detailed for each individual program in Appendix D of this book. These limitations are also contained in the individual license agreements recorded on the Software Media. These limitations may include a requirement that after using the program for a specified period of time, the user must pay a registration fee or discontinue use. By opening the Software packet(s), you will be agreeing to abide by the licenses and restrictions for these individual programs that are detailed in Appendix D and on the Software Media. None of the material on this Software Media or listed in this Book may ever be redistributed, in original or modified form, for commercial purposes.

5. **Limited Warranty.**

    (a) **IDGB warrants that the Software and Software Media are free from defects in materials and workmanship under normal use for a period of sixty (60) days from the date of purchase of this Book. If IDGB receives notification within the warranty period of defects in materials or workmanship, IDGB will replace the defective Software Media.**

    (b) **IDGB AND THE AUTHOR OF THE BOOK DISCLAIM ALL OTHER WARRANTIES, EXPRESS OR IMPLIED, INCLUDING WITHOUT LIMITATION IMPLIED WARRANTIES OF MERCHANTABILITY AND FITNESS FOR A PARTICULAR PURPOSE, WITH RESPECT TO THE SOFTWARE, THE PROGRAMS, THE SOURCE CODE CONTAINED THEREIN, AND/OR THE TECHNIQUES DESCRIBED IN THIS BOOK. IDGB DOES NOT WARRANT THAT THE FUNCTIONS CONTAINED IN THE SOFTWARE WILL MEET YOUR REQUIREMENTS OR THAT THE OPERATION OF THE SOFTWARE WILL BE ERROR FREE.**

    (c) This limited warranty gives you specific legal rights, and you may have other rights that vary from jurisdiction to jurisdiction.

6. **Remedies.**

    (a) IDGB's entire liability and your exclusive remedy for defects in materials and workmanship shall be limited to replacement of the Software Media, which may be returned to IDGB with a copy of your receipt at the following address: Software Media Fulfillment Department, Attn.: *SMIL For Dummies*, IDG Books Worldwide, Inc., 10475 Crosspoint Blvd., Indianapolis, IN 46256, or call 800-762-2974. Please allow three to four weeks for delivery. This Limited Warranty is void if failure of the Software Media has resulted from accident, abuse, or misapplication. Any replacement Software Media will be warranted for the remainder of the original warranty period or thirty (30) days, whichever is longer.

    (b) In no event shall IDGB or the author be liable for any damages whatsoever (including without limitation damages for loss of business profits, business interruption, loss of business information, or any other pecuniary loss) arising from the use of or inability to use the Book or the Software, even if IDGB has been advised of the possibility of such damages.

    (c) Because some jurisdictions do not allow the exclusion or limitation of liability for consequential or incidental damages, the above limitation or exclusion may not apply to you.

7. **U.S. Government Restricted Rights.** Use, duplication, or disclosure of the Software for or on behalf of the United States of America, its agencies and/or instrumentalities (the "U.S. Government") is subject to restrictions as stated in paragraph (c)(1)(ii) of the Rights in Technical Data and Computer Software clause of DFARS 252.227-7013, or subparagraphs (c)(1) and (2) of the Commercial Computer Software - Restricted Rights clause at FAR 52.227-19, and in similar clauses in the NASA FAR supplement, as applicable.

8. **General.** This Agreement constitutes the entire understanding of the parties and revokes and supersedes all prior agreements, oral or written, between them and may not be modified or amended except in a writing signed by both parties hereto that specifically refers to this Agreement. This Agreement shall take precedence over any other documents that may be in conflict herewith. If any one or more provisions contained in this Agreement are held by any court or tribunal to be invalid, illegal, or otherwise unenforceable, each and every other provision shall remain in full force and effect.

Installation Instructions

The *SMIL For Dummies* CD offers valuable information that you won't want to miss. The following sections tell you how to install the items from the CD.

Using the CD with Microsoft Windows

To install items from the CD to your hard drive, follow these steps:

1. **Insert the CD into your computer's CD-ROM drive.**
2. **Click the Start button and choose Run from the menu.**
3. **In the dialog box that appears, type** d:\start.htm.
4. **Read through the license agreement, nod your head, and then click the Accept button if you want to use the CD.**
5. **To navigate within the interface, click any topic of interest to take you to an explanation of the files on the CD and how to use or install them.**
6. **To install software from the CD, simply click the software name.**

Using the CD with a Mac

To install items from the CD to your hard drive, follow these steps:

1. **Insert the CD into your computer's CD-ROM drive.**
2. **Double-click the CD icon to show the CD's contents.**
3. **Double-click** start.html **to open your browser and display the license agreement.**
4. **Read through the license agreement, nod your head, and then click the Accept button if you want to use the CD.**
5. **To navigate within the interface, click any topic of interest to take you to an explanation of the files on the CD and how to use or install them.**
6. **To install software from the CD, simply click the software name.**

For more information, see Appendix D, "About the CD."

IDG BOOKS WORLDWIDE
BOOK REGISTRATION

We want to hear from you!

Visit **http://my2cents.dummies.com** to register this book and tell us how you liked it!

✔ Get entered in our monthly prize giveaway.

✔ Give us feedback about this book — tell us what you like best, what you like least, or maybe what you'd like to ask the author and us to change!

✔ Let us know any other *For Dummies*® topics that interest you.

Your feedback helps us determine what books to publish, tells us what coverage to add as we revise our books, and lets us know whether we're meeting your needs as a *For Dummies* reader. You're our most valuable resource, and what you have to say is important to us!

Not on the Web yet? It's easy to get started with *Dummies 101*®: *The Internet For Windows*® *98* or *The Internet For Dummies*® at local retailers everywhere.

Or let us know what you think by sending us a letter at the following address:

For Dummies Book Registration
Dummies Press
10475 Crosspoint Blvd.
Indianapolis, IN 46256

BESTSELLING
BOOK SERIES